Sensitive Negotiations

SUNY series, Studies in the Long Nineteenth Century
——————
Pamela K. Gilbert, editor

Sensitive Negotiations
Indigenous Diplomacy and British Romantic Poetry

Nikki Hessell

Cover image: Photo by Takeshi Arai from Pexels.

Published by State University of New York Press, Albany

© 2021 State University of New York

All rights reserved

Printed in the United States of America

No part of this book may be used or reproduced in any manner whatsoever without written permission. No part of this book may be stored in a retrieval system or transmitted in any form or by any means including electronic, electrostatic, magnetic tape, mechanical, photocopying, recording, or otherwise without the prior permission in writing of the publisher.

For information, contact State University of New York Press, Albany, NY
www.sunypress.edu

Library of Congress Cataloging-in-Publication Data

Names: Hessell, Nikki, author.
Title: Sensitive negotiations : indigenous diplomacy and British Romantic poetry / Nikki Hessell.
Description: Albany : State University of New York Press, [2021] | Series: SUNY series, studies in the long nineteenth century | Includes bibliographical references.
Identifiers: LCCN 2020048370 | ISBN 9781438484778 (hardcover : alk. paper) | ISBN 9781438484761 (pbk. : alk. paper) | ISBN 9781438484785 (ebook)
Subjects: LCSH: English poetry—19th century—History and criticism. | Politics and literature—Great Britain—History—19th century. | Indigenous peoples—Government relations. | Diplomacy—Language. | Great Britain—Foreign relations—19th century. | Politics and culture—Great Britain—History—19th century. | Romanticism—Great Britain.
Classification: LCC PR590 .H47 2021 | DDC 821/.709145—dc23
LC record available at https://lccn.loc.gov/2020048370

10 9 8 7 6 5 4 3 2 1

For Evan and Chele
Truth—Dignity—Justice

Contents

Acknowledgments — ix

Preface — xiii

Introduction: The Power of (Poetic) Promises — 1

1 Truth and Reconciliation: The Case of "the Monster Brandt" — 21

2 Romanticism and Removal: Elias Boudinot, Felicia Hemans, and the *Cherokee Phoenix* — 61

3 Digressive Diplomacy: George Copway and Byron's Lines on the Rhine — 103

4 "Always Build a Fence around the King's Word": Sol Plaatje and *The Deserted Village* — 143

5 Petitions and Repetitions: Rēweti Kōhere and the Ashes of Byron and Macaulay — 173

Conclusion: Coming to Terms with Romantic Poetry — 203

Coda — 219

Bibliography — 223

Index — 247

Acknowledgments

Diplomacy, by its very nature, generates an enormous global archive. I am very grateful to the librarians and archivists who helped me navigate this material, including those at the Victoria University of Wellington Library, National Library, Alexander Turnbull Library, and National Archives in New Zealand; the British Library, National Archives, Guildhall Library, School of Oriental and African Studies Library, and Special Collections at the University of Glasgow in the United Kingdom; the Beinecke Library, Wisconsin Historical Society, Newberry Library, Stuart A. Rose Manuscripts, Archives and Rare Book Library at Emory University, and American Antiquarian Society in the United States; the Ontario Archives in Canada; and the Australian National University (ANU) Library and National Library of Australia in Canberra.

Some of these places provided very generous fellowship schemes that made the work both possible and enjoyable. My deepest thanks go to the American Antiquarian Society (especially Nan Wolverton and all the wonderful visiting fellows who were there in early 2019); the Stuart A. Rose Manuscripts, Archives and Rare Book Library at Emory University; and the Humanities Research Centre at ANU, whose generous scholarly community, led by Will Christie, provided a home away from home.

My own institution has been similarly generous in both financial and intellectual support. I am grateful to the Joint Research Committee of the Faculty of Humanities and Social Sciences for the grants that made parts of this work possible, especially in the early phases of the project, and to the Enriching National Culture group, led by Lydia Wevers and Maria Bargh, which awarded me an internal Treaty of Waitangi Fellowship and a chance to work at the Stout Centre and Te Kawa a Māui (the School of Māori Studies). These investments in research and collegiality laid the foundation for an application to the Royal Society of New Zealand's Marsden Fund, to which I am likewise exceptionally grateful. The Marsden grant has made this book a reality, and it has generated opportunities to collaborate with colleagues and students that would have been out of the question without such financial support.

The list of places that I visited represents a great deal of travel, and my colleagues in the English Programme at Victoria could not have been more generous in their support for this project, including at times when they needed to take on additional work to make it possible for me to be away. The selflessness of program members, at a time of biting budget cuts and rapidly increasing workloads, was appreciated more than I can say. I was also very fortunate to be able to talk about the ideas underpinning this project with a wonderful group of students in seminars on Romanticism and Indigeneity in 2019 and 2020. The challenges and insights of those students will stay with me for a long time. Of that group, I would particularly like to thank Millie Godfery, who has been an intelligent, skillful, and supportive research assistant, not to mention an exceptional researcher in this area in her own right.

My foremost collegial debts are, as always, to the best writing group anyone could wish for. Ingrid Horrocks, Sarah Ross, and Elizabeth Gray have been, for more than a decade, incisive readers and generous friends. You have read big chunks of this work, and you have provided the support and the laughter that underpinned the whole thing. Much of this book was written as I worked alongside you on the Kāpiti Coast, and I'm very grateful to my Aunt Sally and Uncle Brian for being willing to share their space with us while we wrote. I am lucky also to have a virtual network in my field, in the form of the Bigger6 Collective, which is always there to cheer me on. Special thanks go to Manu Chander and Tricia Matthew for being there during some of the tougher times. Rebecca Colesworthy and James Peltz at SUNY Press, along with series editor Pamela Gilbert, the expert production team, and the two anonymous readers, who provided generous feedback on the manuscript, have all made the experience of finishing this book a great pleasure. An abbreviated version of chapter 1 appeared in *Eighteenth-Century Fiction* 33, no. 1 (2020), and a section of chapter 4 was published in *Modern Philology* 112, no. 2 (2015). An abbreviated version of chapter 5 is forthcoming in a collection edited by Porsca Fermanis and Sarah Comyn, *Worlding the South: Nineteenth-Century Literary Culture and the Southern British Colonies*.

To my "Wilson cousins," thanks so much for your hospitality and the many games of cards in Canberra. And to all my family, especially Carwyn, Kohurangi, Ruaariki, and Te Rauhina, I love you more than you will ever know.

Preface

Perhaps appropriately for a project about quotation, this book was born out of another book. In the years in which I was working on *Romantic Literature and the Colonised World: Lessons from Indigenous Translations*, I would occasionally come across examples where Indigenous intellectuals and writers quoted British Romantic poetry in the original English. Because I was looking for translations and also because I considered the urgent intervention needed in my field of Romantic Studies to be one involving colonial bi- and multilingualism, I didn't think much about what these examples meant.

During the same period of time, my partner was involved, on behalf of his *iwi* (tribe or nation), in negotiations with the government to settle a claim under the Treaty of Waitangi, the 1840 document that ushered in the modern nation-state of Aotearoa New Zealand. Because this process involved an enormous amount of time and frequent travel back to the traditional center of his community, the negotiations became a core feature of our lives. Work and family time were organized around his absences and the gradual process of settling the claim was woven into our timelines and our conversations.

Two things stood out to me as I watched these events unfold. One was that, because the Crown (the term we use for the government in the context of treaty settlements) controls the process, the negotiators always had to make use of the language and what we in literary studies would call the "forms" that the Crown chose to recognize. In order to communicate and connect with the Crown negotiators, *mātauranga Māori* (Māori knowledge) had to be processed via these languages and forms, and being a skilled negotiator meant comprehending how to do this processing. Ideas and histories that came out of this land and its people had to be connected somehow to the Crown's own cultural understandings of the relevant relationships and processes. This involves something more than simply expressing oneself in English; instead it means understanding, at a deep level, what values are cherished by the Crown and what languages and forms from within the Crown's cultural frames of reference can be effectively mobilized to make the necessary arguments. It means knowing which English texts and vocabularies to use, in what form, and when, in order to hold the Crown to account. Mostly, this meant quoting the Crown's words or forms back to itself, whether in order to remind it of past obligations and undertakings or simply to fit a model that will make sense.

However, the second thing that stood out was how narrowly the Crown interpreted what constituted "the negotiation" compared with how capacious it seemed to the other side. It wasn't simply that the Crown controlled all the languages and forms, in other words; it was rather that the range of languages and forms it regarded as relevant and connected was extremely limited. Only some of the words mattered; only some of the talking was important; only some of the texts carried weight. But from where I was standing, everything was diplomacy. Every word and every text formed part of the negotiation.

It was not difficult, then, to look with fresh eyes at the scholarly material I had been collecting and realize that this habit of poetic quotation that I had observed was invariably part of a much wider diplomatic process. Like my partner and his fellow negotiators, these Indigenous writers and leaders were trying to find forms and languages from within settler-imperial worldviews and cultural canons in order to communicate, but they retained the right to include any and all genres in that communication. It was all diplomacy, not just every treaty or every petition, but also every line of verse. It was all geared toward a restitution of land, sovereignty, and self-determination.

On the day that my partner's iwi finally signed a deed of settlement with the Crown, the negotiators asked if any of the *rangatahi* (young people) would like to sign. My eldest child, who was only nine at the time, went up and wrote his name—just his first name, Kohurangi, as if he were a nineteenth-century chief and didn't concern himself with surnames. He was confident, not only in his right to sign the deed, but also in his right to represent himself as he saw fit. That name, Kohurangi, situated him in that place and explained who his ancestors were; the Crown would simply have to accept it. Some months later, Kohurangi brought home a poem he had written in his English class. (This class was the only part of his schooling done in English, as he had been in Māori immersion education since he was a preschooler.) The poem was called "The Moon," and it ended with the line, "In the forests of the night." I was surprised to see a line from William Blake in his work, especially as it was meant to be an original poem. I asked him why he'd included it, and he replied that it was his starting point and his aim; he had decided, before he began writing, that he wanted that particular line to be in there. To him, there was nothing unoriginal about this choice, nor was it something that signaled his assimilation into another literary tradition. It was the line that was needed at the time. Sometimes you write in Māori and sometimes you write in English; sometimes you communicate one way of being and sometimes another; sometimes you sign a settlement deed and sometimes you write a poem. It's all diplomacy. It's all a negotiation.

Introduction

The Power of (Poetic) Promises

What are the situations in which we repeat someone's words back to them? "Can I remind you that under oath you said . . ." "The minutes show that at our last meeting you said . . ." "When you slammed the door as you walked out this morning, what did you mean when you said . . . ?"

We often quote other people's words back to them when we are attempting to resolve a conflict, whether large or small. In fact, the act of quoting someone's exact words back to them may be primarily a sign of conflict, a boundary marker in the borderlands of a relationship that indicates the moment at which old words and new actions no longer correspond, but also a moment at which the resolution of that conflict, the realignment of past language and present action, remains possible.

The sites of the courtroom, the meeting room, and the family home that I conjure up at the start of the chapter are chosen because they demonstrate a potential paradox about the sites of quotation. To focus on verbatim language can generate a paradigm of pedantry, bureaucratic or legalistic in its framing, but such a paradigm also overlaps with intimacies and the basic nature of human communication. Verbatim language, an agreed-on set of words, provides cohesion as well as constriction. It cements the terms on which we can rely, but also those on which we will be judged. It forms the perimeter for trust, and it has all the advantages and disadvantages that a perimeter implies. It marks out a space, and that is a space for law, but it is also a space for love.

It is this mixture of institutionalism and intimacy, and the verbatim language that encodes it, that I want to explore in this book by looking at one of its manifestations: the moments, scattered throughout the nineteenth and early twentieth centuries, in which Indigenous peoples quoted English poetry (and specifically British Romantic poetry) as part of their dialogues with settler states and publics. These moments exist in the complex linguistic, political, and emotional space that I sketched earlier in this chapter. They often occur in the most punitive of contexts, in which cold legal instruments and cruel bureaucratic deceptions are being used to extract resources or land and enforce genocidal policies—and yet, they manifest a faith in the warmest of forms and the kindest of languages. They assume that institutions are intimate and that intimacy can be institutionalized in positive ways; in other words, they assume what we might call an Indigenous view of relationships and community organization.

These moments also assume that settlers and colonial or imperial governments mean what they say; that they are prepared to stand by, not only the formal language of a treaty, a political speech, or a piece of legislation, but also the wider cultural documents that underpin these texts: the Bible, first and foremost, but also the literature that encodes a society's most cherished values. The title of this chapter alludes to the essay collection *The Power of Promises: Rethinking Indian Treaties in the Pacific Northwest*, edited by Alexandra Harmon, but it assumes that poetry also partakes in the promises that were being made across the colonized world in the late eighteenth and early nineteenth centuries.[1] One way in which Indigenous peoples could reasonably expect to understand the values of their settler-imperial counterparts was to consider the latter's most cherished lines of literature; one way to hold settlers and governments accountable for the promises they had made was to keep reminding them of the promises inherent in their own lore. The lines of poems that Indigenous diplomats reproduced and mobilized are, as we will see in the coming chapters, treated as statements of intent, as historical record, and as what we might think of as cultural charters. They are treated, in other words, as diplomatic texts.

Quotation was built into colonial diplomacy.[2] Across the colonized world, as this book will consider, Indigenous peoples and settler-imperial

---

1. Alexandra Harmon, ed., *The Power of Promises: Rethinking Indian Treaties in the Pacific Northwest* (Seattle: University of Washington Press, 2008).

2. See the discussion of the role of repetition in Native American diplomacy in the era of encounter, which emphasizes these patterns and tropes, in Robert A. Williams Jr., *Linking Arms Together: American Indian Treaty Visions of Law and Peace, 1600–1800* (New York: Routledge, 1999), 38.

officials undertook a process of repeating the language of past engagements at each new encounter. Prior speeches and declarations were recalled, excerpts of documents were read out, material objects that encoded past promises were produced and handled. The verbatim language of previous encounters was held, by both sides, to have an apparently unbreakable force. Each side engaged in this process, but the epistemological underpinnings of their activities were entirely different. Settler-imperial officials aimed to narrow and codify the exact terms of exchange between the two sides, to generate documents whose precise language would set out what, and by whom and when.[3] Capturing that language, preferably in the form of a treaty or other official written agreement, laid the foundation for subsequently enforcing settler-imperial law, land acquisition, and sovereignty. When these officials quoted past treaties, declarations, and speeches, they were manifesting an apparent faith in the words themselves as significant, especially when they appeared in written form. But they also, paradoxically, treated the words as editable, revisable, or ignorable. Having established the notion that the words written in legal agreements constituted a sacred trust, they proceeded to treat them as mere instruments, subordinate to the overwhelming desire for land, resources, and power and available as temporary tools to acquire these things. Each new document, each new set of phrases, replaced and erased the old, thus suggesting the bewildering tension between the permanence and the malleability of a written culture and its legal structures.

Indigenous peoples approached the act of quotation similarly, but they perceived the aim of the diplomatic process very differently. For them, quotation operated as part of a much wider set of actions designed to requicken the alliances between peoples. Alongside hospitality, gift-exchange, prayer, games, mourning, song, and dance, the quotation of past exchanges between the two sides helped to make that relationship live and breathe. The latest negotiations did not replace the old ones; rather, they acted instead as a palimpsest, a new layer to, and new performance of, the obligations of the ancestors. They did not establish one side's dominance over the other; rather, negotiations helped to balance and maintain relationships across time and generations. Quotation thus contributed to this requickening by serving as a reminder of the mutual

---

3. For a global discussion of imperial treaty making that is acutely alert to Indigenous actions, needs, and interpretations in these processes, see the essays in Saliha Belmessous, ed., *Empire by Treaty: Negotiating European Expansion, 1600–1900* (Oxford: Oxford University Press, 2014).

obligations that held alliances together and the promises that were providing the architecture of those alliances.

To quote was thus to perform an acknowledged rhetorical maneuver in Indigenous-settler diplomacy, but my point extends farther than that; what I want to suggest in this book is that the act of quotation in these contexts remakes the quoted text into a diplomatic artifact and simultaneously remakes the diplomatic encounter into a collage of genres in which poetry, including English poetry, can find a suitable home. Diplomacy was saturated with quotation, and quotation became, as a device, inescapably diplomatic. Understanding that interplay of quotation and diplomacy allows us to stretch the boundaries of what counts as diplomatic text; genres, rhetorics, canons, and tropes that seem inescapably literary to a reader in the European tradition shift before our eyes into aspects of a wider negotiating, petitioning, and treating culture. What holds together the quotation of the disparate texts of treaties, speeches, and declarations, on the one hand, and poetry, on the other, is what we might call verbatim magic: a belief that exact words matter, that what is codified on the page constitutes an agreement between parties, a settler-imperial belief to be sure, but one that inevitably influenced and in turn was shaped by Indigenous communication.

By incorporating poetry into the framework of diplomacy and quotation, Indigenous writers and diplomats continued a practice that made sense within their own knowledge systems. It was not necessary, on these terms, to make a particular generic distinction between expressions of law and of literature. Poetry, song, proverb, dance, carving, weaving, and any number of other genres were seamlessly interwoven with laws, treaties, and contracts in a wide variety of Indigenous traditions across the Atlantic and Pacific worlds.[4] As John Borrows has demonstrated through

---

4. For discussion of the North American context of artistic expression in treaty negotiations historically, see Williams, 83, and for a similar point made from within literary and rhetorical studies, see Lisa King, Rose Gubele, and Joyce Rain Anderson, "Introduction: Careful with the Stories We Tell: Naming Survivance, Sovereignty, and Story," in *Survivance, Sovereignty, and Story: Teaching American Indian Rhetorics*, ed. Lisa King, Rose Gubele, and Joyce Rain Anderson, 3–16; 8–9 (Boulder: University Press of Colorado, 2015). Penelope Edmonds also talks about the absence of critical interest in Indigenous performance-based responses to reconciliation in modern settler colonies; see Edmonds, *Settler Colonialism and (Re)conciliation: Frontier Violence, Affective Performances, and Imaginative Refoundings* (Basingstoke: Palgrave, 2016), 12. See also Christopher B. Teuton's ideas of "the oral impulse," "the graphic impulse," and the "critical impulse" in Teuton, *Deep Waters: The Textual Continuum in American Indian Literature* (Lincoln: University of Nebraska Press, 2010).

a Canadian example, no single document in Indigenous-settler diplomacy can be read separately from the other documents and wider textual and material forms that supported it.[5] Settler and imperial governments and publics thought differently, drawing a firmer line between bureaucratic and literary genres. A community could theoretically, by settler-imperial logic, be held to the terms of an act of legislation or a signed agreement, but not to the terms of a stanza or a sonnet. While it might be desirable for poetry and policy to be consistent with one another, it was not absolutely necessary: poetry expressed a range of sentiments that, while valuable, were not expected to take on the force of law.

And yet, in the cases I discuss in this book, settlers and imperial actors also abandoned the commitments made via treaties, laws, and other agreements. They did not adhere to the logic I have just articulated: that bureaucratic, legalistic, nonfictional texts manifested and required a type of trust and adherence, not inherent in fictional or literary text, that simply had to be enforced. The explanation for this abandonment might be as simple as the unadulterated greed and hypocrisy of settler colonialism. But without dismissing this fundamental truth about colonialism, I want to contemplate another, related possibility. What if the uncoupling of the literary and the legalistic in the settler-imperial mind actually *facilitated* the betrayal of formal legal agreements? To put it another way, did the colonizers' willingness to treat poetry and poetic promises as fictional, subordinate, and nonbinding actually clear the way for a similarly slippery attitude toward other forms, documents, and vocabularies? Did it become easier to betray legal and political promises once poetic promises had been set aside? And might the Indigenous use of English poetry as a diplomatic tool, with its deployment occurring precisely at the moment that settler-imperial honor and honesty began to fray most explicitly— as the fabric of poetic and political expression was steadily ripping in two—highlight this fact?

The distinction I am drawing here between Indigenous and settler-imperial thinking is more than one of aesthetics or genre. It means that in Indigenous-settler interactions, one side regarded *all* the written or spoken language produced by each of the two parties as expressing an interrelated and mutually sustaining truth, while the other regarded at least *some* of

---

5. John Borrows, "Wampum at Niagara: The Royal Proclamation, Canadian Legal History, and Self-Government," in Aboriginal and Treaty Rights in Canada: Essays on Law, Equality, and Respect for Difference, ed. Michael Asch, 155–72 (Toronto: UBC Press, 1997).

that language as either potentially or actually untrue, implausible, fanciful, or meaningless, by virtue of its genre. This discrepancy has the potential to make achieving authentic and just political relationships almost impossible. It opens up a fraught but potent space between verbatim language and real-life actions, between what you say and what you do. It is in this space that hypocrisy and idealism are thrown into sharp relief, the former representing the falling away from one's promises and the latter, simultaneously, representing the hopeful possibility of rising back up toward them. It is into this dynamic space, I want to suggest, that Indigenous diplomats move when they quote English poetry back to its authors, readers, and devotees. As Chadwick Allen has suggested in his discussion of Indigenous redeployments of treaty discourses, "To rephrase Bhabha's definition of colonial mimicry as 'almost the same, *but not quite*,' we might define indigenous re-recognition as 'exactly the same, *but then some*.'"[6] In using exactly the same words as English poets, and in doing so within diplomatic and treaty-oriented dialogues, Indigenous intellectuals extracted something more, deriving further layers of meaning from words they were not actually altering. Skillfully and strategically, they tried to hold together a matrix of ideas that was, in that long nineteenth-century moment, pulling apart: politics and poetry, words and actions, past and present, as well as the two sides of historical alliances. They attempted a type of diplomacy that we might think of not as bilateral, but rather as biliteral, crossing genre lines and encompassing literary expression in a quest for accountability.

One way to enact this process of accountability was through *captatio benevolentiae*. The phrase literally means "fishing for goodwill," and it describes the way in which a speaker or writer, through a display of good manners, renders their interlocutor attentive, teachable, and well-disposed. Quotation and epigraph are not the only ways to perform *captatio benevolentiae*, but they are effective examples. By quoting literature familiar to their Anglophone audiences, Indigenous diplomats attempted to render their interlocutors attentive, teachable, and most important, well-disposed, and thus to generate the goodwill necessary to requicken alliances. They demonstrated what Tracey Banivanua Mar called "imperial literacy," the ability to understand imperial discourse, adapt it, and do so within an

---

6. Chadwick Allen, *Blood Narrative: Indigenous Identity in American Indian and Maori Literary and Activist Texts* (Durham, NC: Duke University Press, 2002), 19; italics in the original.

emerging system of similar Indigenous communication.⁷ As well as delivering on the oratorical traditions of their own cultures and the repetitive processes of traditional and colonial diplomacy, poetic quotation by these authors and speakers had the added frisson of a perhaps unexpected cosmopolitanism. The *captatio benevolentiae* of Indigenous diplomats was radical, however, because it was not one of homogeneity, in which a member of a group draws on that group's collective knowledge, literature, and lore. Rather, it performed an act of striking cross-cultural communication: fishing for goodwill in someone else's lake.

In that sense, the instances of poetic quotation that this book examines are not simply examples of performing cosmopolitanism, by which Indigenous leaders and intellectuals aim to take their place in the European republic of letters. This latter kind of cosmopolitanism, which was outlined so cogently by Frantz Fanon, aimed to confirm the speaker's taste and education among a white, male elite by demonstrating the requisite literary and classical knowledge.⁸ However, the figures I will examine do not say to their white audiences, "Here is what I know," but rather, "Here is what *you* know." The aim of poetic quotation in these cases is not to perform but rather to remind, to hold the interlocutory audience to *its own* values, ideals, and feelings.⁹ These examples thus differ markedly from the school-based colonial recitation practice sketched by Helen Tiffin, which she calls "a ritual act of obedience, usually by a child performer, who in reciting an English litany speaks as if he/she were the imperial speaker/master rather than the subjectified colonial so often represented in those very passages."¹⁰

---

7. Tracey Banivanua Mar, "Imperial Literacy and Indigenous Rights: Tracing Transoceanic Circuits of a Modern Discourse," *Aboriginal History* 37 (2013): 1–28.

8. Frantz Fanon, *The Wretched of the Earth*, trans. Constance Farrington (New York: Grove Press, 1963), esp. 176, for its discussion of the acquisition of European literature; and Fanon, *Black Skin, White Masks*, trans. Charles Lam Markmann (New York: Grove Press, 1967), 9–40, for its discussion of language.

9. Adela Pinch has explored the connection between quotation and feeling, in the context of early nineteenth-century English practices, in *Strange Fits of Passion: Epistemologies of Emotion, Hume to Austen* (Stanford, CA: Stanford University Press, 1996), 164–92. Her point differs from mine in that it emphasizes the way in which one's own feelings were seen to be captured in a quotation, but her work underlines the fact that poetic quotation was a very familiar form for nineteenth-century Anglophone audiences.

10. Helen Tiffin, "Cold Hearts and (Foreign) Tongues: Recitation and the Reclamation of the Female Body in the Works of Erna Brodber and Jamaica Kincaid," *Callaloo* 16,

The Indigenous diplomat in each of these cases is not presenting their own poetic bona fides, in the modern, plural sense in which we use the term to mean the documentation that verifies a person's qualifications. Rather, they are asking whether their interlocutor is bona fides in the original, singular sense of the phrase, meaning "of good faith."

The Indigenous diplomats were acting, in other words, as early versions of the intellectuals that Dale Turner has called for in Indigenous communities and whom he has dubbed "word warriors":

> Word warriors reconcile the forms of knowledge rooted in indigenous communities with the legal and political discourses of the state. They do this for two reasons. First, our survival as indigenous peoples demands that in order to assert and protect the rights we believe we possess, we must engage the discourses of the state more effectively. Second, indigenous knowledge offers legitimate ways of understanding the world—ways that have never been respected within the legal and political practices of the dominant culture. To make matters worse, these ways have not played a significant role (except in the early treaties) in determining the normative language of the political relationship. Word warriors do the intellectual work of protecting indigenous ways of knowing; at the same time, they empower these understandings within the legal and political practices of the state. Word warriors listen to their "indigenous philosophers" while engaging the intellectual and political practices of the dominant culture.[11]

Turner is talking about a necessary literacy in settler legal and political systems, but this does not, therefore, position cultural knowledge, such as that encoded in poetry, outside the bounds of his overall brief for the word warriors. He begins his book with a poem, "the passing of the pipe," a rhetorical move that, in itself, suggests the ways in which poetry and diplomacy are entwined with each other even in the twenty-first-century versions of Indigenous-settler relations. But the poem also, in its own

---

no. 4 (1993): 909–21; 913.

11. Dale Turner, *This Is Not a Peace Pipe: Towards a Critical Indigenous Philosophy* (Toronto: University of Toronto Press, 2006), 7–8.

words, emphasizes the significance of exact language and its entwinement within poetic and diplomatic discourses; as Turner writes in "the passing of the pipe,"

> we now know you are
> what you say
> and we will
> (to our dying breath)
> hold you to your word. (17–21)

Turner's model of the word warriors seems entirely consistent with the role played by the ancestors discussed in this book, who understood that engaging with the discourses of the state in the nineteenth and early twentieth centuries meant engaging with their cultural discourses as well. And that meant understanding the stories, forms, and lexicons that settler governments and publics claimed to hold dear.

In *Linking Arms Together: American Indian Treaty Visions of Law and Peace, 1600–1800*, Robert A. Williams Jr. discusses what he calls "stories as jurisgenerative devices":[12]

> In Indian diplomacy, stories could be told for a number of educative purposes: to state a grievance, to reinforce a long-standing set of values shared by treaty partners, and to elaborate the norms of behavior expected of those in a relationship of connection. In American Indian visions of law and peace, the telling of a story sought to build and sustain a common life, a life lived in solidarity with different peoples on a multicultural frontier. Through their treaty stories, American Indian diplomats of the Encounter era sought to educate the strange and alien-seeming newcomers to their world as to what was meant by treaty partners behaving as relatives toward each other.[13]

---

12. Williams, 95.

13. Williams, 89. Williams's point resonates with Kwame Anthony Appiah's idea that "evaluating stories together is one of the central human ways of learning to align our responses to the world. And that alignment of responses is, in turn, one of the ways we maintain the social fabric, the texture of our relationships." See Appiah, *Cosmopolitanism: Ethics in a World of Strangers* (New York: W. W. Norton, 2006), 29.

Williams here is describing a process by which Indigenous diplomats used their *own* stories to try to engage settler interlocutors. His extraordinary book ends in 1800, roughly the point at which my book begins, and this change in time frame might explain the shift toward quoting English stories, in the form of poetry, that my project traces. As colonization accelerated, nation-to-nation relationships shifted from being between Indigenous and imperial nations to being between Indigenous and settler nations, and both conflict and Indigenous land loss became more pronounced as the balance of power shifted away from partnership and toward an increasingly exploitative and violent relationship. The "nomos" (or "normative universe of shared meanings") that Williams describes as operating in the seventeenth and eighteenth centuries in North America was, by the beginning of the nineteenth century, mutating into a space in which shared meanings meant meanings from settler thought that Indigenous thinkers grasped hold of, rather than the collaborative, story-woven project of earlier balanced partnerships or Indigenous-led storywork.[14] Methodologically stories remained jurisgenerative devices, but the source of the stories was shifting as power itself shifted.

The year 1800 is both a plausible and a tidy date at which to situate this change, but to a British Romanticist, the date also looms large as a moment of Romanticism's own solidification as a cultural force in the form of the second edition of William Wordsworth and Samuel Taylor Coleridge's *Lyrical Ballads* and Wordsworth's accompanying preface. In other words, Romantic poetry was the poetry of the moment: in North America, Indigenous relationships with the British government and the emerging settler state and federal governments changed dramatically after the American War of Independence, requiring new approaches to diplomatic engagement, in precisely the era we now refer to as Romantic. In the Southern Hemisphere, British settlers began to gain a foothold on Indigenous land in those same years, from the late eighteenth century through to the mid-nineteenth century. Settlers brought Romantic literature with them, read it in the magazines and annuals that were sent from Britain, and taught it in colonial and mission schools. It is not surprising, then, that Indigenous readers and thinkers, both around

---

14. Williams, 47. The importance of nomos in legal discourse is articulated in Robert M. Cover, "Foreword: Nomos and Narrative," *Harvard Law Review* 97, no. 1 (1983): 4–68; Jo-ann Archibald, *Indigenous Storywork: Educating the Heart, Mind, Body, and Spirit* (Vancouver: UBC Press, 2008).

1800 and in the later nineteenth and early twentieth centuries, were also exposed to this literature and saw it as both an encapsulation of settler values and a resource to be incorporated into cross-cultural conversations such as those that happened via treaty councils, petitions, speeches, and letters. Romantic literature was fashionable and timely, and its deployment signaled Indigenous peoples' modern and adaptable approach to engaging settler-imperial audiences.

But Romantic literature was also thematically appropriate. In its focus on justice, sympathy, land, humanity, idealism, kin relationships, and fellow feeling, British Romanticism offered a cultural shorthand for the values that Indigenous negotiators wished to reference and mobilize. This confluence of literature and Indigenous ideas is, of course, not coincidental. One reason why a new generation of British writers became interested in these ideas was precisely that political events around the world had suggested the imminent or actual collapse of these values and the desperate need to reinstate and record them. That collapse was evident in the Lake District and the rapidly enclosing countryside of England, in the industrializing cities of the Midlands and the North, in the subjugation of people in Scotland, Ireland, and Wales, on the streets of London, and in the war-torn and revolutionary centers of the continent. But while the effects were observable in Europe, the cultural force driving them was global colonization along with its associated human and economic exploitation. It is no exaggeration to say that the experiences of Indigenous peoples across the world were precisely the experiences that triggered Romantic literature, as the quest for land, wealth, and cultural and political domination that drove settler-imperial actions globally came to shape British and European life.

This point is related to Lynn Festa's idea of the emergence of sentimental literature in eighteenth-century Europe. As Festa notes, "Sentimental texts helped create the terms for thinking about agency and intent across the geographic expanse of the globe by giving shape and local habitation to the perpetrators, victims, and causal forces of empire. In an era in which imperial reach increasingly outstripped imaginative grasp, sentimental fiction created the tropes that enabled readers to reel the world home in their minds."[15] Global processes undoubtedly generated European literary forms,

---

15. Lynn Festa, *Sentimental Figures of Empire in Eighteenth-Century Britain and France* (Baltimore, MD: Johns Hopkins University Press, 2006), 2. For another account of the role of emotions in Indigenous-settler relationships, this one focused on the Southern

and Festa makes a brilliant and convincing case for the sentimental as "the literary mode of empire in the eighteenth century."[16] I see my project as pivoting away from Festa's in some senses because it focuses on poetry, not the novel; the long nineteenth century, not the eighteenth; and, most especially, on Indigenous rather than European writing. By approaching this task with a methodology that I hope is itself diplomatic in its demands for balance and its commitment to producing better relationships, and by taking the lead, not from what European writers produced or readers consumed, but from what Indigenous writers and thinkers drew from European literature, my book concludes that Romantic literature, with its politically engaged manifestations of sentimentalism, is the most important body of English literature in this global context. Indigenous diplomats were not, of course, especially interested in Festa's "literary mode of empire," given that what they sought was neither to create nor to be subject to an empire, but rather to be in a relationship, and one imagined as a responsible adherence to the terms of past alliances and contacts.[17] They were looking instead for what we might call the literary mode of diplomacy, the genres, texts, and tropes that would speak to the disappointments as well as the opportunities that were available. As Festa points out, sentimental literature is in no way conceived as a meeting of equals: "sentimentality as a crafted literary form moves to locate that emotion, to assign it to particular persons, thereby designating who possesses affect and who elicits it."[18] It is an entirely imperial genre, one that is not, at any level, committed to requickening alliances or reframing relationships equitably. British Romantic poetry, by contrast, was ideal, not simply because it was the poetry of the moment in the sense of fashion and literary trend; it was, for its authors and also for its Indigenous deployers, forged out of the legal, political, military, and diplomatic crisis that is settler colonialism but ostensibly committed to the rebalancing of equitable relations.

In Romantic studies, the Indigenous deployment of this literature has largely been judged to be derivative, a sign of an inauthentic Indigenous expression, which has been victimized by colonial education and is in

---

Hemisphere settler colonies, see Jane Lydon, *Imperial Emotions: The Politics of Empathy Across the British Empire* (Cambridge: Cambridge University Press, 2019).

16. Festa, 2.

17. See Daniel Heath Justice, *Why Indigenous Literatures Matter* (Waterloo: Wilfrid Laurier University Press, 2018), xix.

18. Festa, 3.

line with Tiffin's insistence that "learning by *heart* the culture of others strangles self-expression—the absorption of their aesthetics, indeed their 'tongue,' cuts off one's own."[19] In part, that is because Romantic studies continues to partake in Romanticism's own fetish for individual, organic expression and for some kind of separation between the literary and the nonfictional. As a field, we remain unwilling to acknowledge what Scott Richard Lyons has dubbed "rhetorical sovereignty": "the inherent right and ability of *peoples* to determine their own communicative needs and desires in this pursuit, to decide for themselves the goals, modes, styles and languages of public discourse."[20] Not only is the Romantic position an inappropriate standpoint from which to judge Indigenous communication, which is much less in thrall to the idea of originality as a virtue and has no cultural obligation to Romanticism's values, but it also insists on a *literary* framework for a style of communication that was far more multimodal. Colonial diplomacy was literary, but it was also political, genealogical, material, and physical.[21] It involved the oral and the written, Indigenous and settler objects, land and waterways, animals and ancestors, and cosmologies as well as covenants. Most of all, it involved quotation, a constant referring back to past conversations, documents, alliances, peoples, and times. All manner of texts in what Antoinette Burton and Isabel Hofmeyr have called "the imperial commons" were used to create this web of quotation that would help clarify relationships and obligations.[22] There is no particular reason why the canon of British Romantic poetry should not be one of these texts; in fact, as I have outlined, it was well suited to the task in terms of its preoccupations and its historical moment. Indeed, it could take its place as one of the "hidden transcripts" that

---

19. Tiffin, 918; emphasis in the original.

20. Scott Richard Lyons, "Rhetorical Sovereignty: What Do American Indians Want From Writing?" *College Composition and Communication* 51, no. 3 (2000): 447–68; 449–50; emphasis in the original.

21. See Phillip H. Round's discussion of "hybrid negotiating practices" in *Removable Type: Histories of the Book in Indian Country, 1663–1880* (Chapel Hill: University of North Carolina Press, 2010), 102–15.

22. Antoinette Burton and Isabel Hofmeyr, "The Spine of Empire? Books and the Making of an Imperial Commons," in *Ten Books That Shaped the British Empire: Creating an Imperial Commons*, ed. Antoinette Burton and Isabel Hofmeyr, 1–28 (Durham, NC: Duke University Press, 2014). See also Jane Stafford's delineation of the literary network of empire in *Colonial Literature and the Native Author: Indigeneity and Empire* (Basingstoke: Palgrave, 2016).

Saliha Belmessous has identified as central to understanding Indigenous law and its claims against imperial states.[23]

Vine Deloria Jr. provided a model of Native American communication that is useful in understanding the strategies of these poetry-quoting diplomats. In *We Talk, You Listen: New Tribes, New Turf*, Deloria explained:

> The best method of communicating Indian values is to find points at which issues appear to be related. Because tribal society is integrated toward a center and non-Indian society is oriented toward linear development, the process might be compared to describing a circle surrounded with tangent lines. The points at which the lines touch the circumference of the circle are the issues and ideas that can be shared by Indians and other groups. There are a great many points at which tangents occur, and they may be considered as windows through which Indians and non-Indians can glimpse each other.[24]

There are many texts, concepts, and values that might potentially sit at these tangents, and it is the argument of this book, not simply that British Romantic poetry can be read as constituting one of these "windows" through which Indigenous and non-Indigenous peoples might be able to see and comprehend one another, but that this was precisely the reason why Indigenous diplomats turned to it as a device. In doing so, Indigenous diplomats were both participating in and generating new diplomatic and literary cultures. As Frank Kelderman has explained,

> nineteenth-century Native American writers and orators generated what I term *indigenous publication projects*: mediated forms of indigenous representation that are produced with non-Native collaborators, which take place in institutional and diplomatic networks but also intervene in them. They are *indigenous* not because they authentically give voice to the ideas of indige-

---

23. Saliha Belmessous, "The Problem of Indigenous Claim-Making in Colonial History," in *Native Claims: Indigenous Law against Empire, 1500–1920*, ed. Saliha Belmessous, 3–16 (Oxford: Oxford University Press, 2011).

24. Vine Deloria Jr., *We Talk, You Listen: New Tribes, New Turf* (New York: Macmillan, 1970), 12.

nous actors, but because these mediated forms of publication nevertheless construct indigenous counter-discourses within colonial scenes of interaction. And they are forms of *publication* not because they necessarily hail a potentially unlimited audience, but because they organize politically meaningful publics within existing communication networks. Finally, I define them as *projects* because they are collaborative forms of textual production, directed at some measure of institutional change.[25]

We can see in the examples that this book considers some of the truth of Percy Bysshe Shelley's famous dictum that "poets are the unacknowledged legislators of the world," as British Romantic poets provide the raw material for a particular kind of legal discourse. In *Brown Romantics: Poetry and Nationalism in the Global Nineteenth Century*, Manu Samriti Chander rightly emphasizes the term "unacknowledged" in order to broaden the field of who is to be termed "Romantic."[26] I am likewise interested in thinking about a broader and a browner Romanticism, which has remained largely unacknowledged. But here I am more interested in the idea, to rephrase Shelley, that poetry is the unacknowledged legislation of the world. To these Indigenous diplomats, poetry was assumed to have a legislative force. In a diplomatic relationship, one side could hold the other side to account for its poetry as much as its proclamations, its stanzas as well as its statutes, its lines alongside its laws.

The figures that this book considers are, of course, a tiny sample from the extensive world of colonial Indigenous diplomacy. They represent a type of diplomat who was Anglophone, educated in a settler-dominated schooling system, and personally interested in English poetry. These diplomats were almost always controversial figures in their own communities, partly because of these personal histories, but also because of the inevitable disruptions to processes of mandating and authorizing leaders that arrived with colonization. They represent the type of diplomat that Kelderman has carefully delineated in his idea of "authorized agents" and the texts they produced:

---

25. Frank Kelderman, *Authorized Agents: Publication and Diplomacy in the Era of Indian Removal* (Albany: State University of New York Press, 2019), 12.

26. Manu Samriti Chander, *Brown Romantics: Poetry and Nationalism in the Global Nineteenth Century* (Lewisburg, PA: Bucknell University Press, 2017), 3.

The literatures of Indian diplomacy offer alternative representations of Native agency, re-inscribing the figure of the indigenous diplomat as an agentic subject whose words carried political weight in concrete institutional situations. And no matter how artificial their status as "official" delegates was, these literatures constructed Indian diplomats as the *authors* of texts that were collaboratively produced or sponsored by existing organizations. Indeed, even when they were transcribed or translated by non-Native collaborators, these publication projects established indigenous speakers as the originators of discourse, whose political voice could be constructed as a tribal-national one. To be an "authorized agent," in other words, meant gaining an "author function" that legitimized collaborative texts as the products of indigenous speakers.[27]

A huge number of significant ancestors are thus not discussed in my book: those who conducted their business in their own tongue; those who had no time for English poetry; and, perhaps most tellingly, women, who were vital and equal diplomatic forces but were not usually given access to the literary and classical side of the colonizers' education system in the nineteenth century. I do not wish to suggest that British Romantic poetry formed a dominant or everyday part of Indigenous diplomacy with settler-imperial interlocutors: that is a world of people who, for the most part, had far more urgent concerns in mind. My aim is rather to identify and consider the narrow yet identifiable thread of Indigenous diplomacy that did see some value or significance in Romantic poetry and wove it into the vast fabric of Indigenous diplomatic activity in the nineteenth and early twentieth centuries. While it is only a thread, it is noticeable how much more space Romantic poetry occupies in Indigenous diplomacy than any other type of English verse. For my own field of Romantic studies, then, this thread represents a new way to consider what the poetry said and meant, how it was used, and what those uses and their legacies might tell us about the way in which we read the canon of Romanticism today.

The chapters of this book are organized chronologically, which allows us to track a particular type of moment in Indigenous-settler relations as it moves across the colonized world, following the path of European

---

27. Kelderman, 26.

settlement and usurpation, while also assessing some profound differences in the ways Indigenous leaders globally engaged with Romantic literature and its lessons. The first section of the book focuses on North America in the first half of the nineteenth century. Chapter 1 considers the 1821 encounter between the Haudenosaunee leader John Brant (Grand River Six Nations) and the poet Thomas Campbell, in which Brant challenged Campbell's account of his father, Joseph Brant, in his poem *Gertrude of Wyoming*. Campbell had famously depicted "the monster Brandt [*sic*]" in his poem, and he had passed on a false accusations that Joseph Brant was present at and participated in the massacre of settlers at the Battle of Wyoming. In locating this encounter within the Grand River Six Nations' wider diplomatic efforts, this chapter considers how Campbell's original composition of the poem, as well as his equivocal response to Brant's challenge, reflects the diplomatic history that links the Haudenosaunee and the British. It sets the poem alongside John Brant's letters to the British imperial government and various settler officials to show the ways in which he understood the poem as having the power to influence debates about the Six Nations' sovereignty and took issue with its words as part of a significant diplomatic engagement in the service of his people.

Chapter 2 examines the extensive republication of Felicia Hemans's poetry in the pages of the first Native American newspaper, the *Cherokee Phoenix*, in the late 1820s and early 1830s. The chapter considers the ways in which Hemans's particular preoccupations and modes of expression were mobilized in the newspaper, not only to generate sympathy in white audiences, but also as intertexts for the Cherokee leadership's considerable body of diplomatic textual production. The sixteen Hemans poems that appeared in the *Phoenix* are read alongside the many memorials, letters, editorials, and essays that the Cherokee leadership produced in these years in order to demonstrate the fluid ways in which British Romantic tropes and vocabularies could migrate to and from Indigenous diplomatic discourse in the period. The chapter proposes that the emotional charge that Hemans's poetry produced was seen as especially useful in mobilizing white settlers' sentiment in the context of the Removal Crisis, in which the Cherokees, along with Indigenous groups everywhere east of the Mississippi, were forced to move west and vacate their land. It also grapples with the question of a diplomatic substitution of a white woman's voice for the voices of the Cherokee women.

Chapter 3 focuses on the Ojibwe author George Copway and his hybrid volume *Running Sketches of Men and Places in England, France, Germany, Belgium and Scotland* (1851). Copway is a complex figure in

Indigenous literary and political history: a Methodist minister and early Indigenous autobiographer and ethnographer, he was deeply involved in Ojibwe politics in the mid-nineteenth century, but he had an often troubled relationship with Ojibwe leaders and communities. *Running Sketches* is frequently held up as the weakest and least "authentic" of Copway's major pieces of literary work because of its reliance on quotation and extract. This chapter aims to recuperate the volume by showing the ways in which Copway utilizes the longest of the literary quotations, a section of Lord Byron's description of traveling on the Rhine from *Childe Harold's Pilgrimage* (Canto III). Instead of treating this as a derivative move in which Copway aims to play the Byronic tourist, this chapter sets the long quotation from Byron in dialogue with Ojibwe treaties, Copway's own history and experiences as a diplomat, and European ideas about history and memory as embodied in Byron's lines. The chapter aims to reconsider the much-derided *Running Sketches* as a fundamentally diplomatic text, which was produced at a critical moment in Ojibwe history and embedded in a global vision of Indigenous power and nationhood.

The second section of the book turns to the Southern Hemisphere. Chapter 4 considers what is almost certainly the most widely read figure and the best-known text in my study: Sol Plaatje and his 1916 work *Native Life in South Africa*. While considerable critical work has been done on this central text of African political thought, including discussions of its practice of quotation, *Native Life in South Africa* has not been situated in either global Indigenous networks nor in the rich diplomatic context from which it emerged. The chapter seeks to read across genres of textual production to show the ways in which Plaatje's long-acknowledged attempt to mobilize the British public's sympathy in favor of equitable treatment for his African compatriots has antecedents in the history of Indigenous colonial diplomacy and manifests his own multimodal approach to a Romantic discourse of diplomatic relationships. It explores the ways in which Plaatje uses Oliver Goldsmith's *The Deserted Village* as a particularly effective diplomatic intertext for considerations of displacement, mobility, forced emigration, equal rights, and Indigenous sovereignty.

In my final chapter, I consider the Māori writer Rēweti Kōhere's juxtaposition of extracts from Byron and Thomas Babington Macaulay with his long-running campaign for land rights in part of his Ngāti Porou homeland. The chapter looks at how key ideas from Byron's and Macaulay's verses are linked to metaphors and legal discourses of Māori land tenure and hereditary ownership across Kōhere's many diplomatic articles, letters, and petitions from the 1910s to the 1940s, particularly the ways in which Byron and Macaulay make use of fire imagery as a metaphor for land rights, sovereignty, and ancestry. While this chapter ends the main part of the book because it comes last chronologically, it also allows me to "bring home" some of the reflections in this book by considering how British Romantic poetry shaped diplomacy in my own country and how my own country might have something to say to the field in which I situate myself. This return to the Pacific is the focus of the conclusion, which considers much more recent manifestations of the same phenomenon among Pasifika women poets, who are taking the lead in cultural diplomacy in the twenty-first century, but who are also once again making Romantic poetry, especially that of William Wordsworth, a part of their diplomatic endeavors.

That situatedness is of considerable importance. I am neither Māori nor Indigenous. I have lived a life (scholarly and personal) marked by settler privilege, which in concrete and material ways facilitates my ability to write this book.[28] I operate in a field that is profoundly white, but, led by Chander and the wider Bigger6 collective, one that is slowly diversifying. My aim in this book is thus not to "settle" myself within Indigenous studies, although I hope my citation practice and intellectual engagement with that field manifests respectful interaction and rigor. Instead, my aim is to speak to Romanticists worldwide about the living legacies of the poetry we study and the great array of what Chander has termed "Brown Romantics" of the past, present, and future, who have been writing, speaking, and engaging with that poetry for centuries. For those of us in the settler colonies, the stolen land on which we stand sustains our scholarship, and we must offer our scholarship back in return, however insignificant that offering might be. As Romanticists in the settler colonies, we can remind ourselves that the poetry to which we have dedicated ourselves is an active force in these lands, which is passed back and forth by settler and Indigenous readers, thinkers, and diplomats, and thus woven into, not just our comprehension of the natural beauty that we might associate with Romanticism, but the history and ongoing legacy of injustice and racism on which the settler colonies were built as

---

28. I have outlined some of this personal history in *Romantic Literature and the Colonised World: Lessons from Indigenous Translations* (Basingstoke: Palgrave, 2018), 9, and outlined it in an episode for the podcast *The East Is a Podcast* (at the time of writing, this episode is available here): https://eastisapodcast.libsyn.com/the-tasks-of-indigenous-translators-w-nikki-hessel.

well. We can hold ourselves to the promises that the Indigenous diplomats this book considers asked us to adhere to when they quoted Romantic poetry: respect and oneness with the land, solidarity with the oppressed, and a fairer and more just world. After all, this poetry is what we said, and continue to say, underpins our sense of ourselves and our values. These are the texts *we* brought to the treaty council, the meeting table, the courtroom, and the family home.

Chapter 1

Truth and Reconciliation

The Case of "the Monster Brandt"

In the winter of 1821–1822, the Scottish poet Thomas Campbell made a new acquaintance. John Brant (Ahyonwaeghs) and his cousin, Robert Johnson Kerr, were Mohawk emissaries from Upper Canada who were visiting England to discuss land purchases and treaty violations with the British government. But when Brant contacted Campbell, he was keen to talk poetry.[1] In 1809, Campbell had published *Gertrude of Wyoming*, a narrative poem set in Pennsylvania and based around a real event, the Battle of Wyoming, which was fought by white settlers on the one hand and British troops and their Haudenosaunee allies on the other, during the American Revolution. In the poem, the young settler heroine, Gertrude, and her family, are visited by an old acquaintance, Outalissi, an Oneida man, who warns them of the impending attack by the British forces:

> This is no time to fill the joyous cup,
> The Mammoth comes,—the foe—the Monster Brandt—
> With all his howling desolating band;

---

1. It is usually assumed that Campbell and John Brant met face to face, based on Campbell's remark that he "formed an acquaintance" with Brant and some secondhand recollections of Campbell's friends. I am grateful to a colleague who pointed out that it is difficult to be certain that a meeting took place and that the "acquaintance" may simply have consisted of letters exchanged while Brant was in London. Campbell does appear to have met with Brant's intermediary, the lawyer Saxe Bannister, who was well known for being sympathetic to Indigenous peoples.

> These eyes have seen their blade and burning pine
> Awake at once, and silence half your land.
> Red is the cup they drink; but not with wine:
> Awake, and watch to-night, or see no morning shine!
>
> Scorning to wield the hatchet for his bribe,
> 'Gainst Brandt himself I went to battle forth:
> Accursed Brandt! he left of all my tribe
> Nor man, nor child, nor thing of living birth:
> No! not the dog that watch'd my household hearth,
> Escaped that night of blood, upon our plains!
> All perish'd!—I alone am left on earth!
> To whom nor relative nor blood remains.
> No! not a kindred drop that runs in human veins!" (III, 138–53)[2]

The "Monster Brandt" here is John Brant's father, the eighteenth-century Mohawk leader Joseph Brant (Thayendanegea), who was, from a European perspective, one of the best-known Indigenous figures of that period in the Americas. John Brant contacted Campbell, thirteen years after the publication of his poem and fifteen years after his father's death, to dispute this literary characterization. His father, he pointed out, was not at the Battle of Wyoming, and was not the villain that Campbell had made him out to be.

This chapter differs from the others in my book because it discusses an alternative kind of quotation practice. In the chapters that follow this one, I discuss Indigenous diplomats who typically quoted Romantic poetry to mobilize positive values and elevate sentiments that they believe could help their cause. In this chapter, I am considering an instance in which the exact language of a Romantic poem was regarded by Indigenous diplomats as false, malicious, and in need of correction, not simply because of its inaccuracy, but because of the effect that poetic falsehoods could have on Indigenous sovereignty and land rights. However, the encounter between Thomas Campbell and John Brant still reinforces the significance of quotation, of verbatim language, and of the role that Romantic poetry played in Indigenous diplomacy. It underlines the mismatch between Indigenous and settler-imperial notions of genre divisions, fact and fiction, and poetic license. And it reminds us that the deployment of this poetry by

---

2. Thomas Campbell, "Gertrude of Wyoming," in *The Poetical Works of Thomas Campbell* (London: Frederick Warne, 1874), 57–94, 340–54. References to the poem and its notes are to this edition unless otherwise stated.

Indigenous diplomats was never a flight of fancy or a rhetorical flourish, but rather a quest for accountability and justice.

Gertrude of Wyoming has been read by David Simpson, Kevin Hutchings, Kate Flint, and Tim Fulford in their important interventions in debates about Romanticism and colonization.[3] But scholarship on the poem, coming as it does from within literary studies, has typically located the encounter between Brant and Campbell within a reading of Campbell's intentions and actions. Where Brant's intentions and actions are considered, they tend to be cast as a case of filial duty: Fulford writes that Brant "resented" the portrayal of his father, while Hutchings provides a nuanced reading of Brant's mobilization of discourses of civility and civilization to "defend his father's honour."[4] But these readings dislocate the encounter from the wider diplomatic context in which I would like to read it. Brant was in London to discuss a long-held grievance about the boundaries of the Grand River settlement in Upper Canada, on which his people lived, a grievance that stretched back to Indigenous-British relationships in the eighteenth century and that persists today. Instead of considering the encounter with Campbell as a kind of personal matter taken up in the middle of a diplomatic mission, we should relocate it as an essential element of the diplomacy, in which lines on a map and lines of poetry were never entirely separate. Brant wanted to talk poetry, but poetry, in this era, played a vital role in diplomacy.

Haudenosaunee Diplomacy and Transatlantic Politics

John Brant's mission to London in 1821–1822 was a chapter in one of the richest and best-documented diplomatic relationships of the trans-

---

3. David Simpson, *Romanticism and the Question of the Stranger* (Chicago: University of Chicago Press, 2013), 171–74; Kevin Hutchings, *Romantic Ecologies and Colonial Cultures in the British-Atlantic World 1770–1850* (Montreal: McGill-Queen's University Press, 2009), 134–53; Kate Flint, *The Transatlantic Indian, 1776–1930* (Princeton: Princeton University Press, 2009), 51; and Tim Fulford, *Romantic Indians: Native Americans, British Literature, and Transatlantic Culture 1756–1830* (Oxford: Oxford University Press, 2006), 183–97. See also Sarah Green, "An Icon of the Ignoble Savage: The Content and Consequence of Thomas Campbell's Representation of Joseph Brant as a 'Monster' in 'Gertrude of Wyoming'" (PhD thesis, University of Western Ontario, 1995). Green's dissertation is probably the first modern study of Campbell's poem and its misrepresentation of Joseph Brant. I am grateful to an anonymous reviewer who pointed out this scholarship.

4. Fulford, 192; Hutchings, *Romantic Ecologies*, 151.

atlantic colonial world. British engagement with the Haudenosaunee people, of which the Mohawks are one group, stretched back to the earliest moments of contact in North America and was part of a complex network of connections between the Haudenosaunee and various European powers. The Haudenosaunee, also known by Europeans as the Iroquois or the Six Nations, are a league of sovereign nations who were brought together by a leader known as the Peacemaker in the fifteenth or sixteenth centuries.[5] The original five nations (the Mohawks, Senecas, Cayugas, Onondagas, and Oneidas) were joined by the Tusacaroras in the 1720s to form the Six Nations. In the eighteenth century, they were led by a council of fifty people taken from the different nations, collectively known as the Rotiyanehson, each of whom had a title that would be passed on to a new leader on their death. This political and spiritual framework included a formal process of diplomacy, which was designed to create peace and harmony. Conferences and negotiations could only be held around the designated council fire, and each of the nations played a defined role that maintained political balance and order.[6] Speeches and agreements were recorded and confirmed using strings or belts of wampum beads.[7] The official council meetings were often supplemented by smaller, private meetings, sometimes referred to as meetings "in the bushes," in which interested parties discussed shared concerns before the speeches were delivered in the council setting.[8]

---

5. The history of the Peacemaker's vision and the establishment of the Great Law of Peace is widely documented. Haudenosaunee sources include Susan M. Hill, *The Clay We Are Made Of: Haudenosaunee Land Tenure on the Grand River* (Winnipeg: University of Manitoba Press, 2017), 32–40; Kayanesenh Paul Williams, *Kayanerenkó:wa The Great Law of Peace* (Winnipeg: University of Manitoba Press, 2018); and John Arthur Gibson, *Concerning the League: The Iroquois League Tradition as Dictated in Onondaga*, Algonquin and Iroquoian Linguistics, Memoir 9 (Syracuse, NY: Syracuse University Press, 1992). Another account can be found in Timothy J. Shannon, *Iroquois Diplomacy on the Early American Frontier* (New York: Penguin, 2008), 26–28.

6. See the summary given in Susan M. Hill, 33–34.

7. William N. Fenton, *The Great Law and the Longhouse: A Political History of the Iroquois Confederacy* (Norman: University of Oklahoma Press, 1998), 224–39.

8. Mary Druke Becker, "Linking Arms: The Structure of Iroquois Intertribal Diplomacy," in *Beyond the Covenant Chain: The Iroquois and Their Neighbors in Indian North America, 1600–1800*, 2nd ed., ed. Daniel K. Richter and James H. Merrell, 29–39; 35 (University Park: Penn State University Press, 2003).

One element of this process came to be known as the condolence ceremony. The story of the Great Law explained that the Peacemaker had brought the chief Hiawatha back to health after the death of his daughters by giving him three strings of beads and speaking words of condolence; one string of beads dried his tears, the next cleared his throat, and the last one opened his ears. These actions became part of the Haudenosaunee league's "requickening" practices, to be used in situations where a leader had died and needed to be replaced, but also as the opening ritual of Haudenosaunee councils more generally. The condolence ceremony involves one group, the clear-minded, visiting the mourning group to condole with them. The two sides each perform the act of wiping each other's eyes, unblocking their ears, and clearing their throat, in order to acknowledge past losses, but also to remove barriers to communication. This requickening process is followed by the performance of the "Six Songs," which express the sorrow of the mourners but also the happiness surrounding the meeting of the two sides and their reengagement with the Great Law of Peace.[9] The connection between creative expression and the political communication process is encapsulated in a phrase sometimes translated as "Let me drive it into your mind with a song," which is used to introduce the performance of a song in support of the messages being delivered.[10]

These processes of negotiation and communication, which were formed among the Haudenosaunee themselves, came to characterize their engagements with the European powers, in which the existing

---

9. Gibson, xxxiii–xl. See also William J. Campbell, *Speculators in Empire: Iroquoia and the 1768 Treaty of Fort Stanwix* (Norman: University of Oklahoma Press, 2012), 16–17; Horatio Hale, ed., *The Iroquois Book of Rites* (1883; reprint, New York: AMS Press, 1969). The most detailed schematic of the Condolence Ceremony can be found in Fenton, *The Great Law and the Longhouse*, but I note here the criticism of Fenton's dominance of Iroquois studies and definitions of condolence in Theresa McCarthy, *In Divided Unity: Haudenosaunee Reclamation at Grand River* (Tucson: University of Arizona Press, 2016), 67. For an Indigenous-authored interpretation of issues concerning condolence, see Doug George-Kanentiio, "Atonement among the Haudenosaunee," *Indigenous Policy Journal* (December 16, 2009), https://ipjournal.wordpress.com/2009/12/16/atonement-among-the-haudenosaunee/.

10. William N. Fenton, "Structure, Continuity, and Change in the Process of Iroquois Treaty Making," in *The History and Culture of Iroquois Diplomacy: An Interdisciplinary Guide to the Treaties of the Six Nations and Their League*, ed. Francis Jennings, William N. Fenton, Mary A. Druke, and David R. Miller, 3–36; 29 (Syracuse, NY: Syracuse University Press, 1985).

Haudenosaunee league morphed into a political confederacy. As Timothy J. Shannon has noted, a shared cross-cultural diplomatic language and set of practices emerged in the early eighteenth century, partly to circumvent the difficulties of translation. Stock metaphors, including opening or unblocking paths, burying hatchets, linking arms, tending the tree of peace, and polishing or repairing the chain (a reference to the image of the Covenant Chain that symbolically bound the Haudenosaunee to the Dutch) were used by Haudenosaunee and European speakers alike and accompanied by the exchange of wampum belts and strings.[11] A vital symbol of the relationship between the Haudenosaunee and the European powers was the Two Row Wampum belt, which contains two parallel lines of purple beads. These lines had stood for the Haudenosaunee and the Dutch, traveling side by side in separate canoes, respectful of each other's customs but operating autonomously.[12] Over time, the Two Row Wampum became a more general symbol of the way in which the Haudenosaunee imagined themselves as equal partners to their European allies, and it remains a potent symbol of Indigenous autonomy alongside settler nation-states.[13] These hybrid processes, objects, and lexicons filtered back to Europe via treaties, journals, letters, travelogues, and newspaper accounts. To a large extent, what late-eighteenth-century Europeans imagined as "standard" Native ceremony, oratory, and diplomacy were in fact derived from Haudenosaunee practices.

The condolence ceremony, while still operating as a Haudenosaunee protocol for the replacement of deceased leaders, also became both a model for (and a critical opening activity in) cross-cultural treaty protocols.[14] In 1768, for example, at a council that Joseph Brant attended, the British diplomat Sir William Johnson and his Haudenosaunee counter-

---

11. Shannon, 95–96. See also William J. Campbell, 19–20; Daniel K. Richter, *The Ordeal of the Longhouse: The Peoples of the Iroquois League in the Era of European Colonization* (Chapel Hill: University of North Carolina Press, 1992), 41; Fenton, "Structure, Continuity, and Change," 16–18.

12. Rick Monture, *Teionkwakhashion Tsi Niionkwariho:ten: We Share Our Matters: Two Centuries of Writing and Resistance at Six Nations of the Grand River* (Winnipeg: University of Manitoba Press, 2014), 14.

13. See, for example, John Borrows, *Recovering Canada: The Resurgence of Indigenous Law* (Toronto: University of Toronto Press, 2002), 125–27.

14. Fenton, "Structure, Continuity, and Change," 6; Susan M. Hill, 40.

parts undertook the condolence ceremony before discussing boundary lines. Johnson's son, Sir John Johnson, would perform the same ritual at a meeting in Niagara in July 1783.[15] Similar examples can be found throughout the seventeenth and eighteenth centuries. The condolence ceremony was essential to the process of creating a respectful space in which the two sides could negotiate.

Multiple layers of repetition characterized these cross-cultural diplomatic encounters. The Haudenosaunee elements of the process, including the condolence ceremony, were themselves repetitions of the rituals laid down by the Peacemaker. Negotiations around the council fire involved the repetition of propositions by both sides, first by the proposers, and then by the listeners, in order to ensure that the issues at stake were fully comprehended before debate and negotiation began.[16] Speakers reminded one another of past negotiations, and wampum records as well as written texts were cited as evidence.[17] For the Haudenosaunee, these repetitions were the point of the negotiations; the relationship itself was what mattered, and it required constant renewal or requickening.[18]

Joseph Brant was a central figure in late-eighteenth-century Haudenosaunee diplomacy. A skilled linguist, who had been educated in both Haudenosaunee traditions and the Anglophone colonial education system, Brant served as a captain in the British army in Great Britain's conflicts with other European powers and the emergent American settler population. He was present at the negotiation of the 1768 Treaty of Fort Stanwix, which set the boundary between British and Haudenosaunee

---

15. Isabel Thompson Kelsay, *Joseph Brant 1743–1807: Man of Two Worlds* (Syracuse, NY: Syracuse University Press, 1984), 343. Earlier examples of white officials condoling can be found in Michael K. Foster, "On Who Spoke First at Iroquois-White Councils: An Exercise in the Method of Upstreaming," in *Extending the Rafters: Interdisciplinary Approaches to Iroquoian Studies*, ed. Michael K. Foster, Jack Campisi, and Marianne Mithun, 183–207; 188–89 (Albany: State University of New York Press, 1984).

16. Richter, 42.

17. See, for example, the descriptions of diplomacy given in William J. Campbell, 16–17.

18. Becker, 36; Shannon, 81–82; Mary A. Druke, "Iroquois Treaties: Common Forms, Varying Interpretations," in *The History and Culture of Iroquois Diplomacy: An Interdisciplinary Guide to the Treaties of the Six Nations and Their League*, ed. Francis Jennings, William N. Fenton, Mary A. Druke, and David R. Miller, 85–98 (Syracuse, NY: Syracuse University Press, 1985).

land holdings, and he would refer back to this document when writing to colonial officials in the future. He developed into an important go-between in the ongoing relationship between the British and the Haudenosaunee because of his skills as a linguist and translator, and he may have taken on the role of a "pine tree chief," one of those whom the Rotiyanehson employed because of their particular merits or abilities.[19] In January 1776, Brant went to London on a trip facilitated by his brother-in-law Sir William Johnson, the British superintendent of Indian affairs, where he met King George III, conducted diplomatic business, posed for a portrait by George Romney, and was interviewed by James Boswell.[20] He sat at the heart of a complex network of political and artistic affiliations that stretched across the Atlantic.

The American War of Independence divided the Haudenosaunee.[21] The Mohawks, along with the Senecas, Cayugas, and Onondagas, fought on the British side, after obtaining a guarantee that they could return to their lands at the conclusion of the hostilities.[22] The British defeat and subsequent capitulation to the Americans in the negotiation of the Treaty of Paris, which ended the war, left the Haudenosaunee in limbo; the Treaty contained no reference to Native Americans, and the newly

---

19. Kelsay, 125, 140. Susan M. Hill notes that while it is plausible that Brant was a pine tree chief, there is no confirmation of this in either written or oral records at Grand River (155). In terms of published biographical resources, Kelsay's book is the most comprehensive account of Brant's life. A shorter and more accessible account can be found in James W. Paxton, *Joseph Brant and His World: 18th Century Mohawk Warrior and Statesman* (Toronto: James Lorimer, 2008). Most later accounts, including Kelsay's and Paxton's, draw on William L. Stone, *Life of Joseph Brant (Thayendanegea)*, 2 vols. (Albany, NY: J. Munsell, 1864).

20. Shannon, 170–71; Kelsay, 165–73; Barbara Graymont, *The Iroquois in the American Revolution* (Syracuse, NY: Syracuse University Press, 1972), 105–6; Coll Thrush, *Indigenous London: Native Travelers at the Heart of Empire* (New Haven, CT: Yale University Press, 2016), 121–31. Brant's sister Molly (Konwatsi'tsiaienni), a powerful leader in her own right, was Johnson's common-law wife.

21. For accounts of the Haudenosaunee deliberations concerning the War of Independence, see Fenton, *The Great Law and the Longhouse*, 582–601.

22. The Oneidas and the Tuscaroras fought with the Americans. For a brief summary of the reasoning for this division, see Jack Campisi, "National Policy, States' Rights, and Indian Sovereignty: The Case of the New York Iroquois," in *Extending the Rafters: Interdisciplinary Approaches to Iroquoian Studies*, ed. Michael K. Foster, Jack Campisi, and Marianne Mithun, 95–108; 97–98 (Albany: State University of New York Press, 1984).

formed American government felt no obligation to honor Britain's promises. Thus, a new understanding between the British and the Haudenosaunee was required.

Brant took on a decisive role in these postwar negotiations as the Rotiyanehson and the British colonial officials recognized that he was uniquely placed to act as a broker between them.[23] Under the direction of the Rotiyanehson, Brant negotiated with the governor of Quebec, Frederick Haldimand, to secure the Grand River lands in British Canada (in what is currently known as southern Ontario) as a new homeland for those Mohawks, and those Haudenosaunee more generally, who were willing to relocate.[24] In a speech to Haldimand in 1783, Brant emphasized the ongoing relationship between his people and the British, and the cross-cultural records and repetitions that secured those memories, saying, "Brother, you have books and records of our mutual Treaties and Engagements, which will confirm the truth of what I have been telling, and as we are unacquainted with the art of writing, we keep it fresh in our memory by Belts of Wampum."[25] Haldimand, who was committed to honoring these past agreements, purchased land from the Mississaugas, who were living around Grand River at the time and who were prepared to live under the protection of the proposed Haudenosaunee settlement.[26] On October 25, 1784, Haldimand made the following proclamation (reproduced here in its entirety):

---

23. Susan M. Hill, 134. See also the detailed account of Brant's diplomatic training and experience in Lisa Brooks, *The Common Pot: The Recovery of Native Space in the Northeast* (Minneapolis: University of Minnesota Press, 2008), 106–62.

24. A detailed account of Brant's role in the negotiations that led to the Haldimand grant can be found in Kelsay, 343–71. See also Fenton, *The Great Law and the Longhouse*, 601–21. Some of Brant's speeches and letters to Haldimand at this time can be found in Charles M. Johnston, ed., *The Valley of the Six Nations: A Collection of Documents on the Indian Lands of the Grand River* (Toronto: Champlain Society, 1964), 38–41; 44–45. As Susan M. Hill points out, the Grand River was already part of the western hunting grounds of the Haudenosaunee (132, 137).

25. Charles M. Johnston, 39.

26. For a summary of the postwar negotiations, see Charles M. Johnston, ix–xxxix. The speeches connected to the Mississauga arrangements can be found on 46–48. For detailed Indigenous-authored interpretations of the Mississauga-Haudenosaunee relationship, see Leanne Simpson, "Looking after Gdoo-naaganinaa: Precolonial Nishnaabeg Diplomatic and Treaty Relationships," *Wicazo Sa Review* 23.2 (2008): 29–42.

> Whereas His Majesty having been pleased to direct that in Consideration of the early Attachment to His Cause manifested by the Mohawk Indians, & of the Loss of their Settlement they thereby sustained that a Convenient Tract of Land under His Protection should be chosen as a Safe & Comfortable Retreat for them & others of the Six Nations who have either lost their Settlements within the Territory of the American States, or wish to retire from them to the British—I have, at the earnest Desire of many of these His Majesty's faithfull Allies purchased a Tract of Land, from the Indians situated between the Lakes Ontario, Erie, & Huron and I do hereby in His Majesty's name authorize and permit the said Mohawk Nation, and such other of the Six Nation Indians as wish to settle in that Quarter to take Possession of, & Settle upon the Banks of the River commonly *called Ours* [Ouse] or Grand River, running into Lake Erie, allotting to them for that Purpose Six Miles deep from each Side of the River beginning at Lake Erie, & extending in that Proportion to the Head of the said River, which them & their Posterity are to enjoy for ever.[27]

Brant then led those Haudenosaunee who wanted to move to Grand River, establishing what is now the Six Nations settlement with the help of engineers provided by Haldimand.[28]

Despite the brevity and apparent simplicity of the Haldimand proclamation, Brant and the people who came to be known as the Grand River Six Nations found that it provided them with very limited rights and protections. According to the British, the exact boundaries of the Grand River settlement were not clearly defined since the land had not been fully surveyed before it was granted to the Six Nations. Objections to the proclamation were raised by some in the next generation of British colonial officials, on the grounds that Haldimand had used the wrong seal or that his orders did not trump existing European understandings about Native land tenure, while others sympathized with Brant's points about compromised autonomy but could not see a way to resolve the conflict. The Haudenosaunee assumption that they owned the land outright was

---

27. Charles M. Johnston, 50–51.
28. An account of the development of the Grand River site can be found in Kelsay, 370–71.

challenged when colonial officials argued that Brant should not be able to sell or lease any of the land to settlers, which was itself a controversial issue within the Six Nations community, some of whom did not believe Brant had the right to do so either.[29] In an attempt to clarify the issues of compensation and land boundaries, Brant traveled to England a second time in late 1785. On his return to Upper Canada, he arranged for a survey of the Grand River lands as a first step toward securing an official deed to the Haldimand tract, but this survey suggested that the British had never officially purchased the headwaters of the Grand River from the resident Mississauga people, and therefore could not have granted it to Brant and the Six Nations.[30] When John Graves Simcoe became lieutenant governor of Upper Canada, he relied on this evidence to produce the 1793 Simcoe Patent, which reduced the Grand River lands by a third by cutting out the headwaters, and effectively insisted that the Haldimand grant land conform to the new survey. The Simcoe Patent prompted a furious response from Joseph Brant. He traveled, gave speeches, and wrote repeatedly to colonial and British officials in an attempt to resolve the issue in the Six Nations' favor. In 1804, he sent his adopted nephew, John Norton, to Britain to get the promises of the Haldimand proclamation ratified by the British government.[31] None of these efforts was successful, and Joseph Brant died in 1807 with the issues concerning the Haldimand grant still unresolved.[32]

---

29. For assessments of Joseph Brant and his sometimes controversial role within Six Nations politics, see Elizabeth Elbourne, "Broken Alliance: Debating Six Nations' Land Claims in 1822," *Cultural and Social History* 9, no. 4 (2012): 497–525; and Monture, 32–53.

30. Kelsay, 555–56. See also Charles M. Johnston, xxxxix–xl.

31. Kelsay, 625–37; Timothy D. Willig, *Restoring the Chain of Friendship: British Policy and the Indians of the Great Lakes, 1783–1815* (Lincoln: University of Nebraska Press, 2008), 161–95; Sidney L. Harring, *White Man's Law: Native People in Nineteenth-Century Canadian Jurisprudence* (Toronto: University of Toronto Press, 1998), 39. Many of Brant's letters about the Grand River settlement can be found in the Joseph Brant and Family Papers, Public Archives of Canada, Manuscripts Division, MG19-F6. Simcoe's side of the correspondence, along with some of Brant's letters, can be found in John Graves Simcoe, *The Correspondence of Lieut. Governor John Graves Simcoe*, 5 vols. (North York: Ontario Historical Society, 1923–1931).

32. For an overview of the arrangements at Grand River, see Alan Taylor, *The Divided Ground: Indians, Settlers, and the Northern Borderland of the American Revolution* (New York: Knopf, 2006), 109–407; Robert J. Surtees, "The Iroquois in Canada," in *The History and Culture of Iroquois Diplomacy: An Interdisciplinary Guide to the Treaties of the Six Nations and*

The tensions between the Grand River Six Nations and the British government resurfaced when Peregrine Maitland was appointed lieutenant governor of Upper Canada in 1818. Maitland insisted that the British government could not have intended to give the headwaters of the Grand River to the Six Nations since they had not been officially purchased from the Mississaugas, and his officials were instructed to inform the Grand River residents of his opinion.[33] A council was called at Hamilton in July 1819, at which Maitland's hard-line message was delivered to the assembled Six Nations leadership (including John Brant, who was now in his twenties), who demanded that the Haldimand grant be honored. Maitland refused to change his position, and the Six Nations resolved to send John Brant and his cousin Robert Johnson Kerr to London to speak directly to the British government, although internal tensions and the disruptive effects of colonization on leadership protocols meant (in this instance as in the other cases discussed in this book) that their mandate was not entirely straightforward.[34]

It is in this diplomatic context, one both very recent and centuries old, that John Brant's visit to London, and his correspondence with Campbell, need to be read. His mission was just the latest chapter in a political relationship between the British and the Haudenosaunee, a relationship that was now centered on Grand River, his father's reputation and legacy, and the significance of the exact words the British used when they wrote about the Haudenosaunee, whether in proclamation or in poetry.

Gertrude of Wyoming and the Diplomatic Record

It is worth pointing out that it was not just John Brant who cared about Haudenosaunee diplomacy: Thomas Campbell did as well. Both in its verse and in its extensive notes, where he cites written transatlantic sources, Campbell's poem is steeped in the very detailed and specific field of

---

Their League. ed. Francis Jennings, William N. Fenton, Mary A. Druke, and David R. Miller, 67–98 (Syracuse, NY: Syracuse University Press, 1985); and Willig, 123–60. A selection of some of the most pertinent letters and speeches by Joseph Brant on this subject can be found in Charles M. Johnston.

33. Charles M. Johnston, 66.

34. A letter from Brant to the Duke of York, which was addressed from the Hungerford Coffee House in the Strand, shows that Brant was in London on September 12, 1821. See Joseph Brant and Family Papers, 2:293–96.

European understandings of Haudenosaunee diplomatic practices. This fact is not, on its own, especially surprising, given that the Haudenosaunee had long-standing connections with the European powers due to their position in the Northeast and that many of the officials, settlers, and travelers who wrote accounts of their time in America had engaged with the Haudenosaunee, sometimes to the exclusion of any other Indigenous groups. Moreover, the most common site for cross-cultural dialogue was around the council fire, so white understandings of general Indigenous communication were, in fact, frequently formed within the context of diplomatic discourse. Campbell's poem, by relying on sources like these, reflected an understanding of Indigenous peoples that was unconsciously, but almost exclusively, focused, not simply on the Haudenosaunee confederacy, but rather on the confederacy's diplomatic norms.

This focus can be seen in the way that Outalissi, the only Indigenous character to speak in the poem, conducts and expresses himself. Outalissi arrives at Albert's home to condole with him, and his communication with Albert takes some of the form of the condolence ceremony as Europeans imagined it. Outalissi sets up his intentions early, stressing that "the paths of peace my steps have hither led" (I, 124), before condoling with Albert about the loss of Henry's parents. He uses wampum as part of this address, declaring to Albert, "My words this belt approve [sic]" (I, 123). He then recounts the story of how he came to find the baby Henry, but this story is itself couched in Haudenosaunee diplomatic language and history; Henry has been orphaned because of a violent conflict between the Oneida and the Hurons, the latter having betrayed an existing peace treaty with the Haudenosaunee. This betrayal is described using the metaphors of Haudenosaunee diplomacy, as Outalissi says of the Hurons, "And though they held with us a friendly talk, / The hollow-peace tree fell beneath their tomahawk!" (I, 134–35). These events are relevant to Outalissi's address to Albert, not simply because they explain how he comes to be traveling with the infant Henry, but also because they situate the connection between the white settlers of the Wyoming Valley and the Oneida as part of a longer diplomatic history; instead of giving his name, for example, Outalissi introduces himself to Albert by saying "Christian! I am the foeman of thy foe; / Our wampum league thy brethren did embrace" (I, 127–28). After Albert has acknowledged and recounted his connection with Henry's family, Outalissi takes up his "calumet of peace" (I, 201), before singing what Campbell names a "song of parting" to the baby Henry (I, 215). A similar effect is achieved in the final scene of the poem, when Outalissi reappears to grieve with Henry over the deaths of Albert and Gertrude. Here, within a stereotypical portrayal of a stoic Indigenous figure and an emotional white mourner, Outalissi nevertheless takes on the role of the clear-minded condoler, describing the need for both Henry's and his own tears to be dried in order to proceed to victory in their conflict with the British and their Indigenous allies (III, 307–51).

The degree to which these encounters conform to the realities of the condolence ceremony is obviously debatable, but it is clear that Campbell believed that there was some authenticity to his fictional account. His extensive scholarly notes purport to explain details like the wampum belt, the wampum league, and the calumet, or peace pipe, drawing on named Euro-American sources who correctly situate these details within the context of treaty councils among Indigenous nations and between them and European negotiators. Campbell cites Cadwallader Colden's *History of the Five Nations* in his note about wampum, for example, and notes that wampum accompanies "every formal address" or "treaty of amity."[35] The metaphorical language Outalissi deploys is likewise connected in Campbell's notes to real accounts of diplomatic speeches.[36] Campbell is similarly broadly correct to identify his character as Oneida, since the Oneida, unlike the Mohawks, had sided with the Americans in the War of Independence. When Outalissi speaks in the poem, Campbell appears to treat him as a fictional representation of the real diplomatic engagements and tensions in Haudenosaunee territory.

How then might we read the intervening example of Outalissi speaking, the lines that would later be taken up by John Brant in his correspondence with Campbell, in which Outalissi returns to the Wyoming Valley to warn the family about the "monster Brandt"? While on some level this speech serves as a narrative device, intended to prompt the family to protect themselves and Henry to enter the fray, it also draws on the diplomatic contexts that have already been established in the poem: intra-Indigenous conflict and alliances under strain (in this case, the traditional alliance between the Oneida and the Mohawks) and the requickening of existing alliances between the white settlers and the Oneida, which,

---

35. See the note on wampum belts and strings from Cadwallader Colden's *History of the Five Indian Nations* (Campbell 340), and on the wampum league and calumet from Rogers's Account of North America (Campbell 341, 343–44).

36. See the notes on "the paths of peace" (340–41) and on Campbell's repurposing of the words of the Mingo chief Logan (353–54).

along with his personal connection to the family, motivate Outalissi to warn them. As Campbell remarks in his notes on this speech, he had deliberately attempted to mimic the well-known Anglophone rendition of an address by Logan, a Mingo chief, which was delivered at a 1774 treaty council in Virginia (353–54). While the urgency of Outalissi's second address makes it read differently than the earlier and later examples of his speech, it nevertheless partakes in some of the elements of the condolence ceremony that characterize those examples. Here, it is Outalissi who is the mourner, describing the bloody death of his tribe at Brant's hand, his eyes "bewildered" (III, 155) and affected by the violence they once witnessed in the earlier conflict with Brant's warriors: "These eyes have seen their blade and burning pine" (III, 141). Reading Outalissi's three speeches together within a condolence ceremony model demonstrates the ways in which Campbell repurposes received elements of this central part of Haudenosaunee diplomacy for narrative and poetic effect.

The "Brandt" of Campbell's poem thus emerges. not only as a sinister and violent offstage figure, part of the eighteenth-century tradition of literary representations of Native characters that Robbie Richardson has delineated, but also as a character who is interwoven with the diplomatic history and language of Haudenosaunee country.[37] He is a reference point, even when not present, in a much wider story, one of relationships between the Haudenosaunee and other peoples, including both the British and the Americans, and within the Haudenosaunee confederacy. His role in the poem is to be the negative force that is cited in the condolence ceremony, the murderer of Outalissi's people and quite possibly the murderer of Albert and Gertrude at the poem's conclusion, as described in the following lines:

>—yet there, with lust of murderous deeds,
>Gleamed like a basilisk, from woods in view,
>The ambushed foeman's eye—his volley speeds,
>And Albert—Albert—falls! the dear old father bleeds! (III, 249–52)[38]

---

37. Robbie Richardson, *The Savage and the Modern Self: North American Indians in Eighteenth-Century British Literature and Culture* (Toronto: University of Toronto Press, 2018).

38. The term "foeman" here potentially refers to Brant, since earlier in the poem Outalissi named him in particular as "the foe" (III, 139).

It is because of Brant and his alleged actions that Outalissi and the white family condole in the second and third encounters between them in Campbell's poem. But while these poetic descriptions accurately take the measure of Joseph Brant's political and diplomatic significance, they entirely mistake the detail. As a popular poem with considerable transatlantic influence, *Gertrude of Wyoming* had the power to shape understandings about Indigenous peoples generally, the Haudenosaunee in particular, and Joseph Brant most of all. The poem both enclosed a record of diplomatic practices and contributed to them by acting as a problematic text in the history of communication between the British and the Haudenosaunee. These errors would become clear to Thomas Campbell in 1821, when Joseph Brant's name came up once again at a critical point in Haudenosaunee diplomatic history.

Condoling with Campbell

Historian Elizabeth Elbourne has argued that Brant and Kerr's visit to London was "a key moment of expression of Haudenosaunee political vision" and that John Brant was "a skilled negotiator who tried to deploy a variety of techniques and performances around 'civilization,' modernity and tradition, with the central aim of maintaining Haudenosaunee independence."[39] Elbourne does not discuss the correspondence with Campbell in her evaluation of Brant's diplomatic mission, just as literary critics have not discussed the diplomatic mission in their evaluations of the conversation between the two men about *Gertrude of Wyoming*. But I want to use Elbourne's assessment of Brant's 1821–1822 trip to London to link the literary and political aspects of that visit. Brant's central purpose was certainly the articulation of Haudenosaunee and Six Nations' sovereignty, a fact that requires us to ask what political purpose the correspondence with Campbell might have served and in what ways Brant's engagement with Campbell manifested his understanding of that sovereignty. Might the "techniques and performances" that Elbourne isolates be extended to include an engagement with poetry and poets, as a manifestation of modernity that simultaneously contributed to a performance of Indigenous sovereignty? And what aspects of the existing diplomatic relationship between the Haudenosaunee and the British were being referenced, activated, and requickened in this literary debate?

---

39. Elbourne, 497–98.

John Brant was ideally positioned to move in these diplomatic circles, having emerged as a key figure in the decade after his father's death and being well-versed in the processes of Haudenosaunee-British communication. Following the War of 1812, in which Brant and his adopted cousin John Norton fought alongside their British allies in decisive battles, negotiations concerning the scope and control of the Grand River lands resumed. Brant had a front seat in the resumption of these arguments since he served as an interpreter at a crucial treaty council held in April 1815 at Burlington Heights. The transcript of this council highlights the norms and shared history of Haudenosaunee-British diplomatic language and procedure at this time. William Claus, the deputy superintendent general for Upper Canada, opened his speech by emphasizing the cross-cultural nature of these procedures: "The customs of *our* forefathers have prescribed certain Ceremonies which I would be sorry to omit upon the present occasion. The Ceremony of Condolence for the loss of our near and dearest Relations and Friends must be performed, which I now do very sincerely" (my emphasis).[40] Claus then works his way through the condolence ceremony, using the language and forms of the clear-eyed mourner condoling with the Haudenosaunee and punctuating each remark with the presentation of strings or belts of wampum. Following these formalities, he announces, "I will now repeat to you One of the Articles of the Treaty of Peace which secures to you the peaceable possession of all the Country which you possessed before the late War," and then reads verbatim from the relevant treaty article.[41] The speeches in reply, most of which John Brant interpreted for the British officials, emphasize the singular importance of past promises.[42] One of the Onondaga war chiefs, using the honorific "Father" to refer to the British king, reminds Claus, via John Brant:

> You condoled with us who are in grief, and said you are now come to fulfill promises made to us. Our Ancestors were always assured of our Fathers Love towards them. We never had a doubt of his promises being performed. The Promises made to us were heard by the Great Spirit as well as ourselves. . . . Brother We

---

40. "Minutes of the Indian Council held on Burlington Heights 24 April 1815," National Library of Scotland Adv.MSS.46.6.5, Murray Papers 120, 1814–1815, f. 161a.

41. "Minutes of the Indian Council held on Burlington Heights 24 April 1815," ff. 162a–b.

42. Another interpreter, Samuel Saunders, occasionally takes over, but Brant's name is attached as official interpreter to most of the Indigenous speeches.

address you as the Person appointed by our Father to attend to our Interests—You are not ignorant of the promises made to us—We therefore look to you to see them fulfill'd.[43]

The most senior peace chief, John Brant's uncle, known as Tekarohoken (one of the hereditary names passed down by council members), then tells Claus: "Brother—On the commencement of the War, you told us that you would not consent to a renewal of Peace with the Big Knives unless they would restore the ancient boundary lines.—Now we have peace but you have not told us where the Line is fixed."[44] John Brant's firsthand experience of diplomacy in this period was thus shaped by historical relationships, shared diplomatic language and protocols, the importance of verbatim texts, and the memory of past promises.

Brant and Kerr's correspondence with the British government while they were in London utilizes all of these factors. The Six Nations emissaries had arrived in Britain by early September 1821, and began a series of letters to and meetings with British officials and organizations. The colonial secretary, Lord Bathurst, provided an initial opinion that Lieutenant Governor Peregrine Maitland was essentially correct in saying that the Six Nations had no rights to the headwaters of the Grand River.[45] What followed was a dramatic series of letters in the early months of 1822, in which Kerr and Brant outlined the nature and evidence of their countercase.

The rhetoric of this case draws strongly on the idea that the words themselves matter. In a long response to Bathurst's initial endorsement of Maitland's decision, Brant and Kerr stressed the significance of the specific language of the Haldimand proclamation, informing Bathurst that "with respect to the literal meaning of the proclamation no dispute has ever been made; and we may confidently submit that in such a case plain words should not be departed from unless the fulfilment of them be for ever impossible."[46] After a dismissive reply from Bathurst's secretary,

---

43. "Minutes of the Indian Council held on Burlington Heights 24 April 1815," f. 164a.

44. "Minutes of the Indian Council held on Burlington Heights 24 April 1815," ff. 165a–b. Henry's name is spelled "Tekarihoga" in this manuscript. "Big Knives" is the name typically used to describe the Americans.

45. Charles M. Johnston, 68–69.

46. John Brant and Robert Johnson Kerr, Letter to Lord Bathurst, January 31, 1822, Colonial Office Records, National Archives (UK), CO 42/369, 223a.

Robert Wilmot, Brant and Kerr became more assertive on this point, asking Wilmot bluntly, "Has Lord Bathurst read General Haldimand's proclamation?" before commenting with palpable sarcasm:

> Our habits do not allow us to [investigate?] the distinctions of European subtlety. But General Haldimand's proclamation does not say one word of what you state as to the Indians from whom the territory was purchased. The words of General Haldimand are, "I do hereby in His Majesty's name authorize and permit the said Mohawk Nation, and such other of the Six Nation Indians as wish to settle in that Quarter to take Possession of, & Settle upon the Banks of the River commonly called *Ours* [Ouse] or Grand River, running into Lake Erie, allotting to them <u>for that purpose Six Miles deep from each side of the River beginning at Lake Erie and extending in that proportion to the Head of the Said River, which them and their posterity are to enjoy forever.</u>["][47]

The underlining here was supplied by Brant and Kerr, with a particular flourish of the pen under the final word, "forever." The language of the proclamation was presented by the Six Nations' emissaries as indisputable legal evidence; in a subsequent letter they claimed that they had been "advised that the words of the Proclamation constitute so clear a right that they impose on the Government the burthen of proving that they ought to be construed contrary to their natural meaning."[48]

These points about language were buttressed by a wealth of supporting documentation. Sometimes on their own initiative and other times at Bathurst's request, Brant and Kerr sent the colonial secretary, throughout their correspondence, authorized copies of a wide range of material. These documents included extracts from letters by Lord Dorchester assuring Joseph Brant that the Haldimand proclamation would be honored and a full transcription of the proclamation itself, with a similar underlining of the final phrases to that which had appeared in the earlier letter quoted previously. All these documents were signed by Brant and Kerr to indicate

---

47. John Brant and Robert Johnson Kerr, Letter to Lord Bathurst, February 27, 1822, Colonial Office Records, 231a–232a.

48. John Brant and Robert Johnson Kerr, Letter to Lord Bathurst, March 4, 1822, Colonial Office Records, 233a–b.

that they were verbatim copies of the material in their possession. The exact words of what had been promised, as well as the clear implications of sovereignty and ownership encased in those words, were at the heart of the Six Nations' claim, in much the same way that speeches in treaty councils would carefully recount the former words and undertakings of each party, for the purpose of requickening alliances and committing the parties to honorable action in the future.

The emphasis in Brant and Kerr's discussions of language and their deployment of supplementary documentation typically fell on the words used by the British themselves, as seen in the examples cited previously. Much of the emissaries' argument was designed to hold Britain to account for past promises and dismiss any attempt to construe the language of these documents as anything other than plain English. But woven through their letters was an equally significant emphasis on Indigenous understandings of law and legal language. The Grand River Six Nations held their land, Brant and Kerr argued, "in the Indian manner by hunting on it exclusively."[49] In their view, there had not been any confusion among the Grand River Six Nations, nor between them and the Mississaugas, about the nature of their rights to the land; as Brant and Kerr wrote, "We appeal to Indian history for the truth of these remarks; & which we are confident will be found to contain eloquent confirmation of them."[50] The chiefs had never agreed to a reduced land holding or limited ownership rights, and in fact, "the direct contrary is proved by documentary and living evidence."[51] Joseph Brant, in particular, had consistently disputed any interpretation of the proclamation that curtailed either the extent of the Grand River Six Nations' lands or his right to use and dispose of that land as he saw fit, and letters from Joseph Brant formed part of the evidence that his son and nephew presented. Brant and Kerr thus insisted on the cross-cultural validity of their claim, as manifested in both law and language, that the land "became ours in consequence of the grant according to all law Indian or European."[52]

It is within this well-orchestrated diplomatic engagement that we need to situate John Brant's correspondence with Thomas Campbell.

---

49. John Brant and Robert Johnson Kerr, Letter to Lord Bathurst, March 4, 1822, 223b.
50. John Brant and Robert Johnson Kerr, Letter to Lord Bathurst, March 4, 1822, 225b.
51. John Brant and Robert Johnson Kerr, Letter to Lord Bathurst, March 4, 1822, 228a.
52. John Brant and Robert Johnson Kerr, Letter to Lord Bathurst, March 4, 1822, 232a.

Just as it can be used to interpret the language in *Gertrude of Wyoming*, the condolence ceremony is potentially a productive paradigm for the Brant-Campbell encounter. As Drew Lopenzina has pointed out in his study of eighteenth-century Native American writers, the condolence ceremony is relevant to wider writing and narrative contexts because it "codified the assumption that two parties would have contesting versions of reality, differing accounts of significant events, and personal grievances that might bar the way to reconciliation or constructive deliberation."[53] All Brant's dealings in London could be accommodated within the condolence ceremony model; diplomacy did not occur simply in the official political meetings, but also in the cluster of engagements he undertook in Britain.[54] These engagements can all be understood as meetings "in the bushes," part of the wider smoothening of the diplomatic relationship between the Six Nations and the British, which was designed to bring the two sides to agreement in the formal correspondence.

There was also no reason for literary text or poetic expression to remain outside this model of diplomacy. The condolence ceremony incorporated songs and made them central to the summary of key points and the ratification of agreements: the phrase "Let me drive it into your mind with a song," an English translation of the words that introduced the performance of a relevant song in support of the diplomatic speeches in a treaty council, also manifests the certainty that political agreements are best comprehended and remembered via the literary performance and texts that accompany, underline, and manifest them.[55] John Borrows has demonstrated this point in his reading of the Royal Proclamation of 1763 (the legal instrument by which Britain acquired French territories in North America after the Seven Years' War) alongside the 1764 Treaty of Niagara between the British and First Nations and its associated wampum.

---

53. Drew Lopenzina, *Red Ink: Native Americans Picking Up the Pen in the Colonial Period* (Albany: State University of New York Press, 2012), 22.

54. See "Miscellaneous Epitome," *Norwich Chronicle and Norwich Gazette*, October 13, 1821, 2; "Circulation of the Scripture," *Morning Post*, October 9, 1821, 3; "Sunday and Tuesday's Posts," *Bath Chronicle*, October 18, 1821, 2; "British and Foreign Seamen's Friend Society and Bethel Union," *Morning Post*, October 23–October 25, 1821. Brant and Kerr also made contact with the New England Company; a record of this engagement can be found in the New England Company Minute Book, November 8, 1816–May 11, 1830, London Metropolitan Archives MS7920/2.

55. Fenton, "Structure, Continuity, and Change," 29.

Borrows's intertextual and multimodal reading shows that Indigenous understandings of their relationship with the British Crown went well beyond the limits of a single written document. Formal diplomatic papers only made sense in conversation with other kinds of text, like wampum; in fact, as Borrows demonstrates, comprehending these relationships, both in the eighteenth century and today, is only possible if they are framed by Indigenous understandings of diplomacy and its multiple sites and manifestations.[56] Talking to Campbell in an apparently tangential correspondence, and making poetry the subject and substance of that correspondence, did not, therefore, disqualify the encounter from being part of the diplomatic mission. In fact, in terms of Haudenosaunee-British relationships, these characteristics made it fundamentally diplomatic, as integral to the business at hand as any of the letters to Bathurst.

What the Campbell encounter also shared with those letters was a justified fixation on questions of exact words, supporting documentation, Joseph Brant's character and opinions, and the nature of the stories that were being accepted and transmitted as indisputably true in the transatlantic world. *Gertrude of Wyoming* manifested all the faults that Brant and Kerr identified in British colonial logic when they wrote to Lord Bathurst. Campbell appeared to trust sources whose information was completely contradicted, not only by the "documentary and living evidence" that Brant had emphasized in his correspondence with Bathurst and the poet, but also by numerous European and Euro-American authored texts. His poem had the power, through its popularity on both sides of the Atlantic, to create a dangerous and baseless version of Joseph Brant that undermined Haudenosaunee sovereignty. Its status as poetry was precisely what made it powerful; a memorable, quotable phrase like "the monster Brandt" entered popular consciousness far more readily than the exact words of the Haldimand proclamation. Brant's supposed violence and malevolence had been driven into the transatlantic mind by a song; it was operating diplomatically whether Campbell intended it to or not. This particular piece of verbatim language had to be changed, precisely because the Six Nations' case, and their long-standing alliance with the British more generally, rested on the firm belief that verbatim language was sacred.

The diplomatic significance of John Brant's engagement with Campbell in 1821 becomes even clearer when it is set alongside the often-overlooked point that he had already been involved in disputes

---

56. Borrows, "Wampum at Niagara."

about the poem at moments of political crisis. In May and June 1819, a Canadian periodical called the *Christian Recorder* had published a two-part biographical sketch of Joseph Brant by John Strachan, an adviser to Peregrine Maitland and an influential force in colonial Indigenous policy.[57] Although largely positive, Strachan's sketch maligned Brant's character and career, citing Campbell's poem as evidence that Brant was "one of the principal authors of the cruelties committed" at Wyoming, a point that was also insisted on in a new poem by Joseph McCoy, *The Frontier Maid*, which too appeared in 1819.[58] In March 1820, however, the *Christian Recorder* published the following clarification under the title "Capt. Joseph Brant":

> By a communication lately received from a near relative of this distinguished Chief, the Editor learns with regret, that the biographical sketch in the Recorder, has given offence to his family and friends.
>
> As it was intended to exalt rather than depress the character of the deceased, he begs leave to state, that the materials of the sketch were furnished him, many years ago, by a bosom friend of the late Captain Brant, who knew and loved him for more than forty years, and his motives for putting them in form, were two:
>
>> 1st. Mr. Campbell, the most eminent of the Poets of the present day, in a popular poem, had given a very inaccurate account of the expedition to Wyoming, in which he deeply implicates Capt. Brant. From this the Editor exonerates him by relating the true causes of that expedition.
>>
>> 2d. That from the reports of several religious Societies, it appeared that Captain Brant had been deprived of the honor, and not a small honor, of having translated a portion of the New Testament, and this the Editor likewise sets right.

---

57. I am grateful to the anonymous reviewer of my manuscript, who drew my attention to John Strachan's role in colonial governance in Upper Canada.

58. [John Strachan], "Life of Capt. Brant," *Christian Recorder*, June 1819, n.p.; Joseph J. McCoy, *The Frontier Maid: A Poem* (Wilkes-Barre, PA: Butler and Maffet, 1819).

Truth of History rendered some notice of his failings necessary, but these are touched slightly, and so far was the Editor from supposing that he had given offence to Capt. Brant's friends or relations, that he thought he merited their thanks.

He is however extremely sorry that any thing drawn up by him should have given a moment's uneasiness and the more so that any cause of offence should have been found in a work from which it has been anxiously sought to exclude any discussion that could involve private feeling.[59]

John Brant had apparently written to the *Christian Recorder* to dispute, not just the overall manner in which his father was being characterized, but also the specific depiction in Campbell's poem.[60]

The editor couches this response from the Brant family in personal terms by highlighting the "offence" and "uneasiness" that the biographical sketch had caused by intruding on "private feeling." However, as in the later case of John Brant's correspondence with Campbell, this matter of family honor was playing out in a far broader political and diplomatic arena. The sketch had appeared in the May and June 1819 issues of the *Christian Recorder*; in July 1819, Lieutenant Governor Peregrine Maitland's officials met with the Six Nations at a major council in Hamilton to discuss Maitland's controversial claim that they did not own the headwaters of the Grand River. This council was the first moment at which John Brant is recorded acting in an official diplomatic capacity. His uncle Henry (Tekarohoken) occupied one of the most significant roles in the Haudenosaunee leadership and spoke at this council.[61] Tekarohoken outlined the negotiations between the British and his people after the War of Independence, and he drew heavily on the significance of exact words and the documentation that supported them. At one point, he commented: "We are Surprised to find that Government says, that we own the Lands to the Falls only as we have Writings to prove otherwise. We have them here and are ready to produce them." The transcriber then

---

59. [John Strachan], "Capt. Joseph Brant," *Christian Recorder*, March 1820, n.p.

60. Isabel Thompson Kelsay identifies John Brant as the author of the letter to the *Christian Recorder*, based on evidence in Stone's biography (653), as does F. Douglas Reville in *History of the County of Brant* (Brantford, Ontario: Hurley Printing Company, 1920), 49. Stone appears to have had this confirmed by a Brant relation, William Johnson Kerr (2:523).

61. For detail about the role of the Tekarohoken, see Susan M. Hill, 36.

notes, "The Original Deed from General Haldimand Produced by John Brant."[62] The publication of a critical portrait of Joseph Brant in these three contentious months in 1819 had the potential to swing settler and colonial government support away from the Grand River Six Nations; indeed, it is possible that it was intended to do so.

One way in which John Brant manifested his increasingly significant political and diplomatic role within the Grand River leadership was to tackle the way his father's reputation was being construed, both in Campbell's poem and in the subsequent prose that it buttressed. His 1819 response to the poem has been overlooked in studies of the later encounter with Campbell or, where it has been discussed, has been seen simply as a dress rehearsal for that encounter.[63] But what the events of May–July 1819 show is that John Brant saw *Gertrude of Wyoming* as a piece of literary diplomacy, one that counted against his cause and needed to be addressed whenever he was called on to confront the British government at the council fire, whether in Upper Canada or in Great Britain.

"Restorying" *Gertrude of Wyoming*

We cannot know exactly what information or language was shared between Campbell and John Brant when they discussed *Gertrude of Wyoming* and the latter's father in late 1821. But we do have one rather remarkable source to draw on. Within weeks of corresponding with John Brant, Campbell published a long letter in the *New Monthly Magazine*.[64] In this

---

62. Charles M. Johnston, 68. Johnston identifies Tekarohoken (spelled Tekorihoga in the 1819 council notes) as John Brant, but that seems unlikely. In 1819, the title was still held by his uncle, although Brant would take it on in 1830 at Henry's death. Tekarohoken also appears to refer in his speech to being present at events before John Brant's birth. Moreover, it seems unusual that the transcriber would refer to Tekarohoken as "a Mohawk Chief" without naming him as "John Brant" and then positively identify Brant by name as the person who produced the copy of the Haldimand deed for the British colonial officials to see. The manuscript record of the meeting suggests that these are two different people; see Daniel Claus Papers, Public Archives Canada, MG11-F1, 11:203.

63. See, for example, Kelsay, 653–54.

64. Thomas Campbell, "Letter to the Mohawk Chief Ahyonwaeghs, Commonly Called John Brant, Esq. of the Grand River, Upper Canada, from Thomas Campbell," *New Monthly Magazine*, January 1822, 97–101. Subsequent page references are included in parentheses in the text.

letter, he issued a public apology to Brant for the depiction of his father, conceding that Joseph Brant was not at the Battle of Wyoming, nor did he deserve to be characterized as an especially bloodthirsty individual. But although Campbell accepted that he misrepresented Joseph Brant and appeared to wish to correct the record, his rhetoric and subsequent behavior undermined the reconciliation process in which he seemed to be participating.

I use the word *reconciliation* deliberately here because I want to suggest that one useful way to read the ongoing significance of the encounter between Brant and Campbell is through the lens of a modern Indigenous-settler diplomatic process: the Truth and Reconciliation framework set up in the settler colonies, including Canada. In their work on Canada's Truth and Reconciliation Commission, Jeff Corntassel, Chaw-win-is, and T'lakwadzi established two vital points about the structure of these arrangements. The first is that Truth and Reconciliation processes are controlled by white actors, by settler governments and judiciaries, and thus the forms they take and the responses they engender are often aimed at the political, social, and emotional needs of white participants. As Corntassel, Chaw-win-is, and T'lakwadzi point out,

> A convenient framing of the issue allows political leaders and settler populations to deal with residual guilt on their own terms, which often follows all too familiar scripts of "forgiving and forgetting," "moving on from the past," and "unifying as a country," all the while brushing aside any deeper discussions of restitution or justice. Reconciliation becomes a way for the dominant culture to reinscribe the status quo rather than to make amends for previous injustices.[65]

The second point I am drawing from Corntassel, Chaw-win-is, and T'lakwadzi's work is the need for "restorying" histories with ignored and marginalized truths, which need to replace dishonest historical narratives wherever they are embedded in local or national myths or curricula.[66] Brant's attempt to get Campbell to restory *Gertrude of Wyoming* is part

---

65. Jeff Corntassel, Chaw-win-is, and T'lakwadzi, "Indigenous Storytelling, Truth-telling, and Community Approaches to Reconciliation," *English Studies in Canada* 35, no. 1 (2009): 137–59; 144.

66. Corntassel, Chaw-win-is, and T'lakwadzi, 139.

of a longer conversation between settler and Indigenous populations that is still influential today.

The principal strategy in Campbell's letter of apology is to deflect the blame. He presents himself as a victim of his own scholarly sources, informing John Brant that "with regard to your father's character I took it as I found it in popular history" (97). Indeed, Campbell suggests that there is a degree of unfairness in holding him to account for the portrayal, given the nature of his sources:

> Judge how naturally I adopted accusations against him [Joseph Brant] which had stood in the Annual Register of 1779, as far as I knew, uncontradicted for thirty years. A number of authors had repeated them with a confidence which beguiled at last my suspicion, and I believe that of the public at large. Among those authors were Gordon, Ramsay, Marshall, Belsham, and Weld. (97)

He then goes on to quote from John Adolphus's description of Brant, before declaring:

> When your Canadian friends, therefore, call me to trial for having defamed the warrior Brant, I beg that Mr. John Adolphus may be also included in the summons. And after his own defence and acquittal, I think he is bound, having been one of my historical misleaders, to stand up as my gratuitous counsel, and say "Gentlemen, *you must acquit my client, for he has only fallen into an error, which even my judgment could not escape.*" (98; italics in the original)

Reading these explanations through the lens provided by Corntassel, Chaw-win-is, and T'lakwadzi demonstrates how invested Campbell is in casting himself as a wronged party, allied with the Brants against a history of faulty scholarship and storytelling. The process of testimony, judgment, and, he hopes, acquittal that he envisages imagines a justice system that weighs up the value of stories but is ultimately forgiving in its treatment of white offenders in the storytelling realm, allowing ignorance, error, and the weight of extant scholarship as mitigating circumstances. In other words, Campbell conjures into being the sort of Truth and Reconciliation processes that the twenty-first-century settler colonies have established, in which settler justice systems, in the form of courts, commissions of enquiry, and hearings, delve into storytelling in order, Corntassel, Chaw-win-is, and T'lakwadzi suggest, "to deal with residual guilt on their own terms." Campbell can be absolved, he believes, by engaging with a Truth and Reconciliation process that he is fairly certain will absolve him.

Campbell's rejection of his sources here stands in sharp contrast to how they are depicted in the poem itself. He had equipped *Gertrude of Wyoming* with nearly thirty pages of very detailed source notes, which are designed to explain the references to American flora, fauna, and society, including Indigenous society. These notes, including those documenting Indigenous diplomatic processes that I cited earlier, provide bibliographic references to secondary works where Campbell had found his information, in order to establish the veracity of the picture he was painting.[67] He had, in fact, met Joseph Brant's adopted nephew John Norton when Norton came to England in 1804–1805, and perhaps again in 1816, so he was in the rather remarkable position of having engaged closely with the Grand River Six Nations people and their diplomatic efforts on more than one occasion.[68] The original note about Joseph Brant contributed to the effect of apparent historical detail. Campbell informed his readers that "This Brandt was a warrior of the Mohawk nation, who was engaged to allure by bribes, or to force by threats, many Indian tribes to the expedition against Pennsylvania. His blood, I believe, was not purely Indian, but half German. He disgraced, however, his European descent by more than savage ferocity" (74). In later editions of *Gertrude of Wyoming*, after hearing from John Brant, Campbell replaced that note with this one:

> I took the character of Brandt, in the poem of Gertrude, from the common histories of England, all of which represented

---

67. See Julia Hansen's reading of the notes in her essay, "Viewless Scenes: Vividness and Nineteenth-Century Ideals of Reading in and through *Gertrude of Wyoming*," *ELH* 84, no. 4 (2017): 943–77.

68. For Campbell's account of meeting Norton in 1805, see William Beattie, *Life and Letters of Thomas Campbell*, 3 vols. (London: Moxon, 1849), 1:479–80, 2:51. In 1816, a friend invited Campbell to dine with Norton. Beattie suggests that this meeting occurred and that Norton raised the question of the depiction of Joseph Brant with Campbell at that time, but there is no evidence to support this idea and it contradicts Campbell's 1822 letter to John Brant, which suggests that he had not previously been made aware of the mischaracterization; see Beattie, 2:325n.

him as a bloody and bad man—even among savages—and chief agent in the horrible desolation of Wyoming. Some years after this poem appeared, the son of Brandt, a most interesting and intelligent youth, came over to England, and I formed an acquaintance with him, on which I still look back with pleasure. He appealed to my sense of honour and justice on his own part, and on that of his sister, to retract the unfair aspersions, which, unconscious of their unfairness, I had cast on his father's memory. He then referred me to documents which completely satisfied me that the common accounts of Brandt's cruelties at Wyoming were gross errors; and that, in point of fact, Brandt was not even present at that scene of desolation. . . . Had I known this when I was writing my poem, Brandt should not have figured in it as the hero of mischief. It is but bare justice to say thus much of a Mohawk Indian, who spoke English eloquently, and was thought capable of writing a history of the Six Nations. I ascertained, also, that *he often strove to mitigate the cruelty of Indian warfare. The name of* BRANDT, *therefore, remains in my poem as a pure and declared character of fiction.* (352–53; emphasis in the original)

Nothing about the verses themselves was changed in these later editions; this note simply replaced the earlier note. William Beattie, a close friend of the poet's and the author of *Life and Letters of Thomas Campbell*, said that this note was included in "every subsequent edition," but even that is not correct: the first edition to feature the revised note appeared in 1828, seven years after the encounter between Brant and Campbell, during which at least one edition of the poem was published with the original note in place.[69]

Beattie asks the obvious question here: "why, after so frank an apology, . . . did [Campbell] suffer the *name* to remain in the text?" Campbell's answer, according to Beattie, was that "its suppression would have involved him in the necessity of reconstructing several stanzas; and if the reason

---

69. Beattie, 2:186. The original note was still present in the 1825 edition of the poem, after having also been included in the 1822 edition; see Thomas Campbell, *Gertrude of Wyoming, and Other Poems*, 9th ed. (London: Longman, Hurst, Rees, Orme, Brown, and Greene, 1825), 74–75.

was but indifferent, the *rhyme* was good."[70] The work of rewriting the poem, of restorying the story that it tells, is classified by Campbell as a step too far, simply too much to ask of him as a writer. "Brandt" was, for Campbell, a legible figure for his readers, a kind of symbol of Indigenous peoples rather than an identifiable person. Moreover, the aesthetics of the poem—the fact that the name "Brandt" fortuitously but rather weakly rhymes with "land" and "hand"—is seen as the ultimate value worth protecting, ahead of justice, ahead of truth, and certainly ahead of reconciliation. Campbell had indicated in his 1822 letter to John Brant a certain squeamishness about altering the verse; he refers a couple of times to a division between what he names "false delicacy" and "a sense of honour and justice," and he expressed a particular concern that such false delicacy "would degrade poetry itself if it was adopted" (99–100). Campbell believed, as he stated several times both in the letter and in the revised note to *Gertrude*, that honor and justice had been served by his public acknowledgment that Joseph Brant was not at the Battle of Wyoming and was not the monster he was made out to be in the poem. What Campbell would not concede to, however, was any actual restorying, any retelling of the story itself, the literary form that the story had taken in his poem.

If my critique of Campbell feels like the zealous judgment of the twenty-first-century scholar, I refer you to two nineteenth-century comments. One is from Barry Lancaster, who wrote an article about the events in the Wyoming Valley for the *Allegheny Mail* in 1849. The article opened with the epigraph "the mammoth comes—the foe—the monster Brandt," before proceeding to tell the story of John Brant's visit to England and Campbell's apology. As Lancaster commented, "Every reader is aware that in an interesting, imaginative and highly wrought poem, not one reader in a thousand would perceive a note, or, if they did, would pay but very little attention to it. This is the amount of justice rendered by Campbell to the surviving members of the Brant family."[71] This connection between

---

70. Beattie, 2:185–86, emphasis in the original. See also the exculpatory account given by Cyrus Redding, a friend and fellow editor of Campbell's, in *Literary Reminiscences and Memoirs of Thomas Campbell*, 2 vols. (London: Charles J. Skeet, 1860), 1:95–96, 1:287–89.

71. Barry Lancaster, "Goh-Soh-Gwa-Go, The Indian Commander at Wyoming," *Allegheny Mail*, July 10, 1849. There are many other similar nineteenth-century condemnations of Thomas Campbell's decision to leave the poem untouched. See, for example, the remarks by Anna Jameson, who published an account of her travels in Ontario in the 1830s.

the poem and justice is echoed in an even more telling remark from an anonymous article in an American publication in 1853, in which the author wrote of *Gertrude of Wyoming* and Campbell's decision making concerning the depiction of Brant:

> The world reads the poem, but a few, comparatively, refer to the *prose* of an appendix. This is the misfortune of a correction, thus partially made, and did it not have, in its unfairness, an unbroken series of precedents in its favor, gathered from the white man's intercourse with the Iroquois, it might be a subject of astonishment. Like the Poet's good intentions, our best efforts to do them justice now, are but limited and feeble—a brief, and perhaps, unread appendix to justice to a massive volume of wrong.[72]

The author of this second comment correctly intuits several important points: the hierarchy of different parts of a book and indeed of the literary world; the connection between literal writing and the figurative "volume" of injustice in settler-Indigenous relationships; and the way in which a point as small as the correction of a note in the appendix of a minor poem by someone we would now consider to be a minor author is connected to that "unbroken series of precedents" that leads backward and forward through time to colonization, injustice, the dispossession of land, and the disenfranchisement of people.

It is this "unbroken series of precedents" that makes Campbell's decisions about revising the poem so significant. Julia Hansen has pointed

---

Jameson visited Grand River and heard stories of Joseph Brant. As Jameson wrote: "He is the Brandt whom Campbell has handed down to most undeserved execration as the leader in the massacre at Wyoming. The poet indeed tells us, in the notes to Gertrude of Wyoming, that all he has said against Brandt must be considered as pure fiction, 'for that he was remarkable for his humanity, and not even present at the massacre;' but the name stands in the text as heretofore, apostrophised as the 'accursed Brandt,' the 'monster Brandt;' and is not this most unfair, to be hitched into elegant and popular rhyme as an assassin by wholesale, and justice done in a little fag-end of prose?" Anna Jameson, *Winter Studies and Summer Rambles in Canada*, 3 vols. (London: Saunders and Otley, 1838), 2:106. An Indigenous-authored text from slightly later makes a similar point; see Ke-Che-Ha-Gah-Me-Qua, *Sketch of the Life of Captain Joseph Brant, Thayendanagea* (Montreal: John Dougall, 1873).

72. Anon., *The Saint Nicolas*, 1.4 (July 1853): 126; emphasis in the original.

out the tension between the poem and its notes, remarking that Campbell insists on "an ontological distinction (two Brants exist, one in the poem and one outside the poem), not the ontological priority the Brant family requested and which we as twenty-first century readers expect."[73] But restricting our condemnation to Campbell's privileging of aesthetics and poetic effect risks overlooking the very real political consequences of the ontological distinction on which he insists. It is more than simply distasteful, racist, or unjustified. Joseph Brant's reputation was itself a key factor in the land claim that John Brant had come to England to establish: if one believed that Joseph Brant was an honorable man, it reinforced the need for the British to meet their obligations to the Grand River Six Nations and settle the boundary fairly, since he was a key figure in the original negotiations that led to the Haldimand proclamation and their immediate aftermath and featured heavily in the correspondence between Lord Bathurst and John Brant and Robert Johnson Kerr.[74] If he was, instead, simply the "Monster Brandt," the Six Nations' case was much more easily dismissed on the grounds of generic racist notions of savagery, but also via the logic that Joseph Brant could not be considered an honorable party to the original Haldimand agreement. Joseph Brant was, as Elbourne has suggested, the author of "a theory of Mohawk sovereignty" that was being articulated and embodied by his son and disputed by the Colonial Office in London at just the moment when Campbell made these authorial decisions.[75]

Hansen has pointed out "the strange investments Americans made in a poem they understood to be wrong."[76] But the British had even stronger reasons for investing in Campbell's poem and its errors. The poem had already fixed Brant's character in English minds since its publication in 1809, in ways that had the potential to shape political decisions as Peregrine Maitland and John Brant continued their transatlantic argument a decade later. For example, the portrait that had appeared in the *Christian Recorder* in 1819, which John Brant had disputed, was reprinted without

---

73. Hansen, 964.

74. Haldimand's papers make it clear how central Joseph Brant was to the arrangements that were ultimately included in the Haldimand Proclamation; see, for example, the correspondence between Haldimand and other officials in Charles M. Johnston, 41–52.

75. Elbourne, 499.

76. Hansen, 967.

correction in the 1820 publication *A Visit to the Province of Upper Canada, in 1819*, a book usually attributed to James Strachan but possibly authored by his brother John, who had penned the original sketch.[77] Meanwhile, in Francis Hall's 1818 account of a visit to Grand River, during which he met John Brant, he remarks that the Haudenosaunee had come to Canada "under their chieftain, 'the Monster Brandt.'"[78] Although Hall's account of Joseph Brant is more nuanced than his use of this phrase suggests and although he had a good relationship with John Brant, he nevertheless defaults to Campbell's epithet. Strachan's and Hall's accounts reached readers in Britain and North America at the same moment that British officials in London and Upper Canada were accepting Maitland's interpretation of the Haldimand agreement, and thus Campbell's recirculated phrasing had the potential to influence public opinion on the Grand River matter.[79] This point about the currency of the phrase was recognized by John Brant's British allies; while Brant was in London in early 1822, Robert Gourlay published a statistical account of Upper Canada that noted:

> It is worthy of record, that [Joseph Brant] was not even present at the destruction of Wyoming, as fancied by Mr. Campbell, in his beautiful poem of GERTRUDE OF WYOMING. Several respectable persons are still alive, in Upper Canada, who can testify as to this; and it would be well if Mr. Campbell, in his next edition, would note this, to correct wrong impressions, which his poetical license, in speaking of "the monster Brandt," may create.[80]

---

77. James Strachan, *A Visit to the Province of Upper Canada, in 1819* (Aberdeen: D. Chalmers for J. Strachan, 1820), 149–68. I am grateful to the anonymous reviewer of my manuscript who pointed out John Strachan's role in this 1820 publication.

78. Francis Hall, *Travels in Canada, and the United States, in 1816 and 1817* (London: Longman, Hurst, Rees, Orme, and Brown, 1818), 221. The publishers Wells and Lilly published an edition of Hall's book in Boston in 1818.

79. Kevin Hutchings makes a more general point about the possibility that Campbell's poem shaped public understandings of Native Americans but does not link this to the specific political and diplomatic contexts facing the Grand River Haudenosaunee in the late Regency period; see *Romantic Ecologies*, 153.

80. Robert Gourlay, *General Introduction to Statistical Account of Upper Canada, Compiled with a View of a Grand System of Emigration, in Connexion with a Reform of the Poor Laws* (London: Simpkin and Marshall, 1822), ccv. The phrase remained in literary circulation

Correcting these lines of poetry was not just an aesthetic question, nor even a question of family honor, but rather a question of international diplomacy and Indigenous land rights. The relationship between poetic lines and boundary lines could not have been clearer.

The Campbell-Brant encounter can be profitably read as an early example of the unrealized potential of the restorying process for which Corntassel, Chaw-win-is, and T'lakwadzi advocate. The poem, the events it describes, the events that it leads to, all need to be restoryed, not for their own sake but in order to achieve actual truth and reconciliation. Moreover, achieving truth and reconciliation is not an end in itself, however much settler governments and the colonial governments they replaced would like to believe so; as Corntassel, Chaw-win-is, and T'lakwadzi put it, "Indigenous restorying processes cannot be disentangled from ongoing relationships to their homelands."[81] There are two key points here: in the Truth and Reconciliation context, stories are *always* about land, and they are *always* about ongoing relationships. They are also critical to conflict resolution; as Jill Scott and Alana Fletcher have argued in their discussion of the Canadian Truth and Reconciliation process, a more successful methodology for managing conflict would incorporate "creative means of integrating Indigenous practices and traditions, including Indigenous languages, rituals and ceremonies, storytelling, and peacebuilding traditions," while a Haudenosaunee-specific methodology would highlight "the ways in which storytelling is seamlessly integrated into the materiality of symbolic instruments, sacred traditions, and artistic expression, and how all of these are inseparable from systems of governance, law, and medicine, and from sacred traditions."[82] Campbell might have thought of his "monster Brandt" as an individual, a virtual fiction, a character from the past, but for John Brant and the Grand River Six Nations, the poem inhabited a discourse of land rights, treaty rights, and ongoing relationships. It needed restorying the same way the Haldimand proclamation needed restorying.

---

in later years too; see, for example, the use of "the monster Brandt" in the fictionalized account of the battle in James M'Henry, *The Betrothed of Wyoming: An Historical Tale*, 3rd ed. (Philadelphia, n.p., 1830), 199.

81. Corntassel, Chaw-win-is, and T'lakwadzi, 147.

82. Jill Scott and Alana Fletcher, "Polishing the Chain: Haudenosaunee Peacebuilding and Nation-Specific Frameworks of Redress," in *Arts of Engagement: Taking Aesthetic Action In and Beyond the Truth and Reconciliation Commission of Canada*, ed. Dylan Robinson and Keavy Martin, 157–79; 158, 170 (Waterloo: Wilfrid Laurier University Press, 2016).

From Campbell to Caledonia, from London to Land Back Lane

John Brant's diplomatic mission was ultimately a failure, and his appeals for diplomatic restorying, via poems and proclamations, did not secure the full extent of the promised Grand River lands for the Six Nations in the long term. The relationship between the British and their Native allies had changed significantly in the period after the War of 1812; Elbourne points out that John Brant's visit to England represented the last showing for a particular kind of Indigenous diplomacy, one that could rely on long-standing social bonds between Native leaders and their European counterparts.[83] By 1821–1822, the British no longer saw their Haudenosaunee allies as a powerful force in global diplomacy. Campbell's apparently courteous but superficial response to Brant was in keeping with a wider culture of dismissive British reactions to Indigenous diplomats at this time. Brant himself became the colonial government's superintendent of Indian Affairs in Upper Canada in 1828, and then Tekarohoken in 1830, following his uncle Henry's death. He continued to order surveys of the Six Nations' land and to talk about the injustice of the government's conduct to visiting Europeans and settlers, just as his father had done, in order to assert the rights promised in the Haldimand proclamation.[84] In 1830, he also became the first Indigenous person to be elected to the Upper Canada House of Assembly after he won election in the riding of Haldimand, before being stripped of his office after a complaint about the electoral process. Brant died in a cholera outbreak in 1832 at the age of thirty-eight, leaving Grand River without the benefit of his considerable leadership experience.[85] Settler encroachments on Six Nations'

---

83. Elbourne, 501. A detailed study of the Haudenosaunee contribution to the British cause in the War of 1812, including the military roles played by John Brant and John Norton, can be found in Carl Benn, *The Iroquois in the War of 1812* (Toronto: University of Toronto Press, 1998). Benn makes the same point as Elbourne about the collapse of Haudenosaunee influence with the British after 1815.

84. See, for example, "Diary of Survey of the Indian Surrender in the District of Niagara. Surveyed by order of John Brant, Esquire, Superintendent of the Six Nations Indians," 1831, Archives of Ontario MS 924, RG1-59; and John West, *A Journal of a Mission to the Indians of the British Provinces, of New Brunswick, and Nova Scotia, and the Mohawks, on the Ouse, or Grand River, Upper Canada* (London: L. B. Seeley, 1827), 275–76.

85. Cecilia Morgan, "Site of Dispossession, Site of Persistence: The Haudenosaunee (Six Nations) at the Grand River Territories in the Nineteenth and Twentieth Centuries,"

land continued throughout the nineteenth and twentieth centuries and still continue today; in the twenty-first century, the Six Nations territory in southern Ontario is a tiny fraction of the land promised to them by the Haldimand proclamation.

The power of Haldimand's exact words, and of Joseph Brant's reputation, continues to shape Six Nations communication; official documents on the Six Nations' website prominently display quotations from the Haldimand proclamation, and one, "Six Miles Deep: Land Rights of the Six Nations of the Grand River," features portraits of Governor Haldimand and Joseph Brant.[86] At the fourteenth session of the United Nations Permanent Forum on Indigenous Issues in 2015, Elected Chief G. Ava Hill quoted the Haldimand proclamation again to a global audience: "We are left with less than 5% of our land holdings promised us 'which Them and Their Posterity are to enjoy forever.'"[87] Hill repeated the phrase twice more in her address, once in the context of a formal recommendation that "Canada must be prepared to discuss a resolution based on the terms of our 1784 Haldimand Treaty as granted Six Nations '. . . which them and Their Posterity are to enjoy forever.' Canada must commit to long term arrangements honouring these terms."[88] In July

---

in *Indigenous Communities and Settler Colonialism: Land Holding, Loss and Survival in an Interconnected World*, ed. Zoë Laidlaw and Alan Lester, 194–213; 204–5 (Basingstoke: Palgrave, 2015). In a telling but cruel footnote to his life story, John Brant was himself posthumously fictionalized and defamed as "Captain B—" in an 1835 story by James Hall, which drew on some of the stereotypes that had informed Campbell's poetic version of his father. Steeped in racist typologies, and contrary to all evidence about John Brant, "Captain B—" is depicted as a violent drunk, someone "whose sinister and callous features wore an expression that was anything but attractive. The ferocity of the savage was strongly marked upon his visage, blended with the cunning which is always a characteristic trait in the Indian deportment." See J[ames] H[all], "A Reminiscence," *Knickerbocker* 6 (1835): 13–14.

86. "Six Miles Deep: Land Rights of the Six Nations of the Grand River," http://www.sixnations.ca/SixMilesDeepBooklet2015Final.pdf; see also "Land Rights: A Global Solution," http://www.sixnations.ca/SNGlobalSolutionsBookletFinal.pdf; and "Six Nations of the Grand River: Land Rights, Financial Justice, Resolutions," http://www.sixnations.ca/SNLands&ResourcesBooklet2015Final.pdf.

87. Chief G. Ava Hill, "Six Nations Council: United Nations Fourteenth Session of the Permanent Forum on Indigenous Issues," http://www.sixnations.ca/UnitedNationsApril2015PresentationChiefHill.pdf, 1.

88. Chief G. Ava Hill, 3.

2020, Six Nations protestors began an ongoing occupation of the site of a proposed housing development on their territory, naming the site "1492 Land Back Lane" and referring once more to the exact terms and language of the Haldimand Proclamation. As Audra Simpson noted in a ground-breaking study of Mohawk sovereignty across international boundaries, the Haudenosaunee carry with them the overlapping diplomatic traditions of the Great Law of Peace, the Two Row Wampum, and the various international treaties to which they are a party or by which they are affected, "emphasizing these historical and *intended* meanings of these forms of recognition with them in their day-to-day lives."[89]

Although Joseph Brant is now a widely admired figure in Canadian history and the focus of a range of public commemorations in southern Ontario, Campbell's poetic image of "the monster Brandt" is also still consequential in Indigenous-settler relations in Canada. In 2006, Six Nations residents occupied a site in the southern Ontario town of Caledonia, in protest at a development on land covered by the Haldimand proclamation. As Laura DeVries has pointed out, while the settler public regarded the protest as one that emerged without warning, the Six Nations community saw their actions as part of the history that stretched back to the agreement reached by Joseph Brant and Governor Haldimand.[90] In the bitter public argument that ensued, much of the commentary perpetuated the racist narrative of violent, unjust, and unprovoked action by the Six Nations. This narrative had also been reinforced in an earlier, more famous encounter between settler governments and another group of Mohawks: the 1990 Oka Crisis in Quebec. In her work on Oka, Gail Guthrie Valaskakis has commented that "in all the media coverage, one image emerged as salient: the image of the 'warriors'—bandana-masked, khaki-clad, gun-toting Indians. . . . With few exceptions, the media's warriors were monolithic representations of Indian militants: the military

---

89. Audra Simpson, *Mohawk Interruptus: Political Life across the Borders of Settler States* (Durham, NC: Duke University Press, 2014), 32; emphasis in the original.

90. Laura DeVries, *Conflict in Caledonia: Aboriginal Land Rights and the Rule of Law* (Vancouver: University of British Columbia Press, 2011), 30. See also the discussion in Timothy C. Winegard, "Your Home on Native Land? Conflict and Controversy at Caledonia and the Six Nations of the Grand River," in *Blockades or Breakthroughs? Aboriginal Peoples Confront the Canadian State*, ed. Yale D. Belanger and P. Whitney Lackenbauer, 411–44 (Montreal: McGill-Queen's University Press, 2014).

masculine, criminalized through association with terrorism."[91] Some of the same imagery can be inferred from an October 2020 Ontario Superior Court of Justice ruling against the land defender and Six Nations spokesperson Skyler Williams, in which Justice R. J. Harper wrote that Williams and other land defenders "have shown nothing but a willingness to resort to violence and destruction in order to achieve their goals."[92] This imagery is a modern projection, for the television and internet age, of a long-standing racist representation of Haudenosaunee masculinity as violent and monstrous, a representation that Campbell contributed to and failed to correct at a moment in which it might have made a significant difference.

Did Campbell feel that his letter and his correction of the note were sufficient? The answer is probably yes, as Beattie's comments about the need to preserve the rhyme would suggest. I am intrigued, however, by a notation Campbell appears to have made in his own copy of the 1839 edition of his *Poetical Works*.[93] At the end of the two stanzas in which Outalissi rages against "the Monster Brandt," there is a small cross penciled in the margin. At the back of the volume, next to the revised note published after Campbell engaged with John Brant, which is set out across a two-column page, there are three penciled asterisks: one at the start of the note, one at the bottom of the first column next to the first reference to the *New Monthly Magazine* letter, and one at the top of the second column. In other places in this copy of the *Poetical Works*, Campbell includes similar notations but they are accompanied by penciled notes that explain why he is highlighting a particular moment. The Brant references are not explicated any further; the cross and the asterisks simply stand as mute witnesses to some sort of authorial thought process, perhaps one that was not intended for other eyes. Do they signify some ongoing uncertainty on Campbell's part about his actions? Or perhaps the complete opposite: could they be a reminder to himself, and perhaps to anyone who cared to look at this particular copy of his work, that he had attempted to make amends? Maybe they constitute a settler-imperial version of Scott Richard Lyons's notion of the x-mark, a sign of the

---

91. Gail Guthrie Valaskakis, *Indian Country: Essays on Contemporary Native Culture* (Waterloo: Wilfrid Laurier University Press, 2006), 39.

92. *Foxgate Developments Inc. v. Doe* et al., 2020 ONSC 6529 (CanLII), http://canlii.ca/t/jb9rh.

93. This copy is held at the Beinecke Library at Yale University, among Campbell's personal papers (Thomas Campbell Papers, OSB MSS 106, Box 2, Folder 15).

deeply entangled worlds of European genres and texts with Indigenous peoples and writings.[94]

My final question, then, to settlers, and especially to settler-scholars in literary studies, is this: At what price our aesthetics? What kind of world do we uphold when we say that lines of poetry must not be changed but lines in a proclamation, in a treaty, or on a map are indefinitely editable? Campbell defended poetic license, not simply as an explanation of his original error, but also as a justification for an ongoing failure to redress that error fully, at the same time as he attempted to portray himself as the victim of just such a failure of sources, of fact checking, of scruples concerning written accounts. It seems to me that our work in English literary studies, including Romantic studies, is often engaged in a similar process, which expresses explicit sorrow and shame about past injustices while simultaneously upholding European aesthetics at all costs. Citations favor the sources that we know and that we feel we can access easily, even when they are shown to be flawed. The people about whom we sometimes write, and about whom the Romantics certainly wrote, are assumed to be virtually fictional and certainly not agents to whom one can be accountable; one of the remarks Campbell makes in his letter, a remark that Kate Flint has rightly called the "crux" of the matter, is "I really knew not, when I wrote my poem, that the son and daughter of an Indian chief were ever likely to peruse it, or be affected by its contents" (97).[95] John Brant's interaction with Thomas Campbell might mark, for our field, an important germinal moment, in which Indigenous people came face to face with Romanticism, its authors, and its champions and asked for *actual* truth and reconciliation.

---

94. Scott Richard Lyons, *X-Marks: Native Signatures of Assent* (Minneapolis: University of Minnesota Press, 2010).

95. Flint, 51.

Chapter 2

Romanticism and Removal

Elias Boudinot, Felicia Hemans, and the *Cherokee Phoenix*

When the editor of the first Native American newspaper wanted some apt poetry for his pages, he turned to British Romanticism. The bilingual *Cherokee Phoenix*, which began publication in Georgia in 1828, included English poems on the back page of virtually every issue. A range of popular British and American poets thus were featured in the weekly paper, but one showed up over and over again. Between 1828 and 1831, sixteen poems by Felicia Hemans were chosen for publication by the *Phoenix*'s editor, Elias Boudinot, making Hemans the most prolific poet in the newspaper by a significant margin.

John Brant and the Six Nations had used the exact words of a British Romantic poem as part of their campaign in the late 1810s and early 1820s for honesty and accountability concerning past agreements. A decade later, a new approach to Indigenous deployments of Romantic verse emerged in a very different site and moment. This approach did not focus so much on truth and reconciliation as on related but distinct terms: sincerity and sympathy. It did, however, continue the process of linking Romanticism to Indigenous-settler diplomacy and assuming that the words contained in Romantic poems could serve a political purpose in reminding settler governments and publics about their own purported values.

Like all the diplomats and thinkers that this book considers, Elias Boudinot is a complex figure in his people's history, someone whose legacy is still divisive in the twenty-first century. Born Galagina, he became known by the Anglicized name Buck Watie before adopting the name of the American politician and philanthropist Elias Boudinot, with whom he had stayed on his way to the Foreign Mission School in Cornwall, Connecticut. Educated there and at the Moravian Mission School in Spring Place, Georgia, Boudinot is often read as thoroughly assimilated and colonized, one of a generation of Cherokee leaders who argued for their rights on the basis of their people's "civilized" way of life.[1] As editor of the *Cherokee Phoenix*, Boudinot argued forcefully against Cherokee removal before becoming convinced that it was an inevitability, following the passage of the 1830 Removal Act and President Andrew Jackson's decision to ignore the Supreme Court's findings in *Cherokee Nation v. Georgia* (1831) and *Worcester v. Georgia* (1832), both of which provided some endorsement of Cherokee sovereignty.[2] Boudinot resigned as editor of the *Cherokee Phoenix* in August 1832, having lost the support of the Cherokee National Council leadership over his acceptance of the case for removal. As one of what became known as the Treaty Party, Boudinot signed the 1835 Treaty of New Echota, an act of defiance against the National Council for which he was assassinated in 1839, probably in

---

1. This reading of Boudinot is especially prominent in Theda Perdue, ed., *Cherokee Editor: The Writings of Elias Boudinot* (Knoxville: University of Tennessee Press, 1983), although a sympathetic version of it can also be found in Jace Weaver, *That the People Might Live: Native American Literatures and Native American Community* (Oxford: Oxford University Press, 1997), 70–73, and in Bernd C. Peyer, *The Tutor'd Mind: Indian Missionary-Writers in Antebellum America* (Amherst: University of Massachusetts Press, 1997), 166–223. Theresa Strouth Gaul provides one of a number of important correctives to this interpretation of Boudinot's conduct and attitude in "Editing as Indian Performance: Elias Boudinot, Poetry, and the Cherokee Phoenix," in *Native Acts: Indian Performance, 1603–1832*, ed. Joshua David Bellin and Laura L. Miekle, 281–307 (Lincoln: University of Nebraska Press, 2011), as do Rose Gubele, "Unlearning the Pictures in Our Heads: Teaching The Cherokee Phoenix, Boudinot, and Cherokee History," in *Survivance, Sovereignty, and Story: Teaching American Indian Rhetorics*, ed. Lisa King, Rose Gubele and Joyce Rain Anderson, 96–115 (Boulder: University Press of Colorado, 2015); Gregory D. Smithers, *The Cherokee Diaspora: An Indigenous History of Migration, Resettlement, and Identity* (New Haven, CT: Yale University Press, 2015), 88–90; and Phillip H. Round, *Removable Type: Histories of the Book in Indian Country, 1663–1880* (Chapel Hill: University of North Carolina Press, 2010), 123–49.

2. For details of the Supreme Court cases, see Jill Norgren, *The Cherokee Cases: The Confrontation of Law and Politics* (New York: McGraw-Hill, 1996); Ronald A. Berutti, "The Cherokee Cases: The Fight to Save the Supreme Court and the Cherokee Indians," *American Indian Law Review* 17.1 (1992): 291–308; Clifford M. Lytle, "The Supreme Country, Tribal Sovereignty, and Continuing Problems of State Encroachment into Indian Country," *American Indian Law Review* 8.1 (1980): 65–77; Joseph C. Burke, "The Cherokee Cases: A Study in Law, Politics, and Morality," *Stanford Law Review* 21.3 (1969): 500–531.

accordance with a Cherokee law that forbade anyone to make a treaty without the expressed consent of the council.[3] By the time of his death, the genocidal effects of the 1830 Removal Act were being felt across the southeastern United States and beyond as the Cherokees and other nations were forced west of the Mississippi in the catastrophic journey now referred to in English as the Trail of Tears.

The *Cherokee Phoenix* sat at the center of Cherokee diplomatic efforts in the late 1820s and early 1830s. As Theresa Strouth Gaul has argued, the English poetry in the *Phoenix* was not filler; rather, it served a vital role in communicating the Cherokees' views to Euro-American readers, operating alongside coverage of the events of the late 1820s and early 1830s and thus transforming into a commentary on those events.[4] Gaul points out the general thematic overlaps between the poetry in the paper and the perilous situation of the Cherokees. But within this framework, Hemans serves a particular purpose that deserves further attention. Her prominence in the *Phoenix* suggests Boudinot's sustained intellectual engagement with her ideas and preoccupations, an engagement enhanced by the anti-Removal rhetoric of the newspaper and the texts produced by that rhetoric. A closer examination of Hemans's poems alongside the political content of the newspaper reveals the specific, immediate, and developing ways in which Boudinot sought to align Cherokee diplomatic rhetoric and practices with Romanticism's values, tropes, and forms, and vice versa. In Hemans's work, despite the fact that some of her poems reproduced racist colonial notions of the virtues of appropriating Indigenous land, the Cherokees nevertheless had a powerful repository of English text centered on sincerity, sympathy, women's voices, and the potentially fraught concept of a "home."

Newspaper Diplomacy

Boudinot and the Cherokees of his generation were responding to a long history of diplomatic engagement with European and American powers. Throughout the seventeenth and eighteenth centuries, the Cherokees had negotiated with the imperial forces of Spain, France, and Britain, most

---

3. Rachel Caroline Eaton, *John Ross and the Cherokee Indians* (New York: AMS Press, 1921), 29; see also Colin G. Calloway, *Pen and Ink Witchcraft: Treaties and Treaty Making in American Indian History* (Oxford: Oxford University Press, 2013), 121–63.

4. Gaul, "Editing as Indian Performance," 285–88.

conspicuously in the 1730 Cherokee embassy to London.[5] A bewildering array of overlapping treaties was signed in this period, all of which contributed to the loss of Cherokee land, as pressure from encroaching settlers increased.[6] Following the American War of Independence, the Cherokee leaders signed the Treaty of Long Island at Holston (1777) with treaty commissioners from Virginia and North Carolina, in an attempt to fix permanent boundaries between their own land and white settlements. In 1785, the Cherokees negotiated for the first time with the new American government, signing the Treaty of Hopewell to build a diplomatic relationship with a national powerbroker that they believed would restrain the southeastern states and territories, whose encroachments on the 1777 treaty boundaries had gone unpunished by settler governments. Following a spate of settler violence, another treaty was signed at Holston in 1791, again attempting to set boundaries for the Cherokees' land and jurisdiction and to establish annuity payments for their ceded territory. But the failure of any of these treaties to protect their autonomy or lands led to further violence and a period of protracted disunity among the Cherokees from 1794 onward. In 1802, the year Boudinot was born, Thomas Jefferson composed what came to be known as the Georgia Compact, a document that established Native removal, couched in disingenuously peaceful and voluntary terms, as official government policy, which signaled to the white residents of Georgia and the Southeast that they would soon have access to Native land.

---

5. A useful overview of the diplomatic contact between the Cherokees and Europe can be found in Robert J. Conley, *The Cherokee Nation: A History* (Albuquerque: University of New Mexico Press, 2005), 17–94. The Cherokee embassy to London is discussed in Leonard J. Sadosky, *Revolutionary Negotiations: Indians, Empires, and Diplomats in the Founding of America* (Charlottesville" University of Virginia Press, 2009), 24–28; Coll Thrush, *Indigenous London: Native Travelers at the Heart of Empire* (New Haven, CT: Yale University Press, 2016), 82–94; and Ian Chambers, "The Empire Visits the Metropolis: The Red Atlantic, Spatial Habitus and the Cherokee," *Atlantic Studies* 12.1 (2015): 67–89. Eighteenth-century Cherokee life is covered in Tyler Boulware, *Deconstructing the Cherokee Nation: Town, Region, and Nation among Eighteenth-Century Cherokees* (Gainesville: University Press of Florida, 2011), and an example of eighteenth-century Cherokee engagement with Britain is richly contextualized in Kate Fullagar, "Envoys of Interest: A Cherokee, a Ra'iatean, and the Eighteenth-Century British Empire," in *Facing Empire: Indigenous Experiences in a Revolutionary Age*, ed. Kate Fullagar and Michael A. McDonnell, 239–55 (Baltimore, MD: Johns Hopkins University Press, 2018).

6. Conley, 55.

By the end of the first decade of the nineteenth century, it was clear to the Cherokees that they required a unified response to their constant land losses and the succession of broken treaties. In 1809, a new National Council was formed, drawing on traditional notions of consensus and the role of a wide range of leaders, both men and women, while setting up an executive that could communicate directly and efficiently with the American local and federal governments.[7] These efforts were disrupted by the War of 1812 and the Cherokees' involvement, on the side of the Americans, in the Creek War of 1813–1814. Further treaties followed in 1816, 1817, and 1819, each of which led to greater land cessions in return for unmet promises about secure borders for the Cherokees.[8] Some Cherokees moved west following the 1816 treaties, joining an existing group of emigrants to form a new group known as the Western Cherokees or the Old Settlers, while the remaining Eastern Cherokees declared, following the 1819 treaty, that there would be no more land sales to the United States.[9]

Between 1819 and 1827, the Cherokees adopted a new tactic for communicating with the American state and federal governments. They reorganized their outward-facing political structure to mirror that of the United States, with three branches of government, a separation of powers, a principal chief, and a bicameral legislature.[10] They produced a constitution, which echoed that of the independent United States. And they developed a syllabary, which allowed for the production of Tsalagi (Cherokee-language) material and a sustained push for literacy in their own tongue.[11] The structures of both hard and soft diplomatic power were put

---

7. An excellent overview of Cherokee legal processes generally, and the arrangements made in 1809, can be found in Rennard Strickland, "Address: To Do the Right Thing: Reaffirming Cherokee Traditions of Justice under Law," *American Indian Law Review* 17.1 (1992): 337–46.

8. For background on the 1817 negotiations, see Susan M. Abram, *Forging a Cherokee-American Alliance in the Creek War: From Creation to Betrayal* (Tuscaloosa: University of Alabama Press, 2015), 94–96; and Rennard Strickland, *Fire and the Spirits: Cherokee Law from Clan to Court* (Norman: University of Oklahoma Press, 1975), 61–62.

9. Berutti, 291–308.

10. Conley, 106; Rochelle Raineri Zuck, *Divided Sovereignties: Race, Nationhood, and Citizenship in Nineteenth-Century America* (Athens: University of Georgia Press, 2016), 32–68.

11. The development of the Cherokee syllabary by Sequoyah (George Guess) is covered in Smithers, *The Cherokee Diaspora*, and Margaret Bender, *Signs of Cherokee Culture: Sequoyah's*

in place in the 1820s to help communicate the Cherokees' nationhood and their unwillingness to cede any further land or political control.[12] The *Cherokee Phoenix* was a significant element in this new approach. The National Council voted in 1825 to establish a newspaper and appointed Elias Boudinot its inaugural editor. The paper was to make use of the Cherokee syllabary but also to include English material. Boudinot traveled in the Northeast, raising money and speaking to white audiences about the plan for a newspaper, before producing an English-language prospectus in October 1827. The first issue of the *Cherokee Phoenix* was published on February 21, 1828. Two hundred copies of each issue were printed, and there is evidence of a relatively wide circulation in the United States, with some copies even making it across the Atlantic.[13]

The *Cherokee Phoenix* was published in a diplomatic climate shaped by both Western and Indigenous traditions and by the legacies of negotiations between the two. Throughout colonial history, the Cherokees had, as Gregory D. Smithers has noted, "recognized that it had become a diplomatic necessity to appropriate various forms of Western political discourse if they hoped to be understood by colonial officials."[14] The newspaper itself was one of these forms; so too were official documents like constitutions, essays, and other pieces of nonfictional prose such as memorials, the name given to the official communiqués issued by the Cherokee government to the U.S. government. At the same time, the Cherokee leadership continued their own diplomatic practices. Cherokee diplomacy in the eighteenth century had reflected the long-standing principles of harmony, balance, and consensus. Kinship relationships were emphasized and used as rhetorical devices for creating bonds and recipro-

---

Syllabary in Eastern Cherokee Life (Chapel Hill: University of North Carolina Press, 2002). Its role in the *Cherokee Phoenix* is covered in detail in Ellen Cushman, *The Cherokee Syllabary: Writing the People's Perseverance* (Norman: University of Oklahoma Press, 2011).

12. For summaries of the events from 1809 onward, see William G. McLoughlin, *Cherokee Renascence in the New Republic* (Princeton, NJ: Princeton University Press, 1986); Duane Champagne, *American Indian Societies: Strategies and Conditions of Political and Cultural Survival*, Cultural Survival Report 32 (Cambridge, MA: Cultural Survival, 1989), 45–47; and William G. McLoughlin, *After the Trail of Tears: The Cherokees' Struggle for Sovereignty, 1839–1880* (Chapel Hill: University of North Carolina Press, 1993).

13. Perdue, ed., *Cherokee Editor*, 15–16.

14. Smithers, 17.

cal obligations between parties in a negotiation. The leading negotiators on each side were referred to as "Beloved" men or women, confirming the respect they commanded and the mandate with which they acted.[15] The focus was on creating a peaceful state of mind in which friendly relations could be established or reestablished. Past grievances were put aside in order to reaffirm a present-day relationship that could be carried into the future, which meant that speeches at the treaty grounds were what the Cherokees called "good talks," consisting of declarations of friendship and positive intentions.[16] These speeches aimed at "making the path clear," or clearing the way for peace. In the late eighteenth century, however, this approach was modified in the face of violence, land losses, and persistent treaty breaches. Cherokee speakers began to emphasize pity and justice as key rhetorical elements, and, with some caution, to present grievances in the negotiation process rather than leaving them to one side.[17] Meanwhile, the necessarily repetitive processes of diplomatic negotiation, which involved sitting in a circle, lighting the council fire, smoking the peace pipe, and recording the negotiations' outcome in wampum, were augmented by new repetitive actions and new media that had emerged by the time of the 1791 treaty at Holston: repeating prior treaty promises; recording speeches in writing; and demanding copies of speeches for future reference.[18]

The detailed records of the late eighteenth-century treaty talks demonstrate the characteristics of Cherokee diplomatic rhetoric, and especially the process of repeating the words of earlier negotiations.

---

15. See Daniel Heath Justice, *Our Fire Survives the Storm: A Cherokee Literary History* (Minneapolis: University of Minnesota Press, 2006), esp. 39–40; Smithers, 31; and Joshua B. Nelson, *Progressive Traditions: Identity in Cherokee Literature and Culture* (Norman: University of Oklahoma Press, 2014), 66–71, 140–41.

16. For a broad discussion of Cherokee diplomatic protocols, see Cynthia Cumfer, *Separate Peoples, One Land: The Minds of Cherokees, Blacks, and Whites on the Tennessee Frontier* (Chapel Hill: University of North Carolina Press, 2007), 31–33.

17. Cumfer, 34.

18. Claudia B. Haake, "Civilization, Law, and Customary Diplomacy: Arguments against Removal in Cherokee and Seneca Letters to the Federal Government," *NAIS: Journal of the Native American and Indigenous Studies Association* 4, no. 2 (2017): 31–51; see also Cumfer, 57–58, as well as Round's description of the Cherokees' "hybrid negotiating practices" (102–6).

When Oconostota spoke on July 2, 1777, at the Treaty of Long Island at Holston, for example, he is recorded as saying: "I remember the talk that was lately given at [Williamsburg], and the Belt, I hold it still. The Govr. told me that no man should break the Belt given me by him, whose talk I have now in my mind. He told me that he had hold of one end of the Belt and myself the other." The American treaty commissioners also participated in this cycle of repetition, reading out various letters, treaties, and speeches, before Old Raven replied, using additional quotations from past talks: "The Great beloved man of Virginia spoke to mine who went to see him and said 'Now my friend & Brother I take you by the hand here is my friend who will leat [sic] you to the rest of your people; there the people of North Carolina will meet you likewise, and fix a hard and lasting Boundary between your and their countries for I find you have been much wronged.'"[19] This style of rhetoric was repeated in the negotiations at Hopewell in 1785 and at Holston in 1791, as well as numerous other diplomatic encounters between the Cherokees and settler officials.[20]

By the 1820s, a new generation of leaders expressed themselves in a form more recognizable to Euro-American eyes, but with the same emphasis on the promises of the past. A Cherokee delegation to Washington, D.C., in 1824, for example, told the U.S. Senate: "We appeal to the magnanimity of the American Congress for justice, and the protection of the rights, liberties, and lives of the Cherokee people. We claim it from the United States, by the strongest obligation which imposes it upon them— by treaties; and we expect it from them under that *memorable* declaration,

---

19. Archibald Henderson, "The Treaty of Long Island at Holston, July, 1777," *North Carolina Historical Review* 8, no. 1 (1931): 55–116; 62–81.

20. Records of the talks at Hopewell in 1785 can be found in Benjamin Hawkins, Andrew Pickens, Joseph Martin, and Lachlan McIntosh, "Letter to Richard Henry Lee, President of the Congress, 2 December 1785," *American State Papers: Documents, Legislative and Executive, of the Congress of the United States, Indian Affairs*, vol. 1, ed. Walter Lowrie and Matthew St. Clair Clarke, 40–43 (Washington, DC: Gales and Seaton, 1832). The Draper Manuscripts contain the talks at Hopewell in 1785 (14U1-108) and at Holston in 1791 (15U1-56). See also examples such as "A Talk from the Head-Men and Warriors of the Cherokee Nation, at a Meeting Held at Ustinaire, the Beloved Town, 20th November 1788, addressed to the Honourable Richard Winn, Esquire, Superintendent of the Southern Department, in answer to a Talk sent by him, dated the 12th October, 1788," *American State Papers*, vol. 1, C5, 45–46.

'that all men are created equal; that they are endowed by their Creator with certain unalienable rights; that among these are life, liberty, and the pursuit of happiness.'"[21] Although the repetition of prior documents and agreements had always formed part of the Cherokees' interactions with settler governments, it became a more significant part of their diplomacy as they became increasingly aware that those governments were attempting to interpret existing agreements in self-serving and insincere ways that drifted away from the original promises. The nineteenth-century researcher John Howard Payne recorded a Cherokee comment that encapsulates this awareness: "The President sends a Treaty with a letter to explain it. He then sends [Indian Commissioner] Mr Schermerhorn to re-explain the explained Treaty. The end of it is, the Treaty is so much explained, that it is explained away."[22] Through a mixture of texts, speeches, and material objects, the Cherokees and the Americans rehearsed the terms of their relationship in the past, present, and future, in forms that were predicated on the implicit power of quotation and verbatim language.

As Arnold Krupat has suggested, these new forms of Cherokee communication resulted from

> what are artificial, or, at the least, nontraditional occasions. For the speeches, the occasion for rhetorical performance is an encounter between delegations of whites and Indians for the purpose, in the vast majority of cases, of negotiating Indian land cessions. On these occasions, it should be noted, neither party could proceed in a manner entirely familiar to their culture, although this similarity does not suggest an equality: however necessary innovations of eloquence were to both Native and non-Native peoples, the latter always held the balance of power.
>
> This is to say that Euramericans, on these imperial occasions, had to engage in a manner of formal improvisation, while

---

21. "Views of the Cherokees in Relation to Further Cessions of Their Lands. Communicated to the Senate, April 16, 1824," *American State Papers*, 2:502. Delegations to Washington were a very familiar feature of nineteenth-century Native American diplomacy; for an overview, see Herman J. Viola, *Diplomats in Buckskins: A History of Indian Delegations in Washington City* (Bluffton, SC: Rivlio Books, 1995).

22. William L. Anderson, Jane L. Brown, and Anne F. Rogers, eds., *The Payne-Butrick Papers*, 2 vols. (Lincoln: University of Nebraska Press, 2010), 1:84.

the Native Americans, as colonial subjects, had to improvise in regard to content, a much more radical step.[23]

Innovations like the *Cherokee Phoenix* manifested this challenge, bringing together a new medium with the requirement for new types of content with which to fill it. But as Krupat suggests, these innovations were already predicated on a history of cross-cultural diplomacy, not simply a history of cross-cultural communication.

The diplomatic contexts for the *Cherokee Phoenix* can be sensed in the October 1827 prospectus, which outlined the content readers could expect:

1. The laws and public documents of the Nation.
2. Account of the manners and customs of the Cherokees, and their progress in Education, Religion and the arts of civilized life; . . .
3. The principal interesting news of the day.
4. Miscellaneous articles, calculated to promote Literature, Civilization, and Religion among the Cherokees.[24]

On the surface, this list suggests a typical range of newspaper departments, which are separate in their aims and characteristics. However, the mixture of official, historical, topical, and miscellaneous material can also be read as the elements of a multifaceted diplomatic engagement with white publics. This point might be made most obviously in the case of the second item on Boudinot's list, which was clearly not aimed at Cherokee readers. But it holds true, to some degree, for all the areas that the prospectus highlights. The reason for printing the laws and public documents of the nation in both English and Tsalagi, for example, was only in part to create an official and public record for the nation itself; it was also a strategy for confirming Cherokee nationhood in the minds of Euro-American readers. As Gaul notes, only around 18 percent of Cherokee households included someone who was literate in English,

---

23. Arnold Krupat, *Ethnocriticism: Ethnography, History, Literature* (Berkeley: University of California Press, 1992), 154.

24. Reprinted as Elias Boudinot, "Prospectus," *Cherokee Phoenix*, February 28, 1828, 3.

and thus the English-language content of the paper must have been primarily, although not exclusively, directed at a white audience.[25] This detail about language literacy helps to clarify the fourth point on the list. Boudinot implies here that English poetry was included to help the Cherokees civilize themselves. But the fact that the poems appeared in English suggests that the real purpose of their inclusion was to catch the eye of what Phillip H. Round has called "Removal publics," the white readers who could potentially influence federal and state policy toward the Cherokees.[26]

In part, this strategy would have been adopted to convey Cherokee sophistication to that readership. But it also connected to a wider program of diplomacy in the pages of the *Phoenix* that cited English text as a way to affirm promises, establish precedent, and motivate sympathy. The paper was full of reprinted material, including treaty documents, important speeches, and transcripts of debates in the federal and state legislatures; over and over again, the Cherokees not only emphasized the exact words of the deliberations at Hopewell and Holston and the speeches made by major American political figures, but also the fact that these words had themselves been repeated throughout the history of diplomatic engagement between the Cherokees and white settler officials. A memorial from the Cherokee legislature that appeared in the April 14, 1830, issue of the *Phoenix*, for example, quoted the eleventh article of the 1791 Holston Treaty verbatim.[27] These white-authored texts were included to remind white publics of the promises that had been made in their name.[28] Including English poems in the paper similarly helped

---

25. Gaul, "Editing as Indian Performance," 288–89.

26. Round, 140.

27. See also the August 12, 1829, issue, which quotes from both the 1791 and 1798 treaties and a speech by James Madison. Sometimes this act of diplomatic repetition was also undertaken by settler allies; see, for example, "William Penn [Jeremiah Evarts]," "Cherokee Treaty Rights, from *The New York American*, 15 September 1829," *Journal of Cherokee Studies* 4, no. 2 (1979): 71–74. The wider point about repetition and its role is made in Keri Holt, "'We, Too, the People': Rewriting Resistance in the Cherokee Nation," in *Mapping Region in Early American Writing*, ed. Edward Watts, Keri Holt, and John Funchion, 199–225; 213 (Athens: University of Georgia Press, 2015); and Maureen Konkle, *Writing Indian Nations: Native Intellectuals and the Politics of Historiography, 1827–1863* (Chapel Hill: University of North Carolina Press, 2004), 75–76.

28. Holt has made this point in relation to the Cherokee-authored texts that adopted white rhetorical forms and language, arguing that while these tactics might suggest the

to remind white publics of their own cultural values involving land, loss, and community and to connect those values to the documentation of the unfolding diplomatic crisis in Cherokee country.[29] There was a legal case to be made for Cherokee sovereignty, but this argument was complemented by a moral case, to which texts such as poems could make a major affective (as well as effective) contribution.[30]

Move or Be Moved: Hemans and the Poetics of Cherokee Diplomacy

Hemans owed her prominence in the *Cherokee Phoenix* to Elias Boudinot's rhetorical and diplomatic strategy. During his time as editor, Boudinot was entirely responsible for the newspaper's content, and he gave a lot of thought to the items he included: as he wrote to his wife's parents, "I have no associate in the Management of the paper, so I have to select pieces for publication, & this requires some time in order to be Judicious."[31] He selected poems from other periodicals, especially *Blackwood's*, for republication, and the inclusion of so many of Hemans's pieces thus reflects her contemporary popularity in the United States.[32] Based on

---

U.S. control over Cherokee expression, "using the language and rhetoric of the United States also enabled the Cherokee to control and manipulate public perceptions of the United States, to the point where they were able to rewrite the United States as a dishonorable, hypocritical nation" (201–2).

29. See Nelson's discussion of Boudinot's demand for consistency concerning treaty-based and constitutional arrangements between the U.S. government and Native peoples (179–80).

30. Andrew Demson does not discuss poetry, but he does make the point that one facet of the Cherokee leaders' rhetorical strategy was that they "scrutinized their powerful neighbors' politics and culture for arguments in favor of Indian nationhood" as part of a twofold legal and moral campaign. See Denson, *Demanding the Cherokee Nation: Indian Autonomy and American Culture, 1830–1900* (Lincoln: University of Nebraska Press, 2004), 6, 27–28.

31. Theresa Strouth Gaul, ed., *To Marry an Indian: The Marriage of Harriett Gold and Elias Boudinot in Letters, 1823–1839* (Chapel Hill: University of North Carolina Press, 2005), 161.

32. Hemans was significant because she mattered to Americans, as Myra Cottingham points out: "She was respected in America, and was offered a magazine editorship by Professor Norton of Harvard College. An early biographer says that the Americans regarded her as the head of a new literary school, owing to her influence on Longfellow"; see Cottingham, "Felicia Hemans's Dead and Dying Bodies," *Women's Writing* 8, no. 2 (2001): 275–94. A similar point is made in Paula R. Feldman, "The Poet and the Profits: Felicia Hemans and the Literary Marketplace," in *Women's Poetry, Late Romantic to Late Victorian:*

this popularity, Boudinot had good reason to regard Hemans's verse as especially likely to speak to white readers. But he also seems to have been motivated by the radical sentimentalism of her work, which was in tune with his own appeals to white audiences. As part of a tour of the Northeast designed to raise funds to establish the *Cherokee Phoenix*, Boudinot had given a speech to an audience at the First Presbyterian Church in Philadelphia, which he published as a pamphlet titled *An Address to the Whites*. In this address, Boudinot outlined a case for white sympathy that resonates strongly with Hemans's language, tone, and poetic concerns, especially in its concluding section:

> There is, in Indian history, something very melancholy, and which seems to establish a mournful precedent for the future events of the few sons of the forest, now scattered over this vast continent. We have seen every where the poor aborigines melt away before the white population. I merely speak of the fact, without at all referring to the cause. We have seen, I say, one family after another, one tribe after another, nation after nation, pass away; until only a few solitary creatures are left to tell the sad story of extinction.
>
> Shall this precedent be followed? I ask you, shall red men live, or shall they be swept from the earth? With you and this public at large, the decision chiefly rests. Must they perish? Must they all, like the unfortunate Creeks, (victims of the unchristian policy of certain persons,) go down in sorrow to their grave?
>
> They hang upon your mercy as to a garment. Will you push them from you, or will you save them? Let humanity answer.[33]

Gender and Genre, 1830–1900, ed. Isobel Armstrong and Virginia Blain, 71–101; 80 (Basingstoke: Palgrave, 1999); and Cheryl Walker, *Indian Nation: Native American Literature and Nineteenth-Century Nationalisms* (Durham, NC: Duke University Press, 1997), 25–27. Boudinot's sources for the poems appear to be a range of both American and English magazines or annuals. In some instances he includes the source of the poem when he publishes it; *Blackwood's Magazine* is an especially common source. Hemans's popularity across the colonial world and its effect on settler poetics are expertly described in Jason R. Rudy, *Imagined Homelands: British Poetry in the Colonies* (Baltimore, MD: Johns Hopkins University Press, 2017), 6–8, 43–74.

33. Perdue, *Cherokee Editor*, 79. The full text of the address is included on pp. 65–83. Boudinot's understanding of the limits of sympathy is discussed in Gina Caison's chapter

Boudinot's own political rhetoric contained within it something akin to the tone of Hemans's verse, melancholy and sentimental, yet not entirely pessimistic.

The selection of poems from within Hemans's oeuvre was potentially rather arbitrary; it depended, not on a choice between her work and other examples from the canon of English poetry, but rather simply a choice between her work and other recently published verses in the American periodical press, nor did it necessarily involve a thorough reading of all her poems, from which a selection was then made. Nevertheless, the poems that Boudinot did choose to reprint all worked to augment and strengthen Cherokee diplomatic rhetoric in the paper by echoing key ideas of home, kinship, land, and loss, ideas that had always played a significant part in Cherokee literature and that were the hallmarks of Hemans's poetic preoccupations.[34] They might have been selected from within a narrow range of poems, but they were nevertheless carefully chosen to act as diplomatic communiqués to the *Phoenix*'s white readers.

"The Two Homes" offers a useful example of a poem that is open to this strategy of diplomatic engagement.[35] The poem had first appeared in England in the February 1829 issue of *Blackwood's Edinburgh Magazine*, and it was published in the *Cherokee Phoenix* on June 17 of the same year. It stages a dialogue between two travelers. The first speaker is returning to their home and is physically within sight of it. They describes their home in terms of its natural setting but also in terms of the memories and sentiments that characterize it. The setting and the sentiments come together to create an almost palpable physical sensation:

---

on removal in *Red States: Indigeneity, Settler Colonialism, and Southern Studies* (Athens: University of Georgia Press, 2018), 109–58, esp. 130.

34. See the emphasis on "home" in the discussion of Cherokee textuality in Justice, *Our Fire Survives the Storm*, 46.

35. Felicia Hemans, "The Two Homes," *Cherokee Phoenix, and Indians' Advocate*, June 17, 1829, 4. All references to Hemans's poetry are to the version published in the *Cherokee Phoenix* on the relevant date, unless otherwise noted. Line numbers are included parenthetically in the text. The *Phoenix* was renamed the *Cherokee Phoenix, and Indians' Advocate* from February 11, 1829, onward; in my notes and bibliography I use whichever title was correct for the issue I am citing, but in my prose I have chosen to refer consistently to the *Cherokee Phoenix*, or simply the *Phoenix*, for ease of reading. The paper is not to be confused with a later publication titled the *Cherokee Advocate*, which commenced some years after Boudinot's death.

My home!—the spirit of its love is breathing
In every wind that plays across my track,
From its white walls the very tendrils wreathing
Seem with soft links to draw the wanderer back. (9–12)

In particular, the speaker notes the domestic setting:

There am I loved—there pray'd for—there my mother
Sits by the hearth with meekly thoughtful eye;
. . . .
There, in sweet strains of kindred music blending,
All the home voices meet at day's decline;
One are those tones, as from one heart ascending. (13–14, 17–19)

The ecstatic speaker then asks their interlocutor where *their* home is, to which the second speaker replies: "In solemn peace 'tis lying, / Far o'er the deserts and the tombs away" (21–22). Their home is with the dead, they suggest, but not entirely without consolation: "And what is home, and where, but with the loving?" (27). The poem ends with the second speaker's firm belief that their family continues to watch over them from the afterlife.[36]

In the context of the Removal Crisis of the late 1820s and early 1830s, the poem's title is heavy with significance. The Eastern Cherokees faced a future characterized by "two homes," a stolen homeland (already much reduced from the original, precontact boundaries of Cherokee land) and a new space, both intangible and inhospitable, in which they would be forced to dwell, cut off from the land and ecology that had sustained them. The original poem uses two speakers to give voice to the two notions of home, but, in the context of the *Phoenix*, the voices might be read as present and future expressions of a single Cherokee voice. There is a note of resilience in this poem, however, despite the obvious sorrow that underpins it. If home can be reconstructed anywhere there is "loving," then it is possible to survive, however unsatisfactorily, as the second speaker does, away from the actual scenes of home. But there is

---

36. Although she only deals with this poem briefly, Anne Mellor's reading of the significance of "home" in Hemans's poetry is the foundational reading for this concept; see Mellor, *Romanticism and Gender* (New York: Routledge, 1993), 127–29.

a strong preference in the poem, one shared by Boudinot, for a home that integrates human relationships with physical sites, people with land. Euro-American readers, on encountering this poem in the pages of the *Phoenix*, were being encouraged to remember their own culture's ideas about both home and the removal from home.

However, they were also being encouraged to read these sentiments alongside the political and diplomatic content of that day's paper. The June 17, 1829, issue of the *Cherokee Phoenix*, in which "The Two Homes" appeared, was filled with the rhetoric of resistance. The first item in the paper was a memorial by the Cherokee leadership to the United States Congress protesting against the proposed removal. "The interests of our citizens," argued the memorial's authors, "are permanent in the soil."[37] The memorial was followed in the newspaper by the contemptuous reply of the federal secretary of war, John H. Eaton, dismissing all the Cherokees' claims to nationhood and sovereignty.[38] These documents provided the spur for Boudinot's editorial in the same issue, which drew on the rhetoric of "home" to make its point:

> There is, as would naturally be supposed, a great rejoicing in Georgia. It is a time of "important news"—"gratifying intelligence"—"The Cherokee lands are to be obtained speedily." It is even reported that the Cherokees have come to the conclusion to sell, and move off to the west of the Mississippi—not so fast. We are yet at our homes, at our peaceful firesides . . . attending to our farms and useful occupations.[39]

Boudinot's ideas of hearth and home are not simply poetic stereotypes, since they draw on the considerable spiritual significance of fires and hearths in both Cherokee tradition and the postcontact Cherokee society in which Boudinot lived.[40] But they do find close echoes in the Hemans

---

37. "Memorial of John Ross, Richard Taylor, [E]dward Gunter, and William S. Coody, Representatives of the Cherokee Nation of Indians," *Cherokee Phoenix, and Indians' Advocate*, June 17, 1829, 1.

38. "The Secretary of War to the Cherokee Delegation," *Cherokee Phoenix, and Indians' Advocate*, June 17, 1829, 1–2.

39. Elias Boudinot, Editorial, *Cherokee Phoenix, and Indians' Advocate*, June 17, 1829, 2.

40. See, for example, Smithers's description of "the sacred fire that occupied an important ceremonial place in chiefdom-era culture continued to be incorporated into ceremonial

poem that he chose to include in this issue. "The Two Homes" uses the image of the hearth to indicate both the warmth of home and the family's continuous and stable occupation of a place: "There am I loved—there pray'd for—there my mother / Sits by the hearth with meekly thoughtful eye" (13–14).[41] Boudinot's editorial here draws on the tangible, concrete notion of home that the poem's first speaker describes. But the editorial also gestures toward the idea of a mournfully displaced home, such as that of Hemans's second speaker, which is being conjured into being by the Euro-American settlers' feverish rumormongering. As Boudinot suggests, this displaced home is not yet a reality, and his writings work hard to shut down the possibility that it will manifest itself. But the structure of "two homes," one "permanent in the soil," as the Cherokee leaders wrote in their memorial that day, and one intangible, glides from Hemans's poem to Boudinot's editorial and back again, as Hemans's generalized scene of mingled stability and loss is recontextualized as a moment in Cherokee history.

Hemans's poem also connects home with a united voice. Her first speaker describes his home as a place where "all the home-voices meet at day's decline; / One are those tones, as from one heart ascending" (18–19). The authors of the memorial to Congress, meanwhile, produced a document that manifested the different voices of the Cherokee leaders as a single voice, complemented by Boudinot's editorial. These are analogous to the "home-voices" in Hemans's poem, voices that, as her hyphenated phrase suggests, draw both their unity and their authority from their shared place in the world. Although the Cherokee leaders' memorial and Boudinot's editorial were composed by different people

---

culture in eighteenth-century Cherokee towns. Indeed, to the eighteenth-century Cherokees fire represented warmth, life, and the light of home" (32), as well as the role that rekindling the sacred fire played in helping to create a sense of kinship and home in new settlements (34–35). For a perspective from within Cherokee literary studies, see detailed references to the role of the hearth in Cherokee life in Justice, *Our Fire Survives the Storm*, 25–27. For a historical perspective, see the examples throughout Anderson, Brown, and Rogers.

41. This is a notion that always figures in Hemans's thinking; in a note in her journal, she commented "Our home!—what images are brought before us by that one word! The meeting of cordial smiles, and the gathering round the evening hearth, and the interchange of thoughts in kindly words, and the glance of eyes to which our hearts lie open as the day;—there is the true 'City of Refuge;'—where are we to turn when it is shut from us or changed?"; see [Harriet Hughes], *Memoir of the Life and Writings of Mrs. Hemans. By Her Sister* (Philadelphia: Lea and Blanchard, 1840), 131.

and in different genres, their shared origins in the voices of the Cherokee homeland unites them.

Similarly uniting them is another kind of home: the textual home they find in the pages of the *Cherokee Phoenix* for June 17, 1829. This textual home, however, houses other voices, selected to speak by the Cherokees but not originating in Cherokee discourse. Some of these, like Eaton's or the projected voices of the Georgia settlers that Boudinot quotes, are chosen because of their oppositional qualities; they contribute to the public debate in which the *Cherokee Phoenix* is engaged by articulating what the Cherokees are struggling against. But "The Two Homes" operates differently. It adds a British voice, a poetic voice, a woman's voice to the "home-voices" of Boudinot and the rest of the Cherokee leadership. By occupying the same textual space, the poem becomes recontextualized as part of the Cherokee message that day, with its tropes of hearth, and home, and voice drawn out and echoed, and with the exact words of the poem amplifying the words of the memorial and the editorial and standing against Eaton's exact words. "One are those tones," as Hemans wrote, and "The Two Homes" is thus transformed, temporarily at least, into a piece of Cherokee diplomacy.

A similar effect can be seen in the selection of Hemans's "The Ruined House" for publication in the *Phoenix,* although in this poem the home is unrecoverable.[42] The poem begins with an epigraph from Wordsworth and adopts a rather Wordsworthian tone in its account of a visitor to a long-deserted home. The speaker begins by noting that it does not matter that the place is not the site of "minstrel-tale of harp and sword" (17); for them,

> It is enough to know that here,
> Where thoughtfully I stand,
> Sorrow and Love, and Hope and Fear,
> Have link'd one kindred band. (21–24)

As in "The Two Homes," it is the hearth that stands as the central image, this time memorialized in terms of a lost history of love and affection:

---

42. Felicia Hemans, "The Ruined House," *Cherokee Phoenix, and Indians' Advocate,* September 9, 1829, 4.

Thou hast heard many sounds, thou hearth,
Deserted now by all!
Voices at eve here meet in mirth,
Which eve may ne'er recall.
Youth's buoyant step, and Woman's tone,
And Childhood's laughing glee,
And song, and prayer have well been known,
Hearth of the Dead! to thee. (33–40)

The connection of kinship, voices, ancestors, song, and spirituality combines with the nostalgic tone to clarify and enumerate the costs of leaving, deserting, or being removed from one's home. The hearth not only symbolizes these losses, it also bears witness to them, operating as a legible reminder of the community to whom this place once belonged. While perhaps less optimistic than "The Two Homes," "The Ruined House" still encompasses the idea that a poetic voice that is aware of the history of the place might yet be able to rekindle the deserted hearth.

"The Two Homes" and "The Ruined House" are perhaps the most explicit examples, but almost all the Hemans poems that Boudinot printed dealt with home as a concept that was both idealized and under considerable pressure. "Evening Song of the Tyrolese Peasants," for example, also depicts two homes, one on earth and one in heaven.[43] In the context of the *Cherokee Phoenix*, Hemans's portrayal of heaven reads as a place of refuge from the horrors of removal, its terms eerily evocative of later accounts of the Trail of Tears:

There shall no tempest blow,
No scorching noontide heat;
There shall be no more snow,
No weary wandering feet. (29–32)[44]

---

43. Felicia Hemans, "Evening Song of the Tyrolese Peasants," *Cherokee Phoenix*, July 9, 1828, 4.

44. Cherokee stories about the Trail of Tears told by survivors and their descendants can be found in Lorrie Montiero, ed., *Family Stories from the Trail of Tears* (Little Rock, AR: American Native Press Archives and Sequoyah Research Center, 1937), https://ualrexhibits.org/tribalwriters/artifacts/Family-Stories-Trail-of-Tears.html. For academic accounts of the hardships and tragedies on the Trail of Tears, see McLoughlin, *After the Trail of Tears*, 1–7; Eaton, 80–91.

Hemans's "The Sunbeam," meanwhile, alludes several times to the persistence and also the complexities of home: seeing a sunbeam pleases a sailor in the poem like hearing "words from home" (8), but the image serves as a reminder of his estrangement from that home and the fragility of his link to it, as transient as words or a beam of light.[45] In "Lines to an Orphan," one of the last Hemans poems that Boudinot published in the *Phoenix*, the speaker reminds an orphan of their lost home and the uncertain future that awaits:

> But oh! too beautiful and blest
> Thy home of youth hath been;
> Where shall thy wing, poor bird! find rest,
> Shut out from that sweet scene!" (17–20)[46]

The homes that Boudinot is drawn to in Hemans's poetry are always bittersweet, formed out of memories, losses, imaginings, or departures.

These poetic reflections on the troubled nature of home and the figurative terms in which Hemans expressed them reverberated through the issues of the *Cherokee Phoenix* in which they appeared. "Evening Song of the Tyrolese Peasants," for example, complemented the essay "A Revery" by "Young Beaver" in the *Phoenix* that day.[47] Hemans's verses imagine a peaceful twilight scene at the end of the working day, characterized by a gentle breeze:

> Sweet is the hour of rest!
> Pleasant the wind's low sigh,
> And the gleaming of the west,
> And the turf whereon we lie.
> . . . .
> Yes, tuneful is the sound
> That dwells in whispering boughs,

---

45. Felicia Hemans, "The Sunbeam," *Cherokee Phoenix, and Indians' Advocate*, February 18, 1829, 4.

46. Felicia Hemans, "Lines to an Orphan," *Cherokee Phoenix, and Indians' Advocate*, December 3, 1829, 4.

47. Young Beaver, "A Revery," *Cherokee Phoenix*, July 9, 1828, 2. It is not clear whether the name "Young Beaver" is a pseudonym; for the purposes of this book, I have treated it as an actual name.

Welcome the freshness round,
And the gale that fans our brows. (9–12, 21–24)

Young Beaver almost seems to repurpose some of Hemans's terms, especially this evocation of the peaceful natural world, in the service of a discussion of the Cherokees' past, present, and future. In earlier times, he writes, while Native Americans enjoyed "flowery meads and fragrant groves," settler populations continued to arrive and force their way west. Just as Hemans's restful scene is here depicted as profoundly fragile, Young Beaver informs his readers that "as the gale of quiet repose gently fanned you, the work of destruction was commenced!" The harmony of the breeze can be reclaimed, however, if the white and Native populations can reestablish friendly relations; in a deliberately optimistic reading of a possible future, and one aimed squarely at a sympathetic white audience, Young Beaver writes that "confidence is returning, and the genial influence of friendship has again swelled the breeze." Hemans's poem was similarly echoed in Boudinot's own article that day, which dealt with the Treaty of Washington that had recently been signed by the Western Cherokees and the U.S. government.[48] As Boudinot pointed out, the terms of the Treaty of Washington brought the whole notion of "home" into question, especially the phrase "permanent home" that was used in the text of the treaty itself. Since each new treaty required the Cherokees to move farther and farther west, Boudinot wrote, "What is then the security in this *new, last,* and *permanent home* of our brethren?" (italics in the original).

These compromised homes also feature in Hemans's poems that overtly question the decision to remove oneself from home. "Nature's Farewell," which appeared in the *Cherokee Phoenix* in September 1828, opens with a scene of departure:

A youth rode forth from his childhood's home,
Through the crowded paths of the world to roam,
And the green leaves whispered as he pass'd,
"Wherefore, thou dreamer! away so fast? (1–4)[49]

The poem consists of addresses to the youth by the flora and fauna of his home, and it ends with a melancholy reflection on the costs of removing:

---

48. Elias Boudinot, Editorial, *Cherokee Phoenix*, July 9, 1828, 2.
49. Felicia Hemans, "Nature's Farewell," *Cherokee Phoenix*, September 17, 1828, 4.

"Farewell!—when thou comest again to thine own,
Thou wilt miss from our music its loveliest tone!
Mournfully true is the tale we tell—
Yet on, fiery dreamer!—Farewell, farewell!"
And a something of gloom on his spirit weigh'd,
As he caught the last sounds of his native shade;
But he knew not, till many a bright spell broke,
How deep were the oracles nature spoke! (37–44)[50]

When read in the publication context of the *Cherokee Phoenix*, the poem's rather ominous conclusion, hinting as it does at the lifelong consequences of the youth's decision, underlines the permanence of the decision facing the Cherokees. Departure from their lands would radically alter their relationship to that space, leaving no room for reintegration or resettlement once their bond with the land was broken.

A similar warning about the decision to leave home, which reads as if recast in Cherokee symbolism, can be seen in "The Wounded Eagle."[51] The eagle was an important spiritual leader for the Cherokees and featured in rituals of war and heroism.[52] Its explicit diplomatic significance was its link to the eagle tail dance, a ritual that had been chosen for performance to open the negotiations for the 1791 Treaty at Holston, whose proceedings were often cited in the *Cherokee Phoenix*.[53] In Hemans's poem, the speaker addresses a bird that she has seen on the ground, an event that, in Cherokee terms (which she would not naturally have intended) was an omen of death.[54] The speaker regards the eagle as out of place in this setting, stating: "Eagle! this is not thy sphere! / Warrior-bird, what seek'st thou here?" (1–2). Leaving its natural home in the sky has been fatal to the eagle:

Thou, that hadst ethereal birth:
Thou hast stoop'd too near to earth,

---

50. This is one of the poems that Theresa Strouth Gaul analyzes briefly in her discussion of poetry in the *Cherokee Phoenix*; see Gaul, "Editing as Indian Performance," 293.

51. Felicia Hemans, "The Wounded Eagle," *Cherokee Phoenix*, May 6, 1828, 4.

52. James Mooney, *Myths of the Cherokee* (Washington, DC: U.S. Government Printing Office, 1902), 281–83.

53. Cumfer, 58.

54. Anderson, Brown, and Rogers, 1:239.

And the hunter's shaft hath found thee,
And the toils of death hath bound thee. (18–21)

The realm of the sky has now been surrendered to the mountain lark, which has claimed the space vacated by the eagle, and the poem ends with an overt decoding of the anthropomorphic symbolism, asking: "Wo [sic] for gifted souls on high! / Is not such *their* destiny?" (29–30; emphasis in the original).

These poetic warnings about voluntary removal sat alongside articles making the same point. On the day that "Nature's Farewell" appeared, for example, Young Beaver published an article on Native emigration, arguing that the Eastern Cherokees had progressed so much and the land provided to the Western Cherokees was so inferior that there was no reason for the Eastern group to leave to join them. Urging caution, he noted: "Let us weigh well this momentous subject ere we act, perhaps an age might not undo that which may have been the work of a day."[55] While the addressees of this multigenre message seem to be the Cherokees themselves, the fact that both the poems and articles like Young Beaver's essay appeared in English meant that white readers were also being drawn in to the Cherokees' dilemma, in an explicit attempt to create cross-cultural communities of sympathy.

Generating and meditating on sympathy is perhaps the most significant link between the Hemans texts that Boudinot selects. In a poem simply titled "Song," Hemans works through a series of images of casual or thoughtless destruction, only some of which are reversible.[56] "If thou hast quenched a lamp, / Once more it may be lighted," she remarks (3–4); however,

If upon the troubled sea
Thou hast thrown a gem unheeded,
Hope not that wind or wave shall bring
The treasure back when needed. (13–16)

In the final stanza, Hemans points out that the heart is like the irretrievable gem, and warns against brutal actions that leave emotional attachment beyond repair. "A Parting Song," meanwhile, is structured around repetitions

---

55. Young Beaver, "Indian Emigration," *Cherokee Phoenix*, September 17, 1828, 3.
56. Felicia Hemans, "Song," *Cherokee Phoenix*, August 6, 1828, 4.

of the question "When will ye think of me, my friends? / When will ye think of me?" (1–2).[57] The speaker is on the verge of departure and wants to build a warm, sympathetic connection with those who remain. The *Cherokee Phoenix*'s white readership is being offered, via these poems and their rhetoric and imagery, the chance to construct itself as friendly, careful, and attentive to what another Hemans poem in the newspaper calls "the sick heart that doth but long / for aid, for sympathy" (25–26).[58]

Hemans's images of sympathy are not meant to suggest asymmetrical relationships, however. Through his use of her poems, Boudinot structures one side of a dialogue between two equal partners, one of whom is vulnerable and makes a claim on the sympathy of the other, but does so within a framework of mutual respect and fellow feeling. This symmetry is most obvious in the poem "The Meeting of the Ships," in which

> Two barks met on the deep mid sea,
> When calms had still'd the tide;
> A few bright days of Summer glee
> There found them side by side. (1–4)[59]

The occupants of the two ships create a temporary but profound emotional community, as

> hands were link'd, and answering eyes
> With kindly meaning shone:
> —Oh! brief and passing sympathies,
> Like leaves together blown!" (13–16)

The speaker laments that the rising winds make the ships mobile again and permanently end the connection between the two sets of occupants, "Never to blend in Victory's cheer, / To aid in hours of wo [*sic*]" (24–25). Hemans herself had linked these sentiments to American literature, prefacing the poem with an epigraph from Washington Irving that Boudinot also includes when he prints "The Meeting of the Ships": "We take each other by the hand, and we exchange a few words and looks of kindness,

---

57. Felicia Hemans, "A Parting Song," *Cherokee Phoenix*, October 1, 1828, 4.
58. Felicia Hemans, "Woman and Fame," *Cherokee Phoenix, and Indians' Advocate*, March 25, 1829, 4.
59. Felicia Hemans, "The Meeting of the Ships," *Cherokee Phoenix, and Indians' Advocate*, March 18, 1829, 4.

and we rejoice together for a few short moments;—and then days, months, years intervene—and we see and know nothing of each other." But the metaphor of linking hands had a further Indigenous application, gesturing as it does toward the Haudenosaunee metaphor of "linking arms" in diplomatic negotiations.[60] In the context of the *Cherokee Phoenix*, the poem highlights the fragility of sympathetic relationships and the significance of harnessing their power at the appropriate moment, even if only in the form of temporary claims. The two ships of state, the Cherokee Nation and the U.S. government, need to meet each other in this charged political moment as sympathetic partners in the land in which they find themselves alongside one another, a message that was embodied by the parallel political systems and their formal communications with each other.

The failure to act as sympathetic partners was something that Boudinot also explored through Hemans's work. "The Indian with His Dead Child" is the only one of Hemans's numerous poems about Native Americans that made it into the *Cherokee Phoenix*.[61] In the poem, a Native father carries the body of his dead child away from the white cemetery in which he had been buried to the family's ancestral land. Theresa Strouth Gaul reads this example as one of a group of poems that "resonate with themes of loss, grief, and exile. Indian removal is portrayed as having already been accomplished with Native Americans as (if not willing) at least passive victims."[62] But this interpretation misses the resistance demonstrated by the poem's speaker. The unnamed father is certainly grief-stricken, but his behavior manifests a faith in the practices of his ancestors and, far from passivity, a contempt for the norms of white society. The father deliberately chooses to leave that society following its neglect at his bereavement:

---

60. See the description in Timothy J. Shannon, *Iroquois Diplomacy on the Early American Frontier* (New York: Penguin, 2008), 43, and also the title by Robert A. Williams Jr., *Linking Arms Together: American Indian Treaty Visions of Law and Peace, 1600–1800* (New York: Routledge, 1999), which makes use of the metaphorical implications of the Haudenosaunee term.

61. Felicia Hemans, "The Indian with His Dead Child," *Cherokee Phoenix, and Indians' Advocate*, July 8, 1829, 4. Occasionally other, anonymous poems about Indians were printed in the Phoenix. The most detailed evaluation of Hemans's poems on Native Americans is Nancy Moore Goslee, "Hemans 'Red Indians': Reading Stereotypes," in *Romanticism, Race, and Imperial Culture, 1780–1834*, ed. Alan Richardson and Sonia Hofkosh, 237–61 (Bloomington: Indiana University Press, 1996).

62. Gaul, "Editing as Indian Performance," 295.

> When his head sank on my bosom,
> When the death-sleep o'er him fell,
> Was there one to say—"A friend is near!"
> There was none!—Pale race, farewell! (37–40)

Speaking directly to his child while juxtaposing the two cultural traditions, the father says:

> I have raised thee from the grave sod,
> By the white man's path defiled;
> On to th' ancestral wilderness
> I bear thy dust, my child! (9–12)

In place of the rejected Christian burial, the father chooses to "bear him unto burial, / Where the mighty hunter's gone" (45–46). The child will rejoin his ancestors in an Indigenous death ritual instead. This journey is not portrayed as an exile or a version of removal; instead it is quite explicitly depicted as a return to a home and an Indigenous way of life: "To the forests, to the cedars, / To the warrior and his bow, / Back, back!" (41–43).

The underlying fortitude and consolation of this position can be seen in the careful construction of the poem, whose first, seventh and final stanzas mirror each other but are infused with subtle changes. The poem begins:

> In the silence of the midnight,
> I journey with the dead;
> In the darkness of the forest boughs,
> A lonely path I tread. (1–4)

By the final stanza, the negativity of the first stanza's "lonely" walk disappears:

> In the silence of the midnight,
> I journey with the dead;
> But my heart is strong, my step is fleet,
> My father's path I tread. (49–52)

The positive language of strength and speed has replaced the loneliness of the opening and it is explicitly linked with the speaker's (and the poem's) reorientation to what Hemans sees as a traditional path and the certainty and confidence it brings. Moreover, from a Cherokee perspective, this reference to the "path" might have had clear diplomatic overtones in its unintended allusion to the concept of "making the path clear," which is a central metaphor in Cherokee diplomatic rhetoric.[63]

Gaul suggests that the passivity she perceives in poems such as "The Indian with His Dead Child" is destabilized by their inclusion in a newspaper that resolutely and actively opposed removal, while Tricia Lootens briefly refers to the poem as an example of the ways in which Hemans "acknowledges the violence and racism of imperialism."[64] A more detailed reading of the poem than either Gaul or Lootens offers suggests something more provocative: what is mobilized by the poem's inclusion in the *Phoenix* is its surprising commitment to notions of Indigenous autonomy. Hemans is not the delineator of passive Native suffering that Gaul identifies, nor simply the delineator of imperial violence onto a passive population that Lootens suggests. In the poem the Indigenous father instead asserts his Indigenous autonomy following a pronounced failure in white sympathy, in which the possibility of constructing oneself as a "friend" has been rejected by the white population. In the poem's newspaper incarnation, Boudinot's white readers are being asked to contemplate a different kind of removal from the one proposed by the U.S. government, one in which the Cherokees strategically withdraw from the cross-cultural relationships and communities that were already in place.

A second and related sort of failure, which complemented the poems that dealt with failed sympathy, was on show in the articles that Boudinot chose to publish in the *Cherokee Phoenix*: the failure of white settlers and governments to adhere to their own promises. One characteristic of the newspaper throughout Boudinot's editorship was the reprinting of verbatim speeches, treaty texts, and published correspondence relating to the Cherokee situation. These texts are featured in almost every issue of the newspaper, which meant that Hemans's poetry was typically surrounded by other kinds of white-authored text. Verbatim language clearly mattered to the Cherokee leadership, especially when it concerned past agreements. For example, "Evening Song of the Tyrolese Peasants," was featured in the same issue as Boudinot's article about the Treaty of Washington, which

---

63. Cumfer, 30, 39.

64. Tricia Lootens, "Hemans and Home: Victorianism, Feminine 'Internal Enemies,' and the Domestication of National Identity," *PMLA* 109, no. 2 (1994): 238–53; 250.

was signed by the Western Cherokees.[65] Boudinot included the text of Article 8 of that treaty word for word in his piece, and he pointed out that "in the above article, the new country, to which the Cherokees are to remove, is guarantied [sic] to them nearly in the same language as that used in the 7th article of the treaty of Holston, viz: 'The United States solemnly Guarantie [sic] to the Cherokee Nation, all their lands not hereby ceded.'" Hemans's "Nature's Farewell," meanwhile, appeared alongside the final instalment of a month-long series in which Boudinot had reprinted all the speeches given during a meeting between George Washington, then–secretary for war General Henry Knox, and the Cherokees at a conference in Philadelphia in 1791. This final installment was composed entirely of Washington's words and ended with the president commenting on the importance of the exact language exchanged in this meeting and its significance in both Euro-American and Cherokee diplomatic traditions:

> I shall subscribe my name to this talk which shall be written in your book, in order to be preserved among you as a witness of our transactions together, and to which you may have recourse in the future.
>
> This book you will sacredly preserve and not suffer any thing to be written therein, but in the presence of the United States or their Agent who is Governor Blount, and under him Mr. Shaw.
>
> In this book the treaty between the United States and the Cherokees will be written together with your speeches here, and this answer thereto.
>
> Besides this manner of recording our proceedings, I confirm all I have said to you in your own method, by a White Belt as the emblem of the purity of our hearts towards you.[66]

Whether looking at events of his own time or drawing connections between current crises and past promises, Boudinot returned to the idea of verbatim language as a key component of any negotiation.

The importance of the exact language of past promises became more pressing following the election of Andrew Jackson as president in

---

65. Elias Boudinot, "A New Treaty," *Cherokee Phoenix*, July 9, 1828, 2.
66. "Washington and the Cherokees. Continued," *Cherokee Phoenix*, September 17, 1828, 1.

late 1828, and Hemans's poetry continued to appear alongside increasingly desperate appeals to the sympathies of the *Cherokee Phoenix*'s white readers. "The Treasures of the Sea" was included in one of the first issues published after the election, in which Boudinot, in a typical move, quoted article 14 of the 1791 Treaty of Holston verbatim as part of his editorial against removal.[67] Jackson was the more explicit target a couple of months later, when Boudinot excerpted this remark from the president's inaugural address: "It will be my sincere and constant desire; to observe towards the Indian tribes within our limits, a just and liberal policy; and to give that humane and considerate attention to their rights and their wants, which are consistent with the habits of our government, and the feelings of our people."[68] On the following page, Boudinot published Hemans's "Woman and Fame," with its denunciation of public, implicitly masculine, power, in favor of the feminine power of hearth and home:

> Happy—happier far than thou,
> With the laurel on thy brow,
> She that makes the humblest hearth,
> Lovely but to one on earth.
> . . . .
> Thou hast green laurel-leaves that twine
> Into so proud a wreath;
> For that resplendent gift of thine,
> Heroes have smiled in death,
> Give *me* from some kind hand a flower,
> The record of one happy hour!
> Thou hast a voice, whose thrilling tone
> Can bid each life-pulse beat;
> As when a trumpet's note hath blown,
> Calling the brave to meet:
> But mine, let mine—a woman's breast,
> By words of home-born love be blessed.
> A hollow sound is in thy song,
> A mockery in thine eye,
> To the sick heart that doth but long

---

67. Felicia Hemans, "The Treasures of the Sea," *Cherokee Phoenix*, January 28, 1829, 4; Elias Boudinot, Editorial, *Cherokee Phoenix*, January 28, 1829, 2.
68. Elias Boudinot, "Summary," *Cherokee Phoenix, and Indians' Advocate*, March 25, 1829, 3.

> For aid, for sympathy:
> For kindly looks to cheer it on,
> For tender accents that are gone.
> Fame! Fame! thou canst not be the stay
> Unto the drooping reed,
> The cool fresh fountain, in the day
> Of the soul's feverish need;
> Where must the lone one turn or flee?
> Not unto thee, oh! not to thee. (1–4, 9–32; emphasis in the original)

The addressee of the poem is Fame itself, but in the context of the *Cherokee Phoenix*, it reads as if addressed to President Jackson, with the fleeting trappings of office and the "hollow" sound of his words on the previous page of the newspaper set against the greater virtues of the humble hearth, "kindly looks," "tender accents," and the "words of home-born love." Crucially, what the "sick heart" of the speaker yearns for is "sympathy," the key affective term that guides both Hemans's poetry and Boudinot's strategic decision to publish it in his paper. The repetition of Hemans's poetry sat in conversation with other verbatim words from white authors, its figurative promises in dialogue with the literal promises of white negotiators, governments, and presidents, as potential admonishments to white readers about their failure to adhere to their own stated principles of both settlement and sentiment.[69]

In adopting this approach to quotation and compilation, Boudinot was participating in an emerging, if short-lived, diplomatic strategy deployed by leading Cherokee writers. As Kelly Wisecup has noted in relation to the articles that Boudinot's cousin John Ridge wrote for the *Phoenix* under the pen-name "Socrates,"

> Compilation functions as a key literary and political strategy that transforms what might seem to be imitation into a careful reading of these sources for Cherokee purposes. Compiling

---

69. See Nelson's brilliant reading of Boudinot's insistence on consistency from the United States and its officials (179–80); a similar point is made in Angela Pulley Hudson, "'Forked Justice': Elias Boudinot, the US Constitution, and Cherokee Removal," In *American Indian Rhetorics of Survivance: Word Medicine, Word Magic, Ernest Stromberg* (Pittsburgh: University of Pittsburgh Press, 2006), 50–65.

these excerpts in new contexts requires that readers participate in the process of reinterpreting them, eventually coming to their own understandings of Cherokee sovereignty as they engage with the text. Importantly, compilation allows Socrates to revise the timeline for the end of Cherokee sovereignty as imagined by the United States: he places previously circulated legal documents such as treaties and U.S. law alongside his commentary on recent events, in this way putting the two in conversation and insisting on the continuing relevance of past treaties and constitutional acts in the present.[70]

Boudinot's compiling and quoting of Hemans's poetry achieves a similar effect, demonstrating what Wisecup calls "the process-oriented nature of sovereignty," which requires a range of texts from different sources and different time periods to be reimagined to help validate Cherokee claims with reference to, but not exclusively in terms of, European cultural thought.[71]

However, as well as participating in Cherokee diplomatic discourses, Boudinot's practice was in many ways related to what David Rothstein has called "Hemans's feminine process of remaking history."[72] As Rothstein points out, this process involved "the practice of memorialization, of bearing idealized memories of family and nation, [which] performs a circular function of reorienting subjects toward fictional ideals of heart, home, and nation."[73] Rothstein is using "memorialization" in a general sense, but the echo of the Cherokee memorials is important to any understanding of Boudinot's

---

70. Kelly Wisecup, "Practicing Sovereignty: Colonial Temporalities, Cherokee Justice, and the 'Socrates' Writings of John Ridge," *Journal of the Native American and Indigenous Studies Association* 4, no. 1 (2017): 30–60;, 33.

71. Wisecup, 52.

72. David Rothstein, "Forming the Chivalric Subject: Felicia Hemans and the Cultural Uses of History, Memory, and Nostalgia," *Victorian Literature and Culture* 27, no. 1 (1999): 49–68; 51. A related argument is outlined by Benjamin Kim in his reading of Hemans's deployment of stories of global crises to make "implicit connections between these crises and her present political situation." See Kim, *Wordsworth, Hemans, and Politics, 1800–1830: Romantic Crises* (Lewisburg, PA: Bucknell University Press, 2013), 105. See also Gary Kelly, "Death and the Matron: Felicia Hemans, Romantic Death, and the Founding of the Modern Liberal State," in *Felicia Hemans: Reimagining Poetry in the Nineteenth Century*, ed. Nanora Sweet and Julie Melnyk, 196–211 (Basingstoke: Palgrave, 2001).

73. Rothstein, 51.

editorial practices. All the *Cherokee Phoenix*'s rhetoric was geared toward a repetitive process of recalling—for the Cherokees, but more importantly, for their diplomatic partners—the memories of past words, actions, and concepts. The process of remembering lost homes, lost relations, and lost land in Cherokee rhetorics performs a similar function to those memorializing activities in Hemans's work by returning with even greater force to the ideals of "heart, home, and nation" and the terms under which they can be preserved. Moreover, as Rothstein notes, the strength of Hemans's vision comes from the fact that these ideals are "portrayed either in the process of emergence or under threat of erasure."[74] The energy generated by this powerful undercurrent of threat to domestic and national harmony explains the unmistakable charge that the poems give off in the pages of the *Cherokee Phoenix*. Far from being an unusual choice, Hemans's poetics seem precisely attuned to Boudinot's rhetorical needs.

The emotional tenor of Hemans's poetry contributes to this diplomatic versatility. Cherokee diplomacy depended on a degree of emotional restraint and an expectation that conflict would be avoided and peacefulness would be both established and practiced. As Jason Rudy has written, part of Hemans's appeal to readers of the late Romantic and early Victorian period was her "innate sense of balance," which involved a measured approach to the management of emotion that did not sacrifice passion, but rather controlled it within a formal structure.[75] Cherokee epistemologies were based around *tohi*, the balance of nature and the creation, and *osi*, or individual balance, respectively.[76] In the postcontact period, including the early nineteenth century and the emergence of the National Council, balance and harmony continued to guide the Cherokees' foreign policy and formal diplomatic rhetoric, in the form of the "good talks," with first European and then American governments.[77] Hemans's poetry offered some of the qualities of "good talks," an emotional honesty that did not disturb and that was geared toward peaceful outcomes and reconciliation between parties.

---

74. Rothstein, 55.

75. Jason R. Rudy, "Hemans' Passion," *Studies in Romanticism* 45, no. 4 (2006): 543–62, esp. 544–51. See also Emma Mason, *Women Poets of the Nineteenth Century* (Blackburn, U.K.: Northcote, 2006), 19–24.

76. Heidi M. Altman and Thomas N. Belt, "Reading Cherokee History through a Cherokee Lens," *Native South* 1 (2008): 90–98; 91; Smithers, 56–57.

77. Cumfer, 2–3, 27; Smithers, 20, 35–36.

Or at least it offered these qualities at first. The year following Jackson's election saw a change in the way Boudinot deployed Hemans's work. After the frequent reprinting of her poems from the beginning of the newspaper in February 1828 until mid-1829, there was a sudden tailing off. "The Indian with His Dead Child" appeared in the July 8, 1829, issue. The next of her poems to appear in the *Cherokee Phoenix* was "Lines to an Orphan" in December 1829; the five-month period between this Hemans poem and the previous one was the longest gap between her appearances in the paper since it began.[78] After the publication of "Lines to an Orphan," only two further Hemans poems appeared during Boudinot's tenure as editor. "The Voice of the Waves," which was published in the *Phoenix* in January 1830, depicted the hopelessness of human endeavor against the power of the sea, with the ocean itself speaking of those who had lost their lives: "They are vanished from this place— / Let their homes and hearths make moan!" (21–22).[79] It was then almost another two years before Boudinot included his next Hemans selection, "Dreams of Heaven."[80] In this poem, the speaker asks three characters, a child, a poet, and a woman, to describe their dreams of heaven. The child's bright vision of a happy afterlife is overtaken by the poet's melancholy impression of earthly existence; in heaven, the poet says, "My soul, a wanderer *here*, shall know / The exile thirst no more!" (23–24). The woman's reflections end the poem, describing heaven as a place where "none have heard the knell / That smites the heart with that wild sound— / *Farewell, Belov'd! Farewell!*" (46–48; italics in the original). Hemans's poem structures the world as one marked by what seems like inevitable wandering, exile, and parting, with women among its most obvious victims, and "beloved" figures left behind.

I will return to these notions of women, and the term "beloved," shortly, but it is worth considering why Boudinot abandoned Hemans's poems as rhetorical and diplomatic devices in this moment. The periods between these last three Hemans poems were times of devastation for the Cherokee cause. Three weeks after Boudinot reprinted "The Indian

---

78. Felicia Hemans, "Lines to an Orphan," *Cherokee Phoenix, and Indians' Advocate*, December 3, 1829, 4.

79. Felicia Hemans, "The Voice of the Waves," *Cherokee Phoenix, and Indians' Advocate*, January 13, 1830, 4.

80. Felicia Hemans, "Dreams of Heaven," *Cherokee Phoenix, and Indians' Advocate*, November 19, 1831, 4.

with His Dead Child," reports emerged that gold had been discovered in Georgia, leading to an overwhelming influx of white prospectors. Just five days after Boudinot published "Lines to an Orphan," Andrew Jackson announced to Congress his plans for the long-signaled removal of all the Eastern Nations. The Indian Removal Act was passed in May 1830, clearing the way for the forced relocation of the Cherokees. Lawyers for the Cherokees then launched two crucial legal actions in 1831. The Georgia government chose to ignore the pending Supreme Court decisions and continued to enact legislation designed to take control of the Cherokee land within the state's borders.[81] The Cherokees augmented the Supreme Court cases with ongoing attempts to engage the U.S. government, including delegations to Washington, D.C., the last of which failed around the time "Dreams of Heaven" appeared in the *Cherokee Phoenix* in mid-November 1831. Although Boudinot had access to a considerable amount of Hemans's poetry in late 1831 and early 1832, which could have continued to fill the poetry section of the *Phoenix*, he simply stopped including her verse (at about the same time that John Ridge stopped writing his quotation-filled "Socrates" essays), preferring instead to use other poems, not from Hemans's pen, that dealt specifically with Native American characters.[82] The limits of sympathetic affect that could be drawn from Hemans's verse had been reached.

Nancy Moore Goslee has suggested that in Hemans's poetry, Native Americans stood for ideas of melancholy, exile, and maternal nature.[83] But it is similarly true that, for Native Americans, in Removal-era Cherokee country at least, it was Hemans's poetry that stood for, and provided the English literary gloss on, their lived experiences of nineteenth-century dispossession, in ways that could make some of that experience intelligible for Euro-American readers. If Indigenous peoples provided a useful shorthand for Hemans, her verse similarly provided a useful shorthand

---

81. Theda Perdue and Michael H. Green, *The Cherokee Nation and the Trail of Tears* (New York: Viking, 2007), 83–84.

82. There were at least eight Hemans poems included in *Blackwood's Magazine* between February and June 1829, as well as a similar number in the Boston-based *Atheneum; or, Spirit of the Magazines*, which Boudinot might have included in the paper at a subsequent date (assuming he had access to one of these periodicals, which appear to have been his major sources for poetry). For background on Ridge's decisions about the "Socrates" essays, see Wisecup, 52–53.

83. Goslee, 238.

for them. And while her characterizations of Indigenous peoples are stereotypes, they are nevertheless forged out of the fractured materials of dispossession, loss, alienation, and sorrow, which were unarguably characteristic of nineteenth-century imperialism. We might thus extend our reading of Hemans's "Indian" poems beyond the fourteen discussed by Goslee to suggest that the undertone of Hemans's verse is always "Indian," always concerned with the price to be paid for the imperial project.

Hemans and the Diplomatic Voice of Women

The eventual erasure of Felicia Hemans from the diplomatic endeavors of the Cherokees echoes an earlier and more serious erasure. Prior to the establishment of the Cherokee National Council, women had played a central role in the leadership and diplomatic frameworks of Cherokee life, especially through the Women's Council, which was formed of the most influential Cherokee women, or "Beloved Women."[84] Women's authority was centered on their role as mothers, a role that, as Theda Perdue puts it, "evoked power rather than sentimentality."[85] The Beloved Women were key diplomatic forces, who were consulted during negotiations and on occasion spoke to the American officials.[86] As Tiya Miles has shown, the role of women in Cherokee diplomacy, which was already undergoing considerable change in the late eighteenth century, began to change further during the removal crises of the early nineteenth century.[87] During

---

84. Cumfer, 27. See also Tom Hatley, *The Dividing Paths: Cherokees and South Carolinians through the Era of Revolution* (Oxford: Oxford University Press, 1995), 52–63. For a much wider discussion of Indigenous women and diplomacy, one that takes account of modern developments, see Laura Parisi and Jeff Corntassel, "A 'Revolution within a Revolution': Indigenous Women's Diplomacies," in *Indigenous Diplomacies*, ed. J. Marshall Beier, 79–95 (Basingstoke: Palgrave, 2009).

85. Theda Perdue, *Cherokee Women: Gender and Culture Change, 1700–1835* (Lincoln: University of Nebraska Press, 1998), 101.

86. Smithers, 31. For one such account of a woman speaking at a council, see Hawkins, Pickens, Martin, and McIntosh, 41. This account is further analyzed in Virginia Moore Carney, *Eastern Band Cherokee Women: Cultural Persistence in their Letters and Speeches* (Knoxville: University of Tennessee Press, 2005), 21–27.

87. Tiya Miles, "'Circular Reasoning': Recentering Cherokee Women in the Antiremoval Campaigns," *American Quarterly* 61, no. 2 (2009): 221–43. See also Smithers, 56; Paula Gunn Allen, *The Sacred Hoop: Recovering the Feminine in American Indian Traditions* (Boston: Beacon

the negotiations with then-general Andrew Jackson in 1817, the women, led by the Beloved Woman Nanye'hi (Nancy Ward), convened their own council before the men met, establishing an antiremoval platform based around the power of motherhood.[88] On May 2, 1817, thirteen women signed a petition that was presented to the Cherokee National Council on Nanye'hi's behalf, informing the council that the women "thought it their duty as mothers to address their beloved chiefs and warriors."[89] This case against removal, which was rooted in Cherokee values but was attempting to extend them to include a maternal attitude toward white settlers, was ultimately unsuccessful; some Cherokees signed a removal treaty with Jackson in July 1817, and protests by the mandated Cherokee leadership did not prevent the U.S. Senate from ratifying the treaty. Following this setback, Margaret Ann Scott led the Cherokee women's protests in a different direction, focusing instead on the Bible and Christian values.[90] The women presented another petition to the council on July 3, 1818, which alluded to both Cherokee spirituality and the role of Christianity in the Cherokee community, as part of a wider instruction to the council members, as "our beloved children," to stand firm against removal.[91] The deaths of Scott in 1820 and Nanye'hi in 1822 heralded major changes in the role of Cherokee women in the new Removal-era politics; as Miles points out, no women served on the committee that drafted the 1827

Press, 1986), 36–38; Duane Champagne, *Social Order and Political Change: Constitutional Governments among the Cherokee, the Choctaw, the Chickasaw and the Creek* (Stanford, CA: Stanford University Press, 1992), 131; and Cumfer, 27, 35–39. For a somewhat different account of the evolution of the roles of Cherokee women, see Perdue, *Cherokee Women: Gender and Culture Change.*

88. Miles, 221–43. For a description of Nanye'hi's role in Cherokee diplomacy, see Justice, *Our Fire Survives the Storm,* 31–41; Cumfer, 35–39.

89. Carney, 11, 38. See also Miles, 226; Perdue, *Cherokee Women: Gender and Culture Change,* 156; Theda Perdue, "Cherokee Women and the Trail of Tears," in *Native Women's History in Eastern North America before 1900: A Guide to Research and Writing,* ed. Rebecca Kugel and Lucy Eldersveld Murphy, 277–302 (Lincoln: University of Nebraska Press, 2007); and Laura E. Donaldson, "'But We Are Your Mothers, You Are Our Sons': Gender, Sovereignty, and the Nation in Early Cherokee Women's Writing," in *Indigenous Women and Feminism: Politics, Activism, Culture,* ed. Cheryl Suzack, Shari M. Huhndorf, Jeanne Perreault, and Jean Barman, 43–55 (Vancouver: University of British Columbia Press, 2010).

90. Miles, 229–32.

91. McLoughlin, *Cherokee Renascence,* 240.

Cherokee constitution, which banned women from voting in elections or serving in public office.[92]

However, there was considerable awareness among the Cherokees that white women's sympathy could be harnessed to support their cause. One of the initiatives undertaken by the Cherokee women in their antiremoval platform was to win the support of the sentimental poet Lydia Sigourney.[93] Sigourney's 1822 poem *Traits of the Aborigines* included an excerpt from a letter by Margaret Scott, an inclusion that acts as the mirror image of Boudinot's use of Hemans: in Sigourney's poem, Cherokee diplomacy is used verbatim in the service of sentimental poetry, while in the *Phoenix*, sentimental poetry is used verbatim in the service of Cherokee diplomacy.[94] Sigourney went on to influence the activist Catharine Beecher, whose *Circular Addressed to Benevolent Ladies of the United States* was a prominent instance of white women's attempts to prevent Native removal, and which quoted from the historical treaties and council speeches.[95] Sigourney also wrote "The Cherokee Mother," a poem specifically addressing removal and maternal sentiment that Boudinot included in his newspaper, and a letter opposing removal from "An Association of Ladies" to the Connecticut members of Congress, which accompanied the poem in the *Cherokee Phoenix*.[96] The letter deployed a

---

92. Miles, 225.

93. Miles, 224.

94. Lydia Howard Sigourney, *Traits of the Aborigines: A Poem* (Cambridge, MA: University Press, 1822), 281. Boudinot published an excerpt of this poem in the *Cherokee Phoenix, and Indians' Advocate* on October 7, 1829, and he published several other Sigourney poems during his tenure as editor.

95. *Circular Addressed to Benevolent Ladies of the United States* (Boston: n.p., 1829), 1–2. See also Mary Hershberger, "Mobilizing Women, Anticipating Abolition: The Struggle Against Indian Removal in the 1830s," *Journal of American History* 86, no. 1 (1999): 15–40; 25–26; Janet Dean, *Unconventional Politics: Nineteenth-Century Women Writers and U.S. Indian Policy* (Amherst: University of Massachusetts Press, 2016), 86–99; and Alisse Portnoy, *Their Right to Speak: Women's Activism in the Indian and Slave Debates* (Cambridge, MA: Harvard University Press, 2005). A similar petition can be found in "Memorial of the Ladies of Steubenville, Ohio, against the Forcible Removal of the Indians without the Limits of the United States," February 15, 1830, United States Documents Serial, vol. 200, doc. 209.

96. Lydia Sigourney, "The Cherokee Mother," *Cherokee Phoenix, and Indians' Advocate*, March 12, 1831, 3; "Letter to the Delegation of the State of Connecticut, from an Association of Ladies," *Cherokee Phoenix, and Indians' Advocate*, March 12, 1831, 3; emphasis in the original. See also Dean, 67–70.

feminine rhetoric familiar to any reader of Hemans, which proposed that women, being "accustomed to associate every hope that cheers, every charity that sweetens life with the idea of home, involuntarily sympathize with those who may be exiled from its sanctuary."[97] These rhetorics of shared oppression were pervasive in the discourse of nineteenth-century American white women, as Lauren Berlant has shown, but they were also being activated on the other side of the settler-Indigenous divide.[98] Boudinot's decision to make such extensive use of Hemans's poetry makes much more sense when we consider the extent to which women's voices, activism, and verse were threaded through the Cherokee removal debates, moving between white and Indigenous communities and focusing on the political and diplomatic potential of feminine sympathy.[99]

The dense, entangled nature of women's voices, English poetry, and Cherokee diplomacy can be further gauged in Robert Campbell's pamphlet *The Present State of the Cherokee Indians* (1829). Campbell, a white resident of Savannah, quotes lines from Sigourney's *Traits of the Aborigines* alongside lines from treaties with the Cherokees, the Georgia Compact, and various laws and reports in an attempt to "call forth the sympathies of every man who abhors tyranny and violence" in favor of the Cherokee cause. Boudinot, in his turn, published Campbell's pamphlet verbatim in the *Cherokee Phoenix*.[100] This constant recycling and recitation of literary and diplomatic materials alongside one another and among different media was all designed to evoke a sympathetic response and remind readers of their existing commitments to the Cherokees.

Although Campbell's pamphlet mentions Sigourney and not Hemans, the latter's influence can nevertheless be felt in this particular example

---

97. See also the rhetoric of the *Circular Addressed to Benevolent Ladies of the United States*, which asked, "Those whose hearts thrill at the magic sound of *home*, and turn with delightful remembrance to the woods and the valleys of their childhood and youth, will they allow this helpless race to be forced for ever from such blessed scenes, and to look back upon them with hopeless regret and despair?" (2–3; emphasis in the original)

98. Lauren Berlant, *The Female Complaint: The Unfinished Business of Sentimentality in American Culture* (Durham, NC: Duke University Press, 2008).

99. For a discussion of some of the particular details of white sympathy in the Removal era, see Susan M. Ryan, *The Grammar of Good Intentions: Race and the Antebellum Culture of Benevolence* (Ithaca, NY: Cornell University Press, 2003), 24–45.

100. Robert Campbell, "Memorial to the Honourable the President and Members of the Senate of the State of Georgia," *Cherokee Phoenix, and Indians' Advocate*, April 29, 1829, 1–2.

of affective advocacy. Sigourney was known as "the American Hemans"; she wrote an introduction for an 1853 Boston edition of Hemans's work, and her own poetry reveals an intense engagement with the themes that dominated the poems of her British counterpart.[101] As Tricia Lootens has pointed out, one of the clearest overlaps in the two poets' work was their interest in Native Americans.[102] But a different triangulation of Sigourney, Hemans, and Native Americans can also be discerned, in which the clear link between the three is not a poetic theme nor a question of style but rather women's voices, Cherokee diplomacy, and that diplomacy's mobilization of white sympathy. Sigourney's poem "The Cherokee Mother" certainly imitates the features of Hemans's verse in both its structure as a monologue delivered by the eponymous mother as she departs with her child and the mournful references to exile, crying children, the "native earth" (32), and the "hearth-stone cold" (39). But it also lingers on the specifics of Cherokee diplomacy and the failure of both official settler documents and broader settler sympathy, especially in its final stanza:

> Will a crush'd nation's deep despair,
> *Your broken faith*—our tear-wet sod,
> The babe's appeal,—the chieftain's prayer,
> Find no memorial with our God? (45–48; emphasis in the original)

While Janet Dean suggests that the reference to a "memorial" reminds readers of white women's petitions to their representatives, it also clearly echoes the memorials written by the Cherokee leadership to the federal government.[103] These links to cross-cultural diplomatic text are set alongside less obvious ideas from the world of Indigenous-settler diplomacy, such as the stanza's second-person address and the emphasis on "broken faith,"

---

101. See Tricia Lootens, "Hemans and Her American Heirs: Nineteenth-Century Women's Poetry and National Identity," in *Women's Poetry, Late Romantic to Late Victorian: Gender and Genre, 1830–1900*, ed. Isobel Armstrong and Virginia Blain, 243–60; 245 (Houndmills, UK: Macmillan, 1999). Sigourney's introductory essay on Hemans can be found in Felicia Hemans, *The Poetical Works of Felicia Hemans, Complete in One Volume, With a Memoir, by Mrs. L. H. Sigourney* (Boston: Phillips, Sampson and Co., 1853), 29–46.

102. Lootens, "Hemans and Her American Heirs," 247–48.

103. Dean, 70. This point is also made in the notes to the poem in Paula Bernat Bennett, ed., *Nineteenth-Century American Women Poets: An Anthology* (Oxford: Blackwell, 1998), 7n.

which speak directly to both abstract settler emotions and concrete settler promises.[104] To read the poem in this way is to center the conversation, not around Anglo-American poetic aesthetics per se, but around those aesthetics as a counter to be used in colonial rhetoric, in which many other aesthetic and diplomatic expressions were in play. To place Hemans, not simply alongside Sigourney, but also alongside Margaret Scott and the Cherokee Women's Council, is to realize the extent of the global and politicized femininity in which Hemans participates.

Boudinot's use of Hemans anticipates modern critical reevaluations of her poetry's worth, status, and purpose. It is striking the degree to which he manifests Isobel Armstrong's suggestion about "affective discourse" and the way in which it is estimated. Armstrong suggests that women writers in the nineteenth century

> engaged with two strategies to deal with the problem of affective discourse. First, they used the customary "feminine" forms and languages, but they turned them to *analytical* account and used them to *think* with. Second, they challenged the male / philosophical traditions that led to a demeaning discourse of feminine experience and remade those traditions. They did not take these philosophical traditions—the only traditions they had—as an inert model but reconstructed them through critique.[105]

This assessment can be reframed in terms of Boudinot and the *Cherokee Phoenix* to elucidate the way in which he uses Hemans's poetry both as a guide for thought and to engage a foreign intellectual tradition on its own terms as a form of critique, admonishment, and exhortation. But that is not simply to say that he engages in a project parallel or analogous to Hemans's own poetic aims. Rather, the same forces that shape Hemans's poetics and her approach to affective discourse were also shaping

---

104. John O'Leary reads the poem effectively in terms of settler sympathy in his article "'Unlocking the Fountains of the Heart'—Settler Verse and the Politics of Sympathy," *Postcolonial Studies* 13, no. 1 (2010): 55–70.

105. Isobel Armstrong, "The Gush of the Feminine: How Can We Read Women's Poetry of the Romantic Period?" in *Romantic Women Writers: Voices and Countervoices*, ed. Paula R. Feldman and Theresa M. Kelley, 13–32; 16 (Lebanon, NH: University Press of New England, 1995), emphasis in the original.

his. Hemans's consideration of the affective occurred within the wider scope of nineteenth-century colonialism, and especially within the scope of Indigenous-settler relationships in the United States, a topic about which she often wrote.[106] There is nothing abstract about the connection between Removal-era America and Hemans's poetics, style, and deployment of affect. The global political forces acting on Boudinot were the same as those acting on Hemans. The most obvious sign of Hemans's contemporary relevance to the Cherokees and to Georgia is the fact that Boudinot's deployment of her poetry occurred in real time. He reprinted (and consequently reframed) Hemans's verse as it appeared in English and American periodicals, treating it as part of the live, public, political discourse from which he could draw. His practice both supports and contradicts Susan Wolfson's reading of the forces of Hemans's reception by demonstrating that there was indeed always a powerful sense of critique and protest in Hemans's verse and that these factors were certainly not overlooked by all nineteenth-century readers.[107] In Cherokee country, at the very least, these factors were entirely evident.

Boudinot was right to intuit that Hemans's poems were preoccupied with the fragile status of home. As Anne K. Mellor's work has shown, Hemans's apparently sentimental and stable tropes of home and hearth are, in fact, always under threat, always constructed as mutable, temporary, and subject to destruction and decay.[108] In their moment, these poems spoke to a world threatened by displaced homes and disrupted lives, in which women's voices were made simultaneously vulnerable and powerful by their status as mothers, wives, and onlookers to global conflict. Hemans's poems argue for a feminine recalibrating of the global order, in which sympathy is not cheap sentimentalism but rather a revivifying force for broken social and political bonds. It is the same power, albeit interpreted

---

106. As well as Nancy Moore Goslee's essay on Hemans's "Indian" poems; see Tim Fulford, *Romantic Indians: Native Americans, British Literature, and Transatlantic Culture 1756–1830* (Oxford: Oxford University Press, 2006), 196–204.

107. Susan J. Wolfson, "Felicia Hemans and the Revolving Doors of Reception," in *Romanticism and Women Poets: Opening the Doors of Reception*, ed. Harriet Kramer Linkin and Stephen C. Behrendt, 214–41; 237–38 (Lexington: University Press of Kentucky, 1999).

108. Mellor, 124–43. See also Kate Singer and Nanora Sweet, "Introduction—Beyond Domesticity: Felicia Hemans in the Wider World," *Women's Writing* 21, no. 1 (2014): 1–8, esp. 3; and David Simpson, *Romanticism and the Question of the Stranger* (Chicago: University of Chicago Press, 2013), 177.

from within European tradition, that the Cherokee Women's Council claimed and that the Cherokee leadership wanted to mobilize in its cause.

But to read Hemans in this way is also to realize the ways in which Cherokee women's voices were silenced as white women's voices were endorsed, a strategy that not only participated in colonial violence but also revealed the limits and hypocrisies of white sympathy. These limits have become imposed as canonical limits as well. Hemans's apparent poetic failings, as manifested in the collapse of her reputation up until the late twentieth century, are themselves signs of a world undone by nineteenth-century colonization, patriarchy, and violence, which has rightly led to the suspicion that sympathy and sentiment are weak, patronizing, and manifestly dishonest responses to oppression. But there was a historical moment in which sympathy was treated as a viable political weapon and wielded largely by minority authors and speakers, a moment in which Hemans's work seemed legitimately powerful. In 1787, the Beloved Woman Katteuha had undertaken her own diplomatic endeavor, writing to Benjamin Franklin: "I am in hopes you have a beloved woman amongst you who will help to put her children right if they do wrong."[109] This is one way in which we might read Felicia Hemans, as the Beloved Woman of Euro-American culture, a voice of reason and compassion from within nineteenth-century white settler-imperial ranks whose words and the sympathetic promises they encoded were, in spite of that, never going to be enough to hold back the Trail of Tears.

---

109. Cited in Cumfer, 39.

Chapter 3

Digressive Diplomacy

George Copway and Byron's Lines on the Rhine

The Mississauga Ojibwe author and minister George Copway (Kahgegagahbowh) might be described as someone destined for the world of Indigenous diplomacy. In his autobiography, he noted that his mother gave birth to him in 1818 while at the site of the government annuity payments for the Mississauga Ojibwe at the Trent River in southern Ontario.[1] It is perhaps not surprising, then, to find that on August 19, 1850, Copway boarded a steamer at Cologne to cross the Rhine as one of the delegates to the third World Peace Congress in Frankfurt. He was traveling, not as an official ambassador for his people, but rather at the invitation of the American temperance campaigner Elihu Burritt, who had proposed him as a representative of the "Christian Indians of America," and he was granted the distinct privilege of giving a speech and presenting a resolution at the Congress.[2] Recollecting this part of

---

1. George Copway, *Life, Letters and Speeches: George Copway (Kahgegabowh)*, ed. A. Lavonne Brown Ruoff and Donald B. Smith, 73 (Lincoln: University of Nebraska Press, 1997), 73. The term *Ojibwe* is sometimes spelt "Ojibwa" or "Ojibway," and is also the term that was corrupted into the word *Chippewa* or *Chippeway*, which is often used in the older documents I refer to in this chapter. I use *Ojibwe* in my own prose for consistency's sake.

2. The fullest account of Copway's role at the congress can be found in Bernd Peyer, "A Nineteenth-Century Ojibwa Conquers Germany," in *Germans and Indians: Fantasies, Encounters, Projections*, ed. Colin G. Calloway, Gerd Gemünden, and Susanne Zantop, 141–64 (Lincoln: University of Nebraska Press, 2002). A short account of the delegates' trip from London to Frankfurt can be found in *Report of the Proceedings of the Third General Peace*

his European trip in his 1851 book *Running Sketches of Men and Places, in England, France, Germany, Belgium, and Scotland*, Copway quoted more than 70 lines from the passage in Canto III of Byron's *Childe Harold's Pilgrimage*, in which Harold stands "on the banks of thy majestic Rhine" (3.409) and excavates the history of conflict written in the scenery.[3]

Copway was in the habit of using quotation as part of his rhetorical style. In publications ranging from an autobiography to a history of his people, he often included lines or short extracts of English literary texts, possibly suggested to him by his wife, Elizabeth, including frequent excerpts from Byron.[4] But these examples were usually a few lines or

---

Congress, Held in Frankfort, on the 22nd, 23rd, and 24th of August, 1850 (London: Charles Gilpin, 1851), xii. For details on Burritt, see Merle Curti, *The Learned Blacksmith: The Letters and Journals of Elihu Burritt* (New York: Wilson-Erickson, 1937). A detailed study of the Peace Congresses that took place throughout mid-nineteenth century Europe can be found in Alexander Tyrrell, "Making the Millennium: The Mid-Nineteenth Century Peace Movement," *Historical Journal* 21, no. 1 (1978): 75–95.

3. George Copway, *Running Sketches of Men and Places, in England, France, Germany, Belgium, and Scotland* (New York: J. C. Riker, 1851), 204–6. The quotation begins with the line "On the banks of the majestic Rhine" and ends with the line "Still springing o'er thy banks, though Empires near them fall." Subsequent references to *Running Sketches* are included in the text. Unless otherwise indicated, other references to Byron's poetry are to *The Complete Poetical Works*, ed. Jerome J. McGann, 7 vols. (Oxford: Clarendon Press, 1980–1993), and are included in the text.

4. Donald B. Smith, "The Life of George Copway or Kah-ge-ga-gah-bowh (1816–1869)— and a Review of His Writings," *Journal of Canadian Studies* 23, no. 3 (1988): 5–38; 14. Most scholarship on Copway is restricted to discussion of the 1847 autobiography and the 1850 *Traditional History*; for examples of criticism on these texts in particular, see A. LaVonne Brown Ruoff, "The Literary and Methodist Contexts of George Copway's Life, Letters and Speeches," in *Life, Letters & Speeches: George Copway (Kahgegagahbowh)*, ed. A. LaVonne Brown Ruoff and Donald B. Smith, 1–21 (Lincoln: University of Nebraska Press, 1997); Donald B. Smith, "Kahgegagahbowh: Canada's First Literary Celebrity in the United States," in *Life, Letters and Speeches: George Copway (Kahgegagahbowh)*, ed. A Ruoff and Smith, 23–60; Cathy Rex, "Survivance and Fluidity: George Copway's The Life, History, and Travels of Kah-ge-ga-gah-bowh," *Studies in American Indian Literatures* 18, no. 2 (2006): 1–33; Smith, "The Life of George Copway," 5–38; H. David Brumble III, *American Indian Autobiography* (Berkeley: University of California Press, 1988); Gerald Vizenor, *The People Named the Chippewa: Narrative Histories* (Minneapolis: University of Minnesota Press, 1984); Meghan C. L. Howey, "'The Question Which Has Puzzled, and Still Puzzles': How American Indian Authors Challenged Dominant Discourse about Native American Origins in the Nineteenth Century," *American Indian Quarterly* 34, no. 3 (2010): 435–74; Joshua David Bellin, *The Demon of the Continent: Indians and the Shaping of American Literature* (University Park: Penn State University Press, 2001), 179–99;

sometimes a stanza. The *Childe Harold* quote in *Running Sketches* deserves attention as the longest, most sustained citation of English poetry in Copway's oeuvre, as well as another contribution to the global pattern of Indigenous diplomacy that this book investigates.

The use of other people's words is a particular critical problem for *Running Sketches*, which might be read, as Kate Flint has suggested, as "a collage of tones."[5] Copway's journal entries make up part of the book, but so too do long sections from newspapers, guidebooks, letters to correspondents in America, and texts of his public addresses to European audiences. The result, to readers trained in Romanticism's tenets of authenticity and originality, is disappointing; Bernd Peyer assesses it to be Copway's "least accomplished work," saying it was "patched together haphazardly" and is full of "lengthy, boring passages" and "tedious banalities."[6] Readers in search of the organic voice of the Romantic speaker are left "to sift through redundant pages in order to find the scattered passages with personal impressions."[7] Tim Fulford supplies a more politically informed reading of Copway's fondness for quotation, but still reads it against the Romantic criterion of authenticity:

> Romantic discourse was one of the most empowering yet destructive elements of Victorian culture, a discourse Copway and Elizabeth could never adopt without, at the same time, translating Ojibwa identity into generalized, feminized, infantilized form. This is nowhere better displayed than in the paradox that quoting British poets reveals Copway's adeptness at assimilation and occludes any exploration he might make in his own words. In fact, the frequent recourse to quotation exposes that for Copway even his own words are, to the extent that they are English, foreign. To be a Romantic Indian was a prospect that British literature offered Copway as a better alternative to being a missionary Methodist or a political campaigner. What he could not derive from it was a literary

---

Cheryl Walker, *Indian Nation: Native American Literature and Nineteenth Century Nationalisms* (Durham, NC: Duke University Press, 1997), 84–108; and Peyer, *The Tutor'd Mind*, 224–77.

5. Kate Flint, *The Transatlantic Indian, 1776–1930* (Princeton, NJ: Princeton University Press, 2009), 216.

6. Peyer, *The Tutor'd Mind*, 273, 276.

7. Peyer, *The Tutor'd Mind*, 273.

voice able to represent the experience of Ojibwa identity as an adult social and ontological condition.[8]

It is worth theorizing about the overall effect of Copway's manifold quotations and pastiches. But such an approach risks reducing specific strategic decisions about the incorporation of another's words into a framework that is both generalized and conceptualized from the perspective of a tradition that values originality above all else, as Deanna Reder's critique of Fulford's interpretation has demonstrated.[9] Scott Richard Lyons has likewise provided an important corrective to this dismissive and decontextualized reading of *Running Sketches* by suggesting that it should be read as part of "a genealogy of native modernity, by which I mean simply a native embracement of modern logics and a refusal to 'vanish' before them."[10] In Lyons's analysis, the various voices that Copway adopts in his text are part of a wider project of "ensuring that Indians are included in a rapidly globalizing modern society."[11] There is nevertheless still very little scholarly work that provides a detailed reading of Copway's specific choices of authors or extracts or that analyzes these choices within the context of the wider rhetorical point that Lyons rightly argues Copway

---

8. Tim Fulford, *Romantic Indians: Native Americans, British Literature, and Transatlantic Culture 1756–1830* (Oxford: Oxford University Press, 2006), 289. Bellin makes a similar point from a similarly sympathetic critical position, suggesting that Copway "felt that the mere act of quoting authorities lent his text a scholarly air" (198). Stafford's discussion of Copway is brief and does not specifically tackle *Running Sketches*, but it is much more astute in its reading of Copway's response to and deployment of English literature (1–6).

9. Deanna Reder, "Âcimisowin as Theoretical Practice: Autobiography as Indigenous Intellectual Tradition in Canada," PhD thesis, University of British Columbia, Vancouver, Canada, 2007, 170–72. A similar point is made, in a more general sense, by Lisa Brooks when she notes that "a belief persists that literacy is a mark of coercive colonialism and modernity inherently antithetical to Indigenous traditions." See Brooks, "Writing and Lasting: Native Northeastern Literary History," *The Oxford Handbook of Indigenous American Literature*, ed. James H. Cox and Daniel Heath Justice, 536–58; 536 (Oxford: Oxford University Press, 2014).

10. Scott Richard Lyons, "Migrations to Modernity: The Many Voices of George Copway's Running Sketches of Men and Places, in England, France, Germany, Belgium, and Scotland," in *The World, The Text, and the Indian: Global Dimensions of American Literature*, ed. Scott Richard Lyons, 143–82; 146 (Albany: State University of New York Press, 2017).

11. Lyons, "Migrations to Modernity," 147.

is attempting to make at that moment.[12] Examples like the long quotation from *Childe Harold's Pilgrimage* in *Running Sketches* are thus judged as subpar Romanticism rather than as expressions of Ojibwe print culture and political rhetoric, and they are not considered within their publication context nor within the wider Indigenous diplomatic history that I aim to trace. I would like here to follow Frank Kelderman's reading of *Running Sketches* as a diplomatic text but attend more closely to the role of Byron's verse in Copway's endeavor.[13]

The lines from Byron in *Running Sketches* are followed almost immediately by an abrupt change of tone. Copway's next chapter, "Peace Congress," begins in what might be described as a bureaucratic register: "The proceedings of the Third General Peace Congress, were opened on Thursday, the 22d of August, 1850, at Frankfort-on-the-Maine, in St. Paul's Church, the building made memorable by the recent meetings of the Frankfort Parliament" (208). The chapter goes on to detail or cite the various motions and speeches from the Congress with almost no independent commentary from Copway. The shift from Byronic lyricism to bland reportage is potentially jarring, and it is this sort of stylistic collage that has led both Copway's nineteenth-century readers and more recent scholars to criticize the book.[14] But the decision to juxtapose Byron's lines and the formal report of the Peace Congress suggests that Copway saw some value in placing them side by side. It is not Byron's verse that sets the tone for this juxtaposition, I would suggest, but rather Copway's report. The Congress is not being interpreted through a Byronic lens; rather, *Childe Harold* is being interpreted as a useful diplomatic text. Instead of seeing the move from verse to reportage as awkward, we are being encouraged to read the two texts—Byron's poem and the Copway book that encloses it—as different generic expressions of diplomatic rhetoric.

---

12. A major exception here is Kevin Hutchings's excellent reading of another instance of Copway quoting Byron; see Hutchings, "'The Nobleness of the Hunter's Deed': British Romanticism, Christianity and Ojibwa culture in George Copway's *Recollections of a Forest Life*," in *Native Americans and Anglo-American Culture, 1750–1850*, ed. Tim Fulford and Kevin Hutchings, 217–40 (Cambridge: Cambridge University Press, 2009). Some consideration of this point can also be found in Walker, 99–101.

13. Frank Kelderman, *Authorized Agents: Publication and Diplomacy in the Era of Indian Removal* (Albany: State University of New York Press, 2019), 201–9.

14. See for example the review from the New York–based *Daily Tribune* in Smith, "The Life of George Copway," 23–24.

Touching the Pen:
Ojibwe Diplomacy in the Nineteenth Century

The diplomatic nature of *Running Sketches* comes into focus if we stop thinking of it as an English text and instead locate it in the textual world of the Ojibwe (and the wider group to which they belonged, the Anishinaabeg) in the early nineteenth century. This was a textual world dominated by diplomacy. The written record of Ojibwe expression from this period is composed almost entirely of treaties, petitions, and the transcripts of speeches made in councils of negotiation with the U.S. government. As Bethel Saler has argued, the interactions between the Indigenous and American nations in the Old Northwest created a "treaty polity," in which Ojibwe leaders had to come to terms with and deploy print culture through the formula of treaties and their associated documents.[15] With the exception of translations of scripture, diplomatic text was the primary genre of Ojibwe written discourse in Copway's lifetime.

The dominance of diplomatic text reflects the significant changes in Ojibwe-U.S. relations in the first half of the nineteenth century. Before the War of 1812, the Ojibwe had maintained relatively friendly relationships with the major European powers who had made alliances with them in order to access the fur trade. In long-standing connections, first with the French and then with the British government, the Ojibwe had developed beneficial trading relationships without ceding control of land or resources.[16] Anishinaabewaki, the land occupied by the Ojibwe and their Anishinaabeg allies and kin, was almost entirely controlled by Indigenous peoples whose traditions and lifeways prescribed encounters with Europeans, including the formalities of diplomatic negotiations.[17] Richard White has dubbed this period and the relationships that characterized it "the middle ground," referring to a shared space created by the constant process of negotiation between the Anishinaabeg and Europeans, as both

---

15. Bethel Saler, *The Settlers' Empire: Colonialism and State Formation in America's Old Northwest* (University Park: Penn State University Press, 2014), 83–120.

16. See, for example, the account provided in Timothy D. Willig, *Restoring the Chain of Friendship: British Policy and the Indians of the Great Lakes, 1783–1815* (Lincoln: University of Nebraska Press, 2008).

17. Michael Witgen, *An Infinity of Nations: How the Native New World Shaped Early North America* (University Park: Penn State University Press, 2011).

struggled to assert their own power and cultural values but were forced to accommodate those of the other side. This process had particular implications for diplomacy, as White articulates:

> The middle ground depended on the inability of both sides to gain their ends through force. The middle ground grew according to the need of people to find a means, other than force, to gain the cooperation or consent of foreigners. To succeed, those who operated on the middle ground had, of necessity, to attempt to understand the world and the reasoning of others and to assimilate enough of that reasoning to put it to their own purposes. Particularly in diplomatic councils, the middle ground was a realm of constant invention, which was just as constantly presented as convention.[18]

After the War of 1812, however, the Ojibwe living on the American side of Lake Superior were now required to negotiate with a different sovereign nation. These negotiations began with relatively amicable settlements in the 1820s that did not involve land cessions or loss of sovereignty, although the 1825 Treaty of Prairie du Chien did lay the groundwork for later cessions by fixing the boundaries between the Ojibwe and neighboring Native nations.[19] Even the growing calls for removal, and the subsequent passage of the Removal Act in 1830, which had created monumental political difficulties for groups like the Cherokees, did not initially exert much pressure on the Ojibwe, whose lands were not seen as desirable for settlement.

Ojibwe resources, however, were in growing demand and were the subject of increasingly unethical diplomacy by American officials. In the 1837 Treaty of St. Peters (sometimes called the Pine Tree Treaty), Ojibwe leaders sold lands in what is currently Wisconsin in return for annuity payments over the following twenty years, after American negotiators

---

18. Richard White, *The Middle Ground: Indians, Empires, and Republics in the Great Lakes Region, 1650–1815*, 2nd ed. (Cambridge: Cambridge University Press, 2011), 52.

19. Erik M. Redix, *The Murder of Joe White: Ojibwe Leadership and Colonialism in Wisconsin* (East Lansing: Michigan State University Press, 2014), xiv; Ronald N. Satz, "Chippewa Treaty Rights: The Reserved Rights of Wisconsin's Chippewa Indians in Historical Perspective," *Transactions of the Wisconsin Academy of Sciences, Arts and Letters* 79, no. 1 (1991): 8.

misrepresented the treaty as covering only the rights to timber resources for the growing settler population. The language of the treaty makes it clear that the U.S. government intended to claim the land and to lay a foundation for a future removal; under Article 5 of the 1837 treaty, the Ojibwe were guaranteed "the privilege of hunting, fishing, and gathering the wild rice, upon the land, the rivers and the lakes included in the territory ceded . . . during the pleasure of the President of the United States."[20] This final phrase, however, was not understood by the Ojibwe signing the treaty as implying that they would need to leave their territory. As the linguist John D. Nichols has explained, the likely translation for the word "guaranteed" would have been the term "baataayaakonigaade," an emphatic term meaning something absolutely fixed in law by the authorities. This term would have trumped any sense of restriction implied by the phrase "the pleasure of the President."[21]

Similar problems occurred at the 1842 Treaty of La Pointe, which was driven by American demand for newly uncovered copper resources in Ojibwe territory and by dissatisfaction among the Ojibwe with the terms and implications of the 1837 agreement. The Ojibwe signatories clearly believed that they were only ceding leased mineral rights to the U.S. government, not possession of the land. Hunting, fishing, and other rights in their territories were protected, but the Ojibwe would be able to exercise them only, according to Article 2 of the 1842 treaty, "until required to remove by the President of the United States."[22] This phrasing concerned the Ojibwe signatories, one of whom, White Crow, asked treaty commissioner Henry Stuart whether it meant that he would be required to leave immediately. According to eyewitnesses on both sides, Stuart replied that the land would not be required for a long time; some versions record that he said removal would not occur during White Crow's lifetime, while others suggest an even longer time span, encompassing the lifetimes of the assembled chiefs' children and perhaps as long as a

---

20. *United States Statutes at Large*, 1837, 7 Stat. 536.

21. John D. Nichols, "The Translation of Key Phrases in the Treaties of 1837 and 1855," in *Fish in the Lakes, Wild Rice, and Game in Abundance: Testimony on Behalf of Mille Lacs Ojibwe Hunting and Fishing Rights*, ed. James M. McClurken, 514–24; 518–19 (East Lansing: Michigan State University Press, 2000). See also Satz, 13–31.

22. Redix, 40–43.

hundred years.²³ Stuart's private correspondence indicates that he believed he was telling the truth and had no sense that removal was imminent.²⁴ The effect of this dialogue was that at least two versions of the agreement circulated and interacted with each other: the written text and the various verbal commitments that Stuart made and that were preserved in the oral record alone.

Although the 1837 and 1842 treaties set out the possibility of removal, there was very little pressure on the Ojibwe to leave their land until the late 1840s. In summer 1847, the Indian Commissioner William Medill had begun investigations into removing the Ojibwe west of the Mississippi.²⁵ These efforts were intensified when Alexander Ramsey was appointed governor of the Minnesota territory in 1849. Ramsey wanted to shift the Wisconsin Ojibwe into Minnesota in order to secure the revenue from their annuity payments for traders and merchants in his own region. In response to resolutions in the Minnesota Territorial Legislature that proposed removal, Ojibwe leaders, supported by many local settlers, began to agitate for reservations that would allow them to remain on their land; in 1849, a group of six *ogimaag* (hereditary leaders; the singular is *ogimaa*), led by Naagaanab, Oshkaabewis, and Gezhiiyaash, formally petitioned the U.S. Congress for the establishment of Ojibwe reservations.²⁶

These issues came to a head in February 1850, when President Zachary Taylor issued an executive order to remove the Ojibwe over whom the federal government believed it had jurisdiction. Local officials in Minnesota decided to enact the removal order by requiring Wisconsin

---

23. Charles E. Cleland, "Preliminary Report of the Ethnohistorical Basis of the Hunting, Fishing, and Gathering Rights of the Mille Lacs Chippewa," in *Fish in the Lakes, Wild Rice, and Game in Abundance*, ed. McClurken, 1–140, 38–39. Cleland cites a letter from Leonard Wheeler to David Greene written in May 1843. The same information was recorded in the Ojibwe oral account of the negotiations; see Satz, 42.

24. Cleland, 55; James A. Clifton, "Wisconsin Death March: Explaining the Extremes in Old Northwest Indian Removal," *Transactions of the Wisconsin Academy of Sciences, Arts and Letters* 75 (1987): 1–40, 15–16.

25. Satz, 45.

26. Cleland, 61–66; Redix, 52–53; Satz, 56. For details of the efforts of the white community in support of the Ojibwe cause, see Clifton, 21. For definitions of the different forms of Ojibwe leadership, see Cary Miller, *Ogimaag: Anishinaabeg Leadership, 1760–1845* (Lincoln: University of Nebraska Press, 2010).

Ojibwe to travel to the northern Minnesota settlement of Sandy Lake in order to collect their annuities in the autumn, but they deliberately delayed the payment so that frozen waterways would prevent these Ojibwe returning to their land. Approximately 12 percent of the Wisconsin Ojibwe population died on the dangerous winter journey back to their homes, and others suffered from disease and malnutrition at Sandy Lake, where insufficient resources were available for the length of time they were required to stay.[27] A further but unsuccessful attempt to remove the Ojibwe was undertaken in 1851 despite the fact that local officials had been requested to halt the process, before removal was formally repudiated by the U.S. government in 1853–1854.[28]

The treaty councils leading up to 1850 were multimedia events, controlled, not by the norms of conventional European diplomacy, but rather by the dominant Ojibwe protocols, in which the written text was only one component. Speeches and caucuses on both sides took up a considerable amount of the council time and were considered by the Ojibwe, in keeping with the other Indigenous groups already discussed in this book, to be more significant than the final text. Councils included spiritual rituals, exchanges of gifts, and the smoking of the peace pipe or calumet. The text itself was often altered as the negotiations unfolded. The Ojibwe signatories referred to signing a treaty as "touching the quill" or "touching the pen," a phrasing that captured both the literal act of signing and a more symbolic sense of the power invested in the material object of the pen, which some ogimaag would literally touch as part of signaling their assent.[29] A council brought together text, speech, and object to create a treaty that was far more dynamic than the stable, written document the Americans imagined they had generated.

American accounts of the 1837 and 1842 councils demonstrate the different media through which a treaty was generated. Verplanck Van Antwerp's journal of the 1837 council, for example, moves from apparently verbatim transcripts of the Ojibwe leaders' speeches to the formal treaty text that was read to the chiefs, shifting registers from the rhetoric of Ojibwe oratory (translated into English by Van Antwerp, who spoke

---

27. Redix, xiv; Clifton, 1–40.

28. Bruce M. White, "The Regional Context of the Removal Order of 1850," in *Fish in the Lakes, Wild Rice, and Game in Abundance*, ed. McClurken, 141–328, 147; Cleland, 68–71.

29. Cleland, 33, 38.

the Ojibwe language, Ojibwemowin) to the legalistic prose of an English treaty.[30] Van Antwerp also describes the material objects relevant to the negotiations, such as the map that the treaty commissioner Henry Dodge used to demonstrate the territory he wished to discuss and the sprig of oak the chief Maghegabo placed on the table to signify and clarify the trees the Ojibwe wished to reserve to themselves.[31]

These records also convey the significance (to both sides, but in different ways) of exact wording. The Ojibwe leaders who spoke at the 1837 council repeatedly drew attention to the source of their words, both to convey their mandate and to ensure clarity when they were citing others. Payajik, for example, told Dodge, "What I am going to say to you is not my own language, but the words of Chiefs and others around you," while Maghegabo said, "I have but few words to say, but they are those of the Chiefs, and very important."[32] When he asked the treaty commissioner to speak to the president on behalf of the Ojibwe, Shagobai required Dodge "to repeat my words to our Great Father in Washington."[33] The Americans, meanwhile, emphasized the exact nature of the *written* words, with Dodge telling the Ojibwe to assemble so that he could "read it [the treaty text] by articles, so that every word may be clearly conveyed and understood by you. Three copies of the Treaty are prepared, of which one will be sent to your Great Father The President of the United States for him to keep, one delivered to yourselves, and the other kept by me."[34] As Van Antwerp noted, "The Secretary then read The Treaty in the following words."[35]

The shared belief in the magic of exact words, combined with competing ideas about whether the written or the oral record mattered more and competing interpretations about what certain words meant, led to a diplomatic relationship structured almost exclusively by citation. At each new diplomatic encounter, whether conducted via council, treaty, petition, executive order, or legislation, the Ojibwe and the Americans would cite to each other the exact words that had been used in previous encounters. As Bruce M. White has noted,

---

30. Van Antwerp's journal is included as an appendix to Satz, 131–53.
31. Satz, 140, 142.
32. Satz, 135, 142.
33. Satz, 148.
34. Satz, 150.
35. Satz, 151.

Ojibwe understanding of the treaties was not based on the exact wording in the documents or on white interpretations of what those words meant, but on the statements made to them at the time the documents were negotiated. In many ways such statements were more important than any written words, considering that few could read or write in English. They remembered the words spoken by government officials representing the Great father or president and believed that those words were not spoken lightly.[36]

For example, in a furious speech at Sandy Lake following the death of many Ojibwe who were lured there, Eshkibagikoonzh (Flat Mouth) attacked Minnesota governor Alexander Ramsey, invoking Ramsey's past words and emphasizing the importance of conveying his own words to the governor with precision:

> I lay it all to him. I charge it all to our Great Father the Governor. It is because we listened to his words that we have now suffered so much. . . . I am not one that speaks of another behind his back. I say to his face all that I desire to say at all; and I would say to the Governor, if he were here, all that I say to you. I want you to write down the words I speak and carry them to him. Tell him I blame him for the children we have lost, for the sickness we have suffered and for the hunger we have endured. . . . I speak to our Great Father at a distance: the words that you now hear will be carried to him. When I saw him he spoke to us about farms and other matters of interest to us. I believed his words would be verified in this respect, but instead of this they have been falsified. And I blame him for this.[37]

The Americans, of course, saw the division of oral and written authority differently. In place of the oral record of a long-standing relationship, forged through various encounters in different forms and media, the government substituted a short-term institutional memory that operated on present

---

36. Bruce M. White, 149.

37. Theresa M. Schenck, *William W. Warren: The Life, Letters, and Times of an Ojibwe Leader* (Lincoln: University of Nebraska Press, 2007), 96.

understandings of particular diplomatic terms. President Taylor's 1850 removal order, a brief document composed in the legalistic language of the U.S. government, was careful to cite the exact words of the written agreements with the Ojibwe (using the then-current term "Chippewa" to describe them), with no reference to any verbal undertakings:

> The privileges granted temporarily to the Chippewa Indians by the Fifth Article of the Treaty made with them on the 29th of July 1837, "of hunting, fishing and gathering the wild rice, upon the lands, the rivers and the lakes included in the territory ceded" by that treaty to the United States; and the right granted to the Chippewa Indians of the Mississippi and Lake Superior, by the Second Article of the treaty with them of October 4th 1842, of hunting on the territory which they ceded by that treaty, "with the other usual privileges of occupancy until required to remove by the President of the United States," are hereby revoked; and all of the said Indians remaining on the lands ceded as aforesaid, are required to remove to their unceded lands.[38]

In response, the Ojibwe ogimaag, who were convinced that Taylor had not ordered their removal, asked for confirmation within the government's own frame of reference, turning to the textual in order to communicate more effectively. In a letter addressed to the president, they demanded written proof of the words of the executive order: "We have asked to see the order, and the name of the President affixed to it, but it has not been shown us."[39]

This citation of past words continued in later negotiations that referenced the 1837 and 1842 treaties. In 1852, the ogimaa Buffalo dictated a memorial about the 1842 negotiations, to be sent to President Millard Fillmore, which made it clear that he believed the words spoken in the treaty councils to be just as significant as the words in the treaty documents.[40] In an 1864 bilingual petition to the commissioner of Indian affairs, the signatory chiefs recounted the history of their treaty negotiations with

---

38. No. 5626, in *Indian Affairs: Laws and Treaties*, vol. 5, ed. Charles J. Kappler, 663 (Washington, DC: U.S. Government Printing Office, 1941), 663.

39. Cleland, 65.

40. Bruce M. White, 247.

the U.S. government. Writing of the 1837 treaty council, the chiefs wrote that they were invited to meet at St Peters and "there the words of our Great Father [i.e., the president of the United States] were repeated to us."[41] Their account of the 1842 negotiations at La Pointe includes what appear to be verbatim transcripts of comments made by negotiators on both sides.[42] The entire document is full of examples of what was "said," "told" or "answered," as well as repeated references to the "word" of the President, in the senses of both "language" and "promise." Citation, as a mode of interacting between treaty partners, was ingrained in Ojibwe written and oral discourse in the mid-nineteenth century.

Copway and Ojibwe Diplomacy

Although he was not from the American side of the Great Lakes, Copway had a long history of involvement with Ojibwe-American diplomatic encounters in the years leading up to *Running Sketches*, having moved to the southern shore of Lake Superior in the winter of 1834–1835 to work for the American Methodist mission there.[43] He was certainly present at the negotiations for the 1842 La Pointe Treaty, where his name is recorded as receiving an annuity payment, and he probably also attended the 1837 St. Peters council; at the time of the latter meeting, he was one of a small group of converted Ojibwe Methodists staying with the Reverend Alfred Brunson, and is thus probably one of those to whom Brunson refers when he says, "I attended this treaty with my Chippewas."[44]

---

41. *Statement Made by the Indians: A Bilingual Petition of the Chippewas of Lake Superior, 1864*, ed. John D. Nichols, 13 (London: University of Western Ontario, 1988).

42. *Statement Made by the Indians*, 17–18.

43. Smith, "The Life of George Copway," 9–10. The distinction between the Canadian and American sides of the border would in any case have been meaningless in Anishinaabeg terms; see Phil Bellfy, *Three Fires Unity: The Anishnaabeg of the Lake Huron Borderlands* (Lincoln: University of Nebraska Press, 2011).

44. Alfred Brunson, *A Western Pioneer*, 2 vols. (New York: Arno Press, 1975), 2:81–82. See also Brunson's account book, which details materials given to Copway in 1836 and 1837 (Wisconsin Historical Society Archives, Wis MSS FM Alfred Brunson papers, Correspondence, 1815–82, n.d.). The treaty council might be the event Copway is referring to in his autobiography when he mentions traveling to St. Peters with Brunson; see Copway, *Life, Letters and Speeches*, 116. Smith is confident that Copway was present at the 1837 council; see "The Life of George Copway," 21–22.

Moreover, he was an important participant in the 1845 Saugeen council, at which the Ojibwe of Upper Canada renewed their efforts to obtain a small reservation and elected Copway the council's vice-president.[45]

Copway was well aware of the significance of the exact words of diplomatic documents, and the tensions between what was said in councils and what was written on paper, as he demonstrated in his discussion of the 1818 Rice Lake Treaty, in which the land on which he was born on the Canadian side of the Great Lakes was purchased by the British:

> In 1818, our people surrendered to the British government a large part of their territory, for the sum of £750; reserving, as they had good reason to believe, all the islands. As they could neither read nor write, they were ignorant of the fact that these islands were *included* in the sale. They were repeatedly told by those who purchased for the government, that the islands were *not* included in the articles of agreement. But since that time, some of us have learned to read, and to our utter astonishment, and to the everlasting disgrace of that *pseudo* Christian nation, we find that we have been most grossly abused, deceived, and cheated.[46]

His recollections of his personal experiences of treaty councils, meanwhile, placed emphasis on supporting documents and the citation of language used at the time of the negotiation. In his account of the Saugeen council of 1845 in his autobiography, Copway reproduced speeches given in the council, the text of one of the Ojibwe chiefs' petitions to the government of Canada, and quoted lines from Lord Sydenham's reply.[47]

Copway took on a more independent and unorthodox diplomatic role as pressure for removal intensified in the late 1840s and early 1850s. In some instances, this was entirely textual. *The Traditional History and Characteristic Sketches of the Ojibway Nation,* published in 1850 in Great Britain and in 1851 in the United States, conveys a sense of urgency in its engagement with white readers: in the preface, Copway makes it

---

45. Smith, "The Life of George Copway," 19.
46. Copway, *Life, Letters and Speeches,* 94; emphasis in the original. See also p. 91 for evidence of Copway's familiarity with intertribal diplomacy between the Ojibwe and their Indigenous neighbors.
47. Copway, *Life, Letters and Speeches,* 127–35, 145–49.

clear that he composed the book in order to "awaken in the American heart a deeper feeling for the race of red men, and induce the paleface to use greater effort to effect an improvement in their social and political relations," and that he was "impelled forward by the thought that the nation whose history I here feebly sketch seems passing away, and that unless a work like this is sent forth, much, very much, that is interesting and instructive in that nation's actions, will with it pass away."[48] In other instances, Copway's diplomatic efforts blended text with direct negotiation. Like many Ojibwe leaders and thinkers, but by no means without controversy, Copway had become convinced that the only way for the Ojibwe to retain a portion of their traditional land was to agree to move to a reservation within its boundaries. In April 1848, he announced his proposal for a new Native territory in the Northwest. Having given speeches around the country and gathered support among prominent Americans, Copway formally petitioned the U.S. Congress to accept the idea. His argument and supporting documents were published as *Organization of a New Indian Territory, East of the Missouri River: Arguments and Reasons Submitted to the Honorable the Members of the Senate and House of Representatives of the 31st Congress of the United States* in 1850. The territory was to be named Kahgega, or "Ever-to-Be," a shortened version of his own name, but also, as Scott Richard Lyons points out, the Ojibwemowin word for "forever."[49]

The territory never materialized; in fact, Congress never even discussed the proposal. But it was in this context of diplomatic discourse that Copway undertook the trip to Europe that is memorialized in *Running Sketches*, and it is in this context, stretching back to at least 1837 but brought into sharp focus in 1850–1851, that *Running Sketches* belongs.[50]

---

48. George Copway, *The Traditional History and Characteristic Sketches of the Ojibway Nation* (Boston: Benjamin B. Mussey, 1851), vii.

49. Lyons, "Migrations to Modernity," 164. A summary of Copway's efforts to bring Kahgega into being can be found in Peyer, *The Tutor'd Mind*, 246–49; and Smith, "The Life of George Copway," 19–22. Copway included speeches he had given in promotion of his idea in the 1850 edition of his autobiography; see Copway, *Life, Letters and Speeches*, 165–88. The pamphlet itself was published in New York by S. W. Benedict. For a reading of Kahgega as a pastoral project, see Timothy Sweet, "Pastoral Landscape with Indians: George Copway and the Political Unconscious of the American Pastoral," *Prospects* 18 (1993): 1–27.

50. The same attention to the political situation of the Ojibwe can be seen in William W. Warren's publication of a series of newspaper articles titled "A Brief History of the

Copway left the United States for Europe in the aftermath of President Taylor's executive order to remove the Ojibwe and the publication of his own pamphlet on removal; he returned as the Ojibwe began to travel to Sandy Lake for the disastrous and cynical annuity payment of autumn 1850; and he published *Running Sketches* as new removal initiatives were undertaken in 1851. On the Canadian side of the Great Lakes, where Copway was born, the year 1850 also marked a watershed in terms of land tenure and diplomacy, as the Ojibwe accepted reservations under the Robinson Treaties.[51] This short period was one of intense diplomatic lobbying, in which, I would like to argue, *Running Sketches* played its part, as a text that spoke to American and Canadian settler audiences, in particular, about the role of the Ojibwe and other Indigenous peoples in the international context of the mid-nineteenth century.

Copway's performance at the Peace Congress might mark the final flourish of early nineteenth-century Ojibwe diplomacy.[52] Later, in 1854 and 1855, in an effort to gain some control over their remaining land and resources, the Ojibwe signed further treaties with the Americans, which extinguished their title to their land in Minnesota and Wisconsin in return for reservations, the control of natural resources, and annuity payments, the legacy of which, including ongoing breaches by the federal and state governments, remains a contentious issue for the Ojibwe in the twenty-first century.[53] Meanwhile, Copway himself became an increasingly troubled figure, afflicted by alcoholism and mental health problems, who developed a range of short-lived and ill-conceived projects to make money and regain status.[54]

Ojibwas" in 1851; like Copway, Warren was an American-educated Ojibwe writer who was closely involved in the diplomatic negotiations of the 1840s and was a reluctant champion of removal. See Warren, *History of the Ojibway People*, 2nd ed., ed. Theresa Schenck (St. Paul" Minnesota Historical Society, 2009); and Schenck, *William W. Warren*.

51. Robert Surtees, *Indian Land Surrenders in Ontario 1763–1867* (Gatineau: Indian and Northern Affairs Canada, 1984), 94–100.

52. For another example of Ojibwe diplomats engaging with both American settlers and European interlocutors in Europe, see Elspeth Martini, "Shawundais and the Methodist Mission to Native North America," in *Facing Empire: Indigenous Experiences in a Revolutionary Age*, ed. Kate Fullagar and Michael A. McDonnell, 303–30 (Baltimore, MD: Johns Hopkins University Press, 2018).

53. Cleland, 92; Satz, 83–128.

54. Smith, "The Life of George Copway," 23–28.

But in 1850–1851, there was still some possibility that the early nineteenth-century Ojibwe diplomatic processes could succeed. It is very clear from *Running Sketches* that Copway saw himself as engaged in international diplomacy on behalf of the Ojibwe and other Indigenous groups when he traveled to Europe. He noted that the English periodicals announced both his plans to attend the Congress and his plans for Kahgega when he arrived in Liverpool, writing to an American correspondent: "My cause here is warmly advocated by the papers, and I hope to realize the whole of what I had anticipated from these noble English people" (42–43, 48). He met with a wide range of English politicians and diplomats and spoke to different public gatherings about Kahgega (318–22). His hopes for support from English thinkers and activists were not realized, however; he was particularly disappointed by his encounters with a group that John Brant also met, "the so-called 'Aboriginal Protection Society' . . . I had made a false estimation of this body. A great name indeed without any power. A body without a knowing aim, and less energy of purpose" (278). As Cecilia Morgan has pointed out, by the mid-nineteenth century, liberal British sympathies had begun to drift away from questions of colonial justice and toward stabilizing the politics of Europe. Copway's insistence that negotiations for peace in Europe must include Indigenous peoples was a conscious and public rebuke to this tendency, and his speeches and activities on his European tour testify to his desire to keep Indigenous-imperial relationships on the transatlantic diplomatic agenda.[55]

His mandate to act as a representative of the Ojibwe is ambiguous, however. He was certainly not an ogimaa and had always felt isolated from the Lake Superior Ojibwe community, although he did have strong personal connections to leading figures such as Bagone-giizhig (Hole in the Day) and his son.[56] His relationship with Lake Huron and Rice Lake Ojibwe, meanwhile, had been damaged by allegations of financial mismanagement that also led to his expulsion from the Methodist Church.[57]

---

55. Cecilia Morgan, "Kahgegagahbowh's (George Copway's) Transatlantic Performance," *Cultural and Social History* 9, no. 4 (2012): 527–48; 537.

56. For information on his relationships in the Ojibwe community, see Smith, "The Life of George Copway," 14. Details of his connection to Bagone-giizhig can be found in Anton Treuer, *The Assassination of Hole in the Day* (Nepean, Ontario: Borealis Books, 2011).

57. Smith, "The Life of George Copway," 16–17.

However, the new political environment brought about by the end of the War of 1812, which placed the Ojibwe in a diplomatic relationship with the United States, had seen the emergence of a different kind of leader. Ojibwe Methodists like Copway, who never revealed his break with the Methodist Church, were ideally placed to mediate between their own people and American politicians and settlers. There is some evidence that Copway and others were seen as having a leadership role that worked alongside and overlapped with that of the traditional religious leaders, or *medewijig*.[58] They also stood alongside the civil leaders of their society, many of whom advocated accommodation with the settlers and missionaries and looked to form new alliances with outside groups in order to achieve Ojibwe goals.[59] Figures like Copway could contribute to and develop this range of alliances because they had access to the international Methodist community, its funds, and its influence. Robert Penner sees these figures as a crucial element in what he terms "the Ojibwe renaissance" of the first half of the nineteenth century, which brought Ojibwe life and aspiration into conversation with "a dynamic imperial context."[60]

Copway's role at the Peace Congress, where he moved a resolution, gave a speech, and presented a calumet, or peace pipe, was portrayed to settler and European audiences at the time in heavily exoticized language. Some observers treated him as an impressive if unusual participant in the gathering, as in this translated report from *Illustrierte Zeitung* supplied by Bernd Peyer:

> A truly uplifting scenario took place during the final session. Copway, the Indian Chief, takes the floor. A man in his forties, of light copper complexion, with shiny straight black hair, nearly beardless, the eyes dark and full of compassion, his build slim and proportional. In a speech, delivered in a style of English that frequently manifests lyrical qualities, he correlates

---

58. Miller, 181–82, 217.

59. Rebecca Kugel, *To Be the Main Leaders of Our People: A History of Minnesota Ojibwe Politics, 1825–1898* (East Lansing: Michigan State University Press, 2012), 3–4, 6–7.

60. Robert Penner, "The Ojibwe Renaissance: Transnational Evangelicalism and the Making of an Algonquian Intelligentsia, 1812–1867," *American Review of Canadian Studies* 45, no. 1 (2015): 71–92; 83.

his own noble quest for peace with the peace found in God, as is taught in the Gospel. Still a wandering savage among the Indians of his tribe 15 years ago, he is now tangible evidence for the advancement of civilization.[61]

Other reports expressed more cynicism about Copway's role at the Congress:

> The ladies no longer have eyes for the handsomely bearded men of the Left; it is the beardless Indian chieftain with the noble Roman profile and dazzling long black hair who catches their attention now. He carries a massive, mystically decorated staff, his royal sceptre, and over the plain black suit he wears shiny armlets along with a colourful sash and sword-belt, his badges of distinction, just like the kings of bygone times who bore their scepters and crowns everywhere they went, even to bed. The only thing the Frankfurters regret is that he is wearing a fine, black European hat instead of a crown of feathers and leaves. This mixture of European elegance and Indian pompousness does seem somewhat ludicrous, and yet, there is still something truly unsettling about the appearance of this handsome man, who has just made the transition from the unlimited freedom of his jungle to the perpetual confines of civilization, who has traveled thousands of miles just for the sake of an ideal that must have a deep and practical meaning for him, only to discover that his own enthusiasm hardly elicits an enthusiastic response from the gaping crowds who tend to regard him as little more than a curiosity.[62]

Both responses suggest a lack of respect for Copway's role in proceedings and no discernible sense of the diplomacy in which he was engaged, but this is a misreading of the Ojibwe role in transatlantic politics. Although removal efforts were underway, they remained in control of their own

---

61. This translation from *Illustrierte Zeitung* is provided by Peyer in his "A Nineteenth-Century Ojibwa Conquers Germany," 149–50.

62. This translation from *Allgemeine Zeitung* is provided by Peyer in his "A Nineteenth-Century Ojibwa Conquers Germany," 147. Copway cites a more complimentary translation of these lines in *Running Sketches*, which omits the sense that his appearance was thought ludicrous (223).

land and were still an autonomous people. Any negotiation involving the North American continent ought to have taken into account the independent sovereignty of the Ojibwe in Anishinaabewaki.[63] Moreover, they had long-standing diplomatic relationships with the major European powers, relationships that had already profoundly shaped the Atlantic world. The Frankfurt Peace Congress was a meeting of their own allies about the future of relationships within their own sphere of influence; while contemporary reports mocked the pretensions of Copway and the sentimental naiveté of his supporters in bringing him to Germany, there was every reason for the Ojibwe to consider their presence at the Congress natural, and perhaps even essential.

As Rebecca Kugel has demonstrated, Ojibwe diplomacy in the nineteenth century retained its links to traditional practices while acknowledging new realities. Treaty councils between the Ojibwe and the Americans consisted of the speeches and gift-exchanges that had always, in Kugel's phrase, "reanimated alliances."[64] New aspects of the council, such as negotiations about land sale and tenure, could be accommodated within the existing frameworks of Ojibwe diplomacy.[65] Copway's engagement with the Congress can be read as an international version of the same dynamic diplomatic process; with a speech of goodwill and friendship, he attempted to reanimate alliances with the historical European allies of the Ojibwe on their own soil.

The material culture of diplomacy mattered, in ways that the reports of Copway's appearance and actions in Frankfurt seem to intuit. The calumet that he presented to the Congress at the end of his speech was not a stereotype or empty symbol of Indianness, but rather a fundamental and indispensable element of any serious Ojibwe negotiation.[66] The strategic use of cross-cultural costume, too, which the reporter just cited interpreted as "ludicrous" in Copway's case, was already well established

---

63. Witgen, 220–22. Witgen's work provides the most comprehensive reading of Ojibwe power and sovereignty within the wider Atlantic context.

64. Kugel, 62; see also Redix, 22.

65. Kugel, 62.

66. Miller, 107–8. See also the description of the role of the pipe in Basil Johnston's account of a council in *Ojibway Ceremonies* (Toronto: McClelland and Stewart, 1982), 157–75. For a firsthand account from the mid-nineteenth century, see Johann Georg Kohl, *Kitchi-Gami: Life among the Lake Superior Ojibway, 1860* (Nepean, Ontario: Borealis Books, 1985), 13–26.

in the diplomatic relationships between the Ojibwe and the Americans. Michael Witgen and Cary Miller give marvelous accounts of Copway's contemporary, the Ojibwe leader Eshkibagikoonzh (Flat Mouth), and his deployment of material culture and costume in his negotiations with the Americans, such as his strategic changes of dress, from Ojibwe garb to American, during negotiations with the Indian agent Henry Rowe Schoolcraft in 1832.[67] A leader of the next generation, Copway's friend Bagone-giizhig (Hole in the Day) the younger, conveyed the extent of his cross-cultural diplomatic authority to the Americans in the late 1840s by wearing the otter-skin turban favored by Ojibwe civil leaders, the eagle feathers of a military leader, the beadwork of a religious leader, and a frock coat and trousers.[68] Copway's "fine, black European hat," which disappointed the German crowds hoping to see "a crown of feathers and leaves," operated alongside items of clothing like his armlets as Ojibwe diplomatic markers, signs that one accepted the commitments and obligations brought on by an alliance and expected reciprocity.[69]

But while some of the newspaper reports seem skeptical, there is evidence from the Congress suggesting that Copway's diplomatic role was taken seriously. On the final day, Copway was given the task of proposing the fifth resolution, that "this Congress acknowledging the principle of non-intervention, recognizes it to be the sole right of every state to regulate its own affairs," before delivering his own speech.[70] This resolution had important resonance for the Ojibwe, far more so than the other four resolutions adopted already in the course of the Congress (which dealt with the adoption of measures to end war and facilitate disarmament, the establishment of an arbitration process for disputes, and an end to loans that were used to purchase armaments), or those that would follow (which dealt with lobbying for a code of international law and condemning the practice of dueling), because it suggested that Indigenous peoples' right to self-government and protection from forced removal or coercive land sales should be guaranteed. Unlike the twenty-minute slots allotted to other speakers, Copway was given forty minutes to address the assembled audience. Although Copway himself and his colleagues in the American

---

67. Witgen, 1–5; Miller, 78.

68. Treuer, 86–87.

69. Miller, 79.

70. *Report of the Proceedings of the Third General Peace Congress*, 42. Copway's account of the Congress can be found in *Running Sketches*, 208–58.

delegation were disappointed by his speech, and the English newspapers gave only a brief outline, the German reporters produced full accounts that were generally complimentary and that make it clear that Copway's speech was a self-confident performance of Ojibwe sovereignty.[71] According to the German accounts, Copway was adamant that he was at the Congress in an official capacity, describing himself as "a delegate" who had come to Germany "to assist in establishing peace."[72] Although couched in deferential language, Copway's case for an Indigenous role within existing and developing diplomatic relationships was clear: "We are surrounded by prejudice on all sides, by the prejudice of governments and nations; the prejudice towers over us like hills upon hills. But the time is not far off when Italy, when Rome, the eternal city, when all the nations of the world will send their representatives to us [the Peace Congress]. That is impossible, they object. But who in the past could have imagined the wonders of the telegraph and the railroad?"[73] By connecting with a common theme in the Congress speeches (the rise of technology and communication as instruments of peace), Copway presents Indigenous diplomacy as a natural part of the Peace Congress and thus a fact of nineteenth-century life.[74] It is characterized as a modern and evolving practice, not a relic of the past.[75]

It is also a practice rooted in the existing relationships between Europeans and Native Americans on the "middle ground," which were alluded to several times in the proceedings. Copway's speech followed those of delegates earlier in the Congress who presented a version of engagement with Native Americans that relied heavily on the structures

---

71. Copway remarked "I have made my poorest speech" (*Running Sketches*, 221). He did not include a copy of the text in *Running Sketches*. Copway's sponsor, Elihu Burritt, described the speech as "ungrammatical, and incoherent"; see Morgan, "Kahgegagahbowh's (George Copway's) Transatlantic Performance," 546n.47. For details of the speech's coverage in the German newspapers, see Peyer, "A Nineteenth-Century Ojibwa Conquers Germany," 149–53.

72. Peyer, "A Nineteenth-Century Ojibwa Conquers Germany," 150.

73. Peyer, "A Nineteenth-Century Ojibwa Conquers Germany," 151–52.

74. See for example Girardin's speech, *Report of the Proceedings of the Third General Peace Congress*, 9.

75. Cecilia Morgan reads *Running Sketches* in this way, as "testimony to the complicated manoeuvres and strategies [Copway] employed in claiming both indigeneity and modernity, not as two separate domains but as entangled and intertwined realms of thinking and being"; see Morgan, "Kahgegagahbowh's (George Copway's) Transatlantic Performance," 542.

of Indigenous rather than European diplomacy, such as Richard Cobden, who linked the peaceful settlement of disputes with Indigenous diplomatic practices in a rather patronizing reference to Copway in his speech to the Congress:

> I see before me a gentleman representing the Indian tribes of America. . . . [Y]ou will have the opportunity of listening by-and-by, and of learning by his talents and accomplishments, how capable that interesting but injured race is of taking a part in the intelligent movements of civilized men. It will inspire you with hope for the future for the aborigines of America, and fill you with sentiments of shame for the wrongs inflicted upon that people. But what is the custom of the Red Indians of America? Why, when they make peace, they bury the hatchet. And it is dug up again only when war begins. But what had he (the Indian chieftain), seen in England? He had paid a visit to the arsenal at Woolwich, and there, in a time of peace, he had seen all the resources of the most inveterate war.[76]

The practice of "burying the hatchet" belonged to the Haudenosaunee, but it had already come to be used, both literally and symbolically, in other examples of treaty making between Americans and Indigenous peoples, in both literal and textual forms, such as the inclusion of the phrase "the hatchet shall be forever buried" in the text of the 1785 Hopewell Treaty between the United States and the Cherokees.[77]

Copway's reading of the fifth resolution, his speech, and his presence in Europe can thus be contextualized as part of a series of diplomatic exchanges, which date back to the earliest contacts in North America, and take their form, at least in part, from Indigenous diplomatic processes. His visit to the Peace Congress is completely consistent with Ojibwe understandings of alliances as, in Rebecca Kugel's phrase, "organic processes" whereby the Ojibwe "invested much effort and time into maintaining the cycle of events—the visits, gift exchanges and expressions of mutuality and good will—that kept an alliance alive."[78] It is on the basis of his

---

76. *Report of the Proceedings of the Third General Peace Congress*, 35.
77. "Treaty with the Cherokee, 1785," in *Indian Affairs: Laws and Treaties: Volume 2—Treaties*, ed. Charles J. Kappler, 8–11; 10 (Washington, DC: U.S. Government Printing Office, 1904), 8–11; 10.
78. Kugel, 10.

involvement with the Congress, and especially with the fifth resolution, that Jace Weaver includes Copway as one of the "Red Diplomats" who shaped the Atlantic world.[79] And it is in his capacity as a "Red Diplomat" that we should reconsider Copway's decision to quote Byron's words in *Running Sketches*.

Byron's Rhine as Diplomatic Artefact

Copway's journey down the Rhine to the Congress seems like an obvious moment for what Bernd Peyer has described as "the inevitable citation from Byron's *Childe Harold*."[80] Like many mid-century tourists, Copway appeared to use Byron's lines as shorthand for a certain kind of culturally sanctioned reaction to European travel that reiterated a borrowed point while attempting to gesture toward an authentic inner feeling.[81] In *Running Sketches*, Copway describes his reaction to traveling on the Rhine, noting that "before night, I set [sic] down to read again the description which Byron by the following lines had immortalized this as well as himself, in writing the following description of this beautiful and strange river. The whole day I have spent in looking over these ruins, and the crags everywhere to be seen" (203–4). But what the reader is presented with next is not an undigested chunk of *Childe Harold*, but rather a carefully selected and crafted citation of precedent. In this long passage, which takes up several pages of his narrative, Copway omits stanzas 52–58, which feature the most autobiographical lines of this section of the poem, as Byron reflects on his own exile, addresses his sister Augusta in the Drachenfels lyric, and discusses the specifics of recent European history in his lines on Marceau. By doing so, Copway also omits quoting the lines most often deployed by mid-century tourists: the stanza on "The castled crag of Drachenfels" (3.496).[82] Copway is not simply attempting to cast himself as Byronic, then, nor is he interested in the particularities of Byron's personal experiences or in following his itinerary as a tourist; in

---

79. Jace Weaver, *The Red Atlantic: American Indigenes and the Making of the Modern World, 1000–1927* (Chapel Hill: University of North Carolina Press, 2014), 182.

80. Peyer, "A Nineteenth-Century Ojibwa Conquers Germany," 146.

81. James Buzard, "The Uses of Romanticism: Byron and the Victorian Continental Tour," *Victorian Studies* 35, no. 1 (1991): 29–49; 39.

82. Buzard, 30.

fact, Copway's trip from Cologne to Mainz does not map neatly on to the area of the Rhine that Byron was writing about in Canto III.[83] Like other nineteenth-century readers who remediated Byron, Copway has a particular use to which he wishes to put the poetry.[84] The appeal of the lines on the Rhine in this case is their place-based lessons about history, peace, and land, and the ways in which they can reframe Copway's own diplomatic text and make it intelligible to white readers.

Byron's lines provide an important conceptualization of history as a matrix of textuality, territory, and materiality, as he contemplates the bloody past of the now-peaceful Rhine. It is a historical projection littered with the material culture of war.[85] The ruined "chiefless castles" (3.413) are the tangible manifestations of the history of conflict, but the poem also contains references to a range of other, imagined artefacts. "Banners on high" (3.420) are "shredless dust ere now" (3.422), as are the shields, "With emblems well devised by amorous pride" (3.436). The symbols that marked out past European allegiances and martial endeavors have proved insubstantial, lacking both in form and in legibility as time has passed, requiring a new material culture for peacetime. Pondering the vagaries of political posterity, Harold asks of the forgotten leaders of the Rhine: "What want these outlaws conquerors should have / But History's purchased page to call them great? / A wider space, an ornamented grave?" (3.429–31). In order to assert one's political identity and to make it durable in a world gripped by conflict, it was necessary, Byron suggested, to establish legitimacy simultaneously on the page, on the "wider space" of the land,

---

83. Details of the area Byron was writing about in his lines on the Rhine can be found in Jerome McGann, "The Composition, Revision, and Meaning of Childe Harold's Pilgrimage III," *Bulletin of the New York Public Library* 71, no. 7 (1967): 415–30.

84. See, for example, Tom Mole's case study in "Spurgeon, Byron, and the Contingencies of Mediation," *Romanticism and Victorianism on the Net* 57–58 (2010), http://www.erudit.org/revue/ravon/2010/v/n57-58/1006518ar.html?lang=en; and Andrew Elfenbein, *Byron and the Victorians* (Cambridge: Cambridge University Press, 1995), esp. 49.

85. Byron was perpetually interested in the technologies and material culture of Regency warfare; see, for example, *Don Juan*, Canto VII, 78.621–24:
But now, instead of slaying Priam's son,
We only can but talk of escalade,
Bombs, drums, guns, bastions, batteries, bayonets, bullets,
Hard words, which stink in the soft Muses' gullets.
The wider issue of Byron's representation of war are analyzed in Philip Shaw, *Waterloo and the Romantic Imagination* (Basingstoke: Palgrave, 2002), 165–91.

and on the material relics that stood for personal and collective memory. This matrix contains unintended echoes of the protocols of Indigenous diplomacy in engaging Europeans and then settler governments on the "middle ground," in which sovereignty and enduring historical claims were asserted through a cross-cultural combination of treaty texts, habitation of the land, and the symbolism of gift exchange and material objects. For a diplomat attempting to reanimate British and French alliances with the Ojibwe, in the face of the threat of removal, these lines provide poignant evidence of the possibilities of political extinction.

Byron's lines thus have resonances with Copway's thinking that go well beyond geographic affinities. The Rhine stanzas of Canto III are deeply invested in the same questions of peace, history, and diplomacy that concerned Copway at this moment, as he traveled to a diplomatic engagement that was entirely concerned with the establishment and maintenance of peace. This connection is perhaps unsurprising. The earlier cantos of *Childe Harold's Pilgrimage* had been composed following Byron's own diplomatic endeavors during his 1809 travels in Europe, and the poem was thus initially conceptualized as part of a diplomatic experience.[86] Canto III, meanwhile, was composed against the backdrop of what Paul Stock has called "Congress Europe," the post-Waterloo diplomatic arrangement that led to a system of regular meetings between the major powers from 1815 to 1825, and out of which the later Peace Congresses emerged.[87] Byron himself had paid close attention to the Congress movement, composing "The Age of Bronze," with its caustic critique of post-Napoleonic Europe, in the aftermath of the 1822 Congress of Verona. With a political agenda of his own that aimed for the settlement of conflict between the Ojibwe and the Americans, Copway chooses to cite lines with a particular diplomatic resonance, lines that articulate both the futility of petty and violent ambition (the symbols of which decay and are reclaimed by an all-conquering Nature) and the dangerous ongoing threat posed by the ambition of such "ceaseless vultures" for the peoples whose lands and lives they would appropriate (3.567). He offers back to the white American

---

86. Roderick Beaton, *Byron's War: Romantic Rebellion, Greek Revolution* (Cambridge: Cambridge University Press, 2013), 3–5.

87. Paul Stock, *The Shelley-Byron Circle and the Idea of Europe* (Basingstoke: Palgrave, 2010), 151. Byron's skepticism about these arrangements is on show in the dedication to *Don Juan*, where he writes of "States to be curb'd, and thoughts to be confined, / Conspiracy or Congress to be made— / Cobbling at manacles for all mankind—" (108–10).

readers of *Running Sketches*, not what Peyer calls the "tedious banalities of plagiarized touristic trivia," generated by a Victorian pseudo-Byron observing the Rhine, but rather, in their own language and their own tradition, the most apt parallel to the Ojibwe situation in the English canon that he could supply.[88]

Copway's citation of Byron might be termed digressive diplomacy. The sudden switch from his own prose to verse and then to the impersonal reportage of the Congress allows him to bring multiple genres, registers, and rhetorics to bear on his reader and their experience of the text. His account of the Peace Congress in *Running Sketches* offers very little personal reflection, consisting instead of quotation and summary from the speeches, largely gathered from contemporary newspaper reports, and almost entirely effacing the content of his own speech (217–18). The intention is not to dilute the diplomatic purpose of the text, however, but rather to enhance it; Copway aims to persuade through a range of overlapping but distinct textual practices. The transition from quoting Byron to quoting speeches only feels jarring to a reader if we privilege genre and regard the transition as one from the literary to the reportorial. But if we read within the frameworks of colonial diplomacy, the transition is more seamless; the rhetoric and the practice of quotation provide the link between fragments of text, with the effect that Byron's lines are drawn into the wider diplomatic narrative.

This collage effect inhabits the structure of Ojibwe diplomacy, with its use of different languages, tones, speakers, media, and objects, to repeat a central message. It was an approach Copway had deployed in the past; while advocating for the new Kahgega territory, he had given lectures that combined a description of his proposal with songs and anecdotes.[89] But it also mimics a characteristic feature of Byron's own writing. As Jane Stabler has persuasively argued, to understand Byron, critics need "to recover the abruptness and discontinuity of [his] generic deflections on the printed page before we can appreciate the reader's response to moments of textual indeterminacy as a crucial part of the meaning of

---

88. Peyer, *The Tutor'd Mind*, 276.

89. See for example the broadsides for his lectures in the eastern United States in 1849 (American Antiquarian Society, BDSDS, 1849). The importance of song for the Ojibwe, and the adaptation of European hymns, is covered in detail in Michael D. McNally, *Ojibwe Singers: Hymns, Grief, and a Native Culture in Motion* (Oxford: Oxford University Press, 2000), with some discussion of Copway included.

the poem."[90] Byron's digressions are central to the experience of reading his work, since they involve the reader in an active, dynamic relationship with the movement of the text and its argument; the reader has to stay engaged with the overall purpose of the poem while simultaneously following a line of thought, or a formal innovation, that seems to digress from the central theme. The challenge is to integrate the digression into one's overall impression of the poem, to appreciate the ways in which Byron's theme might still be shaping apparently marginal moments. Copway's diplomatic endeavors, I would argue, are similarly fluid. They are obvious in the episodes in which he meets politicians, gives lectures to public audiences, and attends the Peace Congress. But they are also evident in the digressions, the swerves into adopted voices, and the citation of others' words. Copway, like Byron, asks his reader to hold in their head the purpose and theme of the text and to read each digression as an additional layer of argument.

The power of this digressive approach and its connection to both Byron and to diplomacy can be seen in the laudatory poem that concludes *Running Sketches*. Written by a Philadelphia-based friend of Copway's who signs himself A. W. H., the poem imagines Copway as the cosmopolitan European traveler that Byron and Childe Harold symbolized. But crucially, A. W. H. portrays this cosmopolitanism as fundamentally diplomatic, informed by European history and culture, but nevertheless directed toward the maintenance of alliances and the establishment of peace:

To George Copway, of the Ojibway Nation

Hail to thee, chief, from the far forest land!
Hail to thee, prince, of the wild wood-land!
From the sun-crowned hills of the glorious west,
Where wild winds billow Superior's breast,
Thou hast travelled o'er broad Atlantic's foam,
Where sages of peace to their councils come;
Thou hast trodden in halls of ancient glory
And traced the records of olden story;—
Thou hast seen grim relics of ruthless ire,
And tortures unknown at thy camping fire.
The war-fiend was worshipped by pale-faced men,

---

90. Jane Stabler, *Byron, Poetics and History* (Cambridge: Cambridge University Press, 2002), 11.

> As well as by braves in the forest glen;
> And torrents of heart-warm, human blood
> Have poured over Europe, as wasting flood.
> But the worship and honor of carnage is past,
> Earth's glorious jubilee soundeth at last;
> Child of the forest! to thee it is given
> To speak in rich cadence the message of heaven;
> And bid the paleface with the Indian combine
> The oak of our country with olive to twine;
> To bid the wild war-notes forever be still,
> While angels are chanting, "On earth good will,
> And glory to God in the highest above,
> The Father of all, the fountain of love." (*Running Sketches* 346)

By including this poem at the end of his volume, Copway mobilizes yet another digressive quotation in the service of his diplomatic project. Although part advertisement and part self-aggrandizement, the poem also provides a bridge between Copway and Byron, turning Copway himself into a versified Byronic figure and plotting his path to the Peace Congress. This path has provided lessons in precisely the violent European history that Byron sketches in his lines on the Rhine, here depicted as Copway witnessing the "grim relics of ruthless ire" (9) that have led to "torrents of heart-warm, human blood" (13) soaking European ground. From those lessons and that scenery, Copway is shown as one of the "sages of peace to their councils come" (6), whose specific role is not to provide color to the international meeting but to speak, as if in a treaty council, for an end to hostilities between Indigenous peoples and settlers. This depiction includes an apparently direct reference to the fact that Copway moved the fifth resolution at the Congress ("to thee it is given / To speak in rich cadence the message of heaven" [17–18]) and a reframing of that resolution as one that specifically addresses violence in North America ("And bid the paleface with the Indian combine / The oak of our country with olive to twine" [19–20]). The common trope of the Native "war whoop" is here reimagined as an image of international, bilateral conflict; the "wild war-notes" (21) that must cease, in both A. W. H.'s and Copway's view, are not simply those produced by the Ojibwe and other Indigenous peoples, but those of settlers and their European allies as well. By reimagining Byron's lines on the Rhine in an entirely topical Ojibwe context, this final digression in *Running Sketches* adds another layer to the complex interweaving of poetry and diplomacy, the Indigenous and the European, and Byron and Copway.

Byron had also featured, albeit in a more scattered form, in another Copway production of this period. *The Traditional History and Characteristic Sketches of the Ojibway Nation* was published in 1851 and was, alongside *Running Sketches* and the Kahgega pamphlet *Organization of a New Indian Territory*, one of a triumvirate of texts that appeared in 1850–1851 as Copway attempted to secure his people's survival. In *Traditional History*, Byron's poetry is frequently associated with conflict and warfare. Copway uses one epigraph from *Don Juan*, for example, when describing the Ojibwe battles with the Santee Dakota, whom he refers to as the "Siouxs" ("'was blow for blow, disputing inch by inch, / For one would not retreat, nor t'other flinch" [8.615–16]), and another from *The Giaour* when discussing Ojibwe-Haudenosaunee conflict: "The death shot hissing from afar, / The shock, the shout, the groan of war" (639–40).[91] A short quotation from the same section of *Childe Harold's Pilgrimage* that features in *Running Sketches* also features here; in the chapter about war with the Haudenosaunee, Copway noted, "Slaughter heaped on high its weltering ranks" (3.453).[92] Surrounding these Byronic quotations are descriptions of the riverside fighting that seem themselves to be channeled through Byron's poem and its depiction of the violent history of the Rhine:

> The waters of Menesotah have been crimsoned with the blood of both nations, and the upper Mississippi has witnessed their unrewarded contest; and their shouts and groans have alike resounded among the mountain passes, and echoed from cliff to cliff on the rock-walled shore.
> The rivers which flow into the Mississippi have floated hundreds of the canoes of the Ojibways, freighted with resolute warriors against the Siouxs. While the Siouxs have passed up the same streams, and finding the smoke of the "*Ah-ah-to-won*" rising from wig-wam, have suddenly startled them with their war-cry. The heights of Lake Superior have been used as towers by the Siouxs, from which to watch the sky across

---

91. Copway, *The Traditional History*, 61, 73.

92. Copway, *The Traditional History*, 93. I have presented the lines as Copway presents them; McGann's text has "heap'd" for "heaped."

the Lake, while the barrier ridges of the North were used by the Ojibways for the same purpose. Thus Nature furnished her children with watch-towers and fortresses.[93]

These digressive quotations and evocations of Byron in *Traditional History* help to weave together the different texts that Copway was producing in 1850–1851. *Traditional History* is full of depictions of Indigenous diplomacy, including references to councils, peace pipes, and treaties. The book ends, meanwhile, with the account of the plan for Kahgega. Copway's intellectual interests, in other words, range across this group of writings, bringing diplomacy, poetry, and Indigenous sovereignty into dialogue with one other within the pages of an individual text, as well as across the range of texts. Byron—and especially the Byron who was concerned with peace and war—is a constant touchstone in these discussions, not because Copway requires Byron's words to think with, but because his audience is white American, British, and European readers, including politicians in all three locations with whom he is diplomatically engaged and who have the power to support his land claims, and for whom this solemn and reflective Byron is himself a major cultural touchstone. The quotations and the mixture of genres may read as digressive, but they aim, as Scott Richard Lyons has argued, at a powerful and modern form of Indigenous nationalism.[94]

Reading Copway's digressive diplomacy requires the same attention to history that Stabler requires in our reading of Byron. Keen to ensure a focus on contextualized reading experiences, Stabler suggests that "one important feature of Byronic digression is that it offers its readers the experience of an encounter with awkward historical particulars coupled with the experience of conflicting textual worlds."[95] Both these elements might also shape our responses to *Running Sketches*. The historical particulars matter; Copway's trip to Europe marked perhaps the last moment in which the Ojibwe could be seen as major political players in the Atlantic world. From the 1850s onward, Ojibwe influence on settler and European policies would fade, becoming what Robert Penner calls "an isolated ghetto of Canadian and American national histories, rather than

---

93. Copway, *The Traditional History*, 61–62.
94. Lyons, "Migrations to Modernity," 143–82.
95. Stabler, 18–19.

a connective element of the imperial."[96] Copway himself would fall into obscurity; as the Ojibwe scholar Gerald Vizenor has noted, "He was ahead of his time in understanding land problems and cultural conflicts, but he had no political constituencies to embrace his ideas. His mission was applauded but not enacted."[97] But in 1850, the potential Ojibwe influence on global politics, via their role as treaty partners with the United States, was still considerable. In just the same way that one must read Canto III of *Childe Harold's Pilgrimage* as a product of the particular circumstances of post-Waterloo Europe, one also needs to see *Running Sketches* as part of the dynamic world of Ojibwe international engagement in the mid-nineteenth century. These are like Stabler's "awkward historical particulars" because they do not sit easily with a simplistic imagined notion of a colonized people being paraded at international events like the Peace Congress for little reason and with little effect. Copway's digression into Byronic verse highlights the awkwardness of this history and the ways in which it licensed an Ojibwe intellectual to draw on multiple traditions in engagements with a global audience.

The "conflicting textual worlds" of Byronic digression are perhaps even more significant than these particulars. What Copway attempts to achieve in *Running Sketches* is the synthesis of the two textual traditions in which he was steeped, but, as in the case of Byron, his work foregrounds the collision of different textual worlds. Oral Ojibwe texts collide with written European ones, poetry with reportage, autobiography with history, personal travelogue with formulaic guidebook. The collage of texts draws attention to the multiple textualities available to Copway and the uncomfortable way such textualities rub up against each other. What links them, however, is the overarching shape of Ojibwe writing. The written textuality of the Ojibwe was almost entirely diplomatic at this moment. It encompassed any number of conflicting textual worlds, but it remained a distinct genre, directed toward the consistent political goal of sovereignty and continued independence. What is thus especially Byronic about *Running Sketches* is not so much the direct citation of Byron, nor the adoption of a Byronic traveler persona, nor even the geographical coincidence of Copway's trip on the Rhine. What links Copway to Byron is a shared awareness of textuality, history, materiality, and the role of digression in

---

96. Penner, 85.
97. Vizenor, 64.

the articulation of these ideas. Copway's digressions, like Byron's, were able to release the energy of the world of print.[98]

From an Ojibwe perspective, however, this energy came in part from the dynamic interaction of the written and the oral, which had become a distinct feature of the treaty councils and their attendant documents. The diplomatic significance that Copway gives to Byron's lines is enhanced when they are placed in conjunction with the oral texts he produced at this time and read alongside his speech at the Congress. The audience in St. Paul's Lutheran Church in Frankfurt did not hear Copway quote Byron, and the readers of *Running Sketches* were not supplied with a copy of his speech. But the two texts, Harold's ruminations on the Rhine and Copway's plea for peace, were nevertheless in a constant, multimedia dialogue with each other, in a manner that echoes the intertextual dialogue that John Borrows has argued is central to Indigenous understandings of diplomacy.[99] The accounts published in the European newspapers make it clear that Copway brought his speech into conversation with Byron's lines. At one point, for example, he made a comment on what he had observed in Frankfurt since his arrival; as one German newspaper reported it, "Where shady green trees now grow and children play under a canopy of flowers, there once stood embrasures, towers, ramparts and the instruments of war."[100] Childe Harold's Rhine is evoked and updated here; like Byron in 1816, Copway sees a European landscape reclaimed by peace and nature, but only barely concealing a material history of war.

As a replacement for these martial symbols and the cycle of violence they represented, Copway offered the Congress the material manifesta-

---

98. For a reading of Byronic digression in terms of rhetorical energy, see Paul M. Curtis, "Byron and the Politics of Editing," in *Palgrave Advances in Byron Studies*, ed. Jane Stabler (Basingstoke: Palgrave, 2007), 60–80.

99. John Borrows, "Wampum at Niagara: The Royal Proclamation, Canadian Legal History, and Self-Government," in *Aboriginal and Treaty Rights in Canada: Essays on Law, Equality, and Respect for Difference*, ed. Michael Asch, 155–72 (Vancouver: University of British Columbia Press, 1997).

100. In another first-person account, Copway says, "Yesterday I walked through the streets and surroundings of this city for the first time; once the city and its neighbourhood was formidably fortified, surrounded by ramparts and walls and mighty towers. How many times have the citizens of this city been exposed to devastating war, how many times have the women and children lamented and wailed because of it? Now I see wonderful gardens in the place of fortifications, and in their midst stands a memorial dedicated to the one who planted them" (cited in Peyer, "A Nineteenth-Century Ojibwa Conquers Germany," 151).

tion of Ojibwe diplomacy, peace, and renewed alliances. As the European newspaper accounts noted, the most striking aspect of his performance was his presentation of a peace pipe to the congressional president, Carl Jaup. According to one account of his speech at the congress, Copway commented:

> Long and frequently have my ancestors fought yours, the blood of my tribe and your tribe has flown and been shed in streams. With great pleasure I announce to you that a new and better spirit has come over us, inspires us, the spirit of peace. I close. As I set forth from the West to visit my European brothers, my father said to me: "Take something with you that you can present as a gift to the strange, pale nation." He gave me this. (The speaker holds it up and unwraps it.) Often as I sat down at a table, it was mistaken for a sword; but it is a calumet, the peace pipe, which we present to those with whom we wish to establish friendship. (Loud, repeated ovation.) I hand it over to the President. (The President rises and displays it—thundering ovation.)[101]

As he noted elsewhere in *Running Sketches*, Copway intended to conduct himself in Europe in an Ojibwe manner: "I will uphold my race. . . . In this land of refinement I will be an Indian" (55). His behavior and rhetoric during his speech to the Peace Congress was entirely consistent with Ojibwe diplomatic practices, as he well knew; his autobiography contains a description of the role of the peace pipe in Ojibwe negotiations.[102] Acknowledging the violence that had characterized European-Indigenous relations in the past, he nevertheless proposed a negotiated peace, embodied by what was not simply the ubiquitous symbol of Ojibwe diplomacy and mediation, but, as Robert A. Williams Jr. has noted, an actual legal text for Native Americans.[103] It was an object that was very easy to misread in the context of the violent history of colonization, as Copway signals

---

101. This is the version of the speech from the German newspapers given in Peyer, "A Nineteenth-Century Ojibwa Conquers Germany," 150–52. A much briefer version can be found in the English-language *Report of the Proceedings of the Third General Peace Congress*, 42.

102. Copway, *Life, Letters and Speeches*, 91.

103. Williams, 94. Williams also gives a wider discussion of the role of the peace pipe at pp. 44–47.

when he notes that it had been mistaken for a sword, but it could in fact replace the material culture of war with one of peace, and it did so within an Ojibwe diplomatic framework.

However, Copway's comments also hint at a Byronic framework. The bloodied Rhine and the simultaneously distant and recent history of war that it symbolized for Byron is replaced here with an equally bloodstained Mississippi and its tributaries.[104] Troubled and violent relationships between the European powers in the Romantic era are implicitly compared with the equally troubled and violent relationships between the Ojibwe and the Europeans and Americans. In order to establish a newly invigorated diplomatic relationship between the Ojibwe and their former allies, in which what Byron calls in *Childe Harold's Pilgrimage* "the blood of yesterday" (3.455) can be overcome, the Byronic castles, banners, and shields will need to be usurped by the peace pipe. The speech embeds one of the most canonical European meditations on war and peace within the conventional Ojibwe rhetoric of tribes, brothers, spirits, and the relationship with "the strange, pale nation." This combination might make the speech seem like a pastiche of both Indigenous and Romantic stereotypes, but to read it this way is to read it with Romanticism's own eyes. It is equally true that it represents the authentic voice of the Ojibwe diplomat, engaging a foreign intellectual tradition on its own terms in the hope of producing reconciliation and peace. Byron's influence on Copway is part of what was, in that moment, a confident imagining of the past, the present, and the international future of the Ojibwe.

Copway's multimedia use of Byron in *Running Sketches* offers Romanticists a compelling example of Byronic remediation. In his case study of the clergyman C. H. Spurgeon, Tom Mole has argued for "a capillary model of cultural transmission that pays attention to previously unexamined moments of citation, appropriation and redeployment" and that is not dismissive of the way in which Byron's texts were "broken into fragments, placed in new contexts, spliced with other people's words, misremembered, misattributed and rendered strange."[105] Copway's apparently derivative and

---

104. In one account of Copway's speech, the listener records hearing Copway refer to the local German people as "the children of the valley of the Rhine and the Danube"; see [John Passmore Edwards?], "Frankfort Peace Congress," in *The Public Good; Devoted to the Advocacy of Great Principles, the Advancement of Useful Institutions, and the Elevation of Man*, vol. 1, supplement (London: Charles Gilpin, 1850): 1–16; 16.

105. Mole, par. 24.

unimaginative use of Byron's lines on the Rhine is an important example of the capillary model, since it allows us to rethink why we place so much value on European-sanctioned modes of citation and transmission. It also allows us to reconsider whether such examples of remediation are as depoliticized as we might imagine. In an example directly related to Canto III and the lines on the Rhine, James Buzard reads another instance of nineteenth-century Byronic remediation, John Murray III's use of snippets of Byron's verse in his line of guidebooks, as packaging the poetry's sentiment but not its politics: "What might then remain was the appropriatable and exciting form of rebelliousness without the content of rebellion. . . . The abstracting of Byronic qualities from the specific political and historical contexts that figured in Byron's poetry enabled travelers to adopt Byronic gestures without any consideration of what might seem to us now the insistent, inherently political character of Byron's verse."[106] This criticism, which Buzard specifically directs toward European travelers, is one that is sometimes leveled at Copway in relation to his abstraction of Byron's words. Yet the example of the Canto III citation in *Running Sketches* might lead us to ask not simply the question just posed about why we place so much value on European-sanctioned modes of citation and transmission, but also why we place so much value on particular culturally sanctioned modes of rebellion and politics. What other political traditions might be at play when Byron is invoked? In what other ways might a writer express rebellion? And might diplomacy, with its simultaneous gestures toward self-determination and recognition, or rebellion and reconciliation, offer a different framework for considering the potential of Romantic citation?

Ojibwe tradition offers a culturally sanctioned use of poetry that is entirely different from that endorsed by Romanticism and the European and settler traditions that derive from it. What might be thought of as literary text in other traditions was, for the Ojibwe, ultimately utilitarian. One cited poetry for practical ends, not in order to strike a pose. The German writer Johann Georg Kohl, who lived with the Lake Superior Ojibwe in the mid-1850s, gives a valuable account of Ojibwe attitudes to poetry at precisely the time Copway was writing:

> In my inquiries after poetry and pictured writing among the Indians, I at length grew weary of the eternal dream-stories

---

106. Buzard, 40.

and magic spells that crossed my path. I would so gladly have met with purely poetic outbursts of a free and disinterested enthusiasm, in which poetry might appear for itself, and without the secondary intention of catching fish or deer.

But such songs are a *rara avis* among the Indians. It seems as if they only possess "poetry with a purpose." As in revolutionary times all the poetry assumes a political tone, though it may be published under the name of spring or autumn songs, or love strains or elegies (in the same way as among the old English Puritans every poem, even the war-songs, was a species of hymn), so among these superstitious Indians, whose entire poetry moves amid dreams, visions, fear of spirits, and magic, every song is at once a magic spell, specially designed to ensnare beavers and bears. Every sorrowful or joyful emotion that opens their mouth is at once wrapped up in the garb of a "wabano-nagamowin" (chanson magicale). If you ask one of them to sing you a simple, innocent hymn in praise of Nature, a spring or jovial sporting stave, he never gives you anything but a form of incantation with which, he says, you will be enabled to call to you all the birds from the sky, and all the foxes and wolves from their caves and burrows. If, again, you ask him for a love-song, he will give you a philter, or a powder with the proper form of incantation, and assure you that this is a most effective love-song.[107]

Kohl views Ojibwe poetry as a kind of failed Romanticism, a misdirection of creative energy into the banality of "poetry with a purpose," and an obsession with outcomes and material things. But for twenty-first-century readers, that need not be our view. We can ensure that we read a text like *Running Sketches* within its own intellectual tradition, in which one cited poetry in order to make things happen. Copway wanted to see Ojibwe independence and the creation of Kahgega; Byron's lines might have been just those required in order to reanimate the old alliances with the European and American powers and to call Kahgega into being.

The long quotation in *Running Sketches* is thus, as Peyer says, "the inevitable citation from Byron's *Childe Harold*," but with a twist. It is

---

107. Kohl, 394–95.

more than self-aggrandizement, and it is not simply Copway's projection of a Byronic self-image. It is inevitable that Copway draws on these lines not because they are English literature's most famous evocation of the Rhine, but because they mark out a particular, place-based theorization of war, peace, history, and diplomacy that Copway wishes to channel. His deployment of Byron belongs in a lineage that includes John Brant and Elias Boudinot, rather than one centered on European tourists. The lines themselves, meanwhile, are a diplomatic artefact, to be deployed when a gesture is required that is, to one's audience, both dramatic and unexpected on the one hand and predictable and convincing on the other. The lines complement Copway's performance at the Peace Congress. They constitute another kind of peace pipe, which is offered to an Anglophone audience as the legible, reassuring version of an ongoing diplomatic conversation.

Chapter 4

"Always Build a Fence around the King's Word"

Sol Plaatje and *The Deserted Village*

In May 1914, a ship called the *Norseman* departed from Cape Town on the long sea voyage to England. Among the passengers was a group of African diplomats, who were heading to London to launch a last-ditch appeal to the British government to intervene in recent South African legislation that aimed to alienate Africans from their land. While on board, one of the diplomats wrote to a friend that he was working on a related project: "I am compiling this little book on the Natives' Land Act and its operation, which I hope to get through the press immediately after landing in England."[1] This throwaway comment was made by Solomon T. Plaatje, and his "little book" became the landmark publication *Native Life in South Africa* (1916).

Plaatje was one of the most prominent African intellectuals of the early twentieth century. A translator, court interpreter, journalist, and editor, he was a leading contributor to African print culture and, like many similar intellectuals, a significant political figure and one of the founding members of the South African Native National Congress (SANNC), which was the forerunner to the African National Congress.[2] In 1914, Plaatje was chosen as one of the group of officials who traveled to London to

---

1. Brian Willan, "Introduction," in Sol. T. Plaatje, *Native Life in South Africa* (1916; reprint, New York: Picador, 2007), 1–13; 4.

2. Background on the formation of the SANNC can be found in Peter Walshe, *The Rise of African Nationalism in South Africa: The African National Congress 1912–1952* (London: Hurst, 1970), 30–42.

convey to the British government the SANNC's concerns about the 1913 Natives' Land Act, a piece of legislation that would deprive Africans of land rights and set the foundation for apartheid policies. *Native Life in South Africa* was specifically designed as a companion publication to the diplomatic mission to England and served as an extended plea to the British public and parliamentarians to oppose the punitive legislation proposed by the South African government. Each chapter began with an epigraph, with examples culled from the Bible, English poetry, and recent political writings. But there was one much more extensive verse extract. In the chapter titled "The Passing of Cape Ideals," Plaatje included a long section of Oliver Goldsmith's *The Deserted Village*.

Janet Remmington has described *Native Life in South Africa* as "a portable protest book."[3] There is a sense in which this is literally true: the book was composed during Plaatje's travels and was designed to be used as a kind of mobile manifesto on the injustices of the Natives' Land Act that he could distribute in Britain. But it is also worth considering the portability of Plaatje's rhetoric more generally, and especially the decisions that he makes in his writing that create networked communities of readers and thinkers across time, space, and genre. One aspect of this portability is the connection between eighteenth-century enclosure in Britain and the global system of colonization. While Plaatje's twentieth-century South Africa might seem about as distant as it is possible to be from Goldsmith's eighteenth-century Britain, it is closely linked by the processes of colonial dispossession that both men documented in their writing. It is hardly a surprise, in that case, that the form and content of their writings also proves portable; Goldsmith's verse can travel to South Africa and back again, replicated but repurposed in Plaatje's prose. But a second aspect to consider is the portability of genre—the way in which genres are mobile, diffusing and recombining as needed. *Native Life in South Africa* demonstrates the way in which British poetic language and forms could be uplifted and resituated to participate in what is perhaps the ultimate portable mode of communication: diplomacy and its textual productions.

---

3. Janet Remmington, "Going Places: Native Life in South Africa and the Politics of Mobility," in *Sol Plaatje's Native Life in South Africa: Past and Present*, ed. Janet Remmington, Brian Willan, and Bhekizizwe Peterson, 54–80; 55 (Johannesburg: Wits University Press, 2016).

This chapter situates Plaatje's deployment of Goldsmith's verse within both his own people's diplomatic traditions and activities and within a constellation of texts that Plaatje authored around the same time that he was working on *Native Life in South Africa*. While Goldsmith is usually considered to be a pre-Romantic author and *The Deserted Village* (1770) was published well before the French Revolution, the poem is nevertheless often included in discussions of Romanticism because of the specific links between its themes of enclosure, dispossession, marginalization, and the thematic concerns we label as Romantic, and it is in this context that I intend to read it. Placing Goldsmith's poem in this way (both in the Romantic canon and in Indigenous diplomatic discourse) reveals the literal afterlife of enclosure in the wider British Empire, but also the rhetorical possibilities of "enclosure" as a concept, as depicted in the ways in which specific slices of literary language become enveloped within unexpected genres and forms, acquiring and producing, but also demanding, meanings as they are enclosed.

Plaatje and Chiefly Diplomacy

Plaatje was born in 1876 in the Orange Free State and was a descendant of the Rolong chief Morolong.[4] His family settled at the Berlin mission station in Pniel, where Plaatje remained when his parents moved farther north. A Setswana speaker, Plaatje was educated in English and Cape Dutch by the Westphal family at the mission school. He left Pniel in 1894 to work as a messenger in Kimberley and then he worked as an interpreter in the British-controlled Cape Colony town of Mafeking in 1898, where he became a successful newspaper editor and local political figure.

For much of Plaatje's lifetime, the Tshidi branch of the Rolong had been led by Montshiwa and his brother Molema, who had resolutely defended Rolong land claims in negotiations with settler officials in southern Africa, while remaining loyal to Britain.[5] The Rolong held

---

4. The most comprehensive account of Plaatje's life can be found in Brian Willan, *Sol Plaatje: South African Nationalist 1876–1932* (London: Heinemann, 1984). Older texts often use the term "Barolong" instead of "Rolong."

5. A detailed account of Montshiwa, his diplomatic efforts and leadership, and the wider context of Rolong politics in the nineteenth century can be found in Seetsele Modiri Molema, *Montshiwa 1815–1896: Barolong Chief and Patriot* (Cape Town: Struik, 1966).

land in common, with chiefs allocating areas to people to use seasonally.[6] The conflict between this conception of land tenure and settler notions of private holdings and exclusive use led the Rolong to take refuge in British law and legal processes in the mid-nineteenth century. As tensions grew between the emerging southern African settler governments and the imperial British government later in the century, Montshiwa urged loyalty to the British Crown, and was dismayed when the 1881 Pretoria Convention that ended the first Boer War led to his people falling under the jurisdiction of the Transvaal government. He continued to petition British officials through the early 1880s, eventually ceding jurisdiction of his people's lands to Queen Victoria in 1884 in an attempt to make them safe from the encroachment of settlers. He also devised a new system of land tenure for the Tshidi Rolong, dividing land into individual parcels in order to use the concept of enclosure of the commons to secure land title for his people.[7] In the 1890s, however, pressure increased on the Rolong to annex their lands to the Cape Colony, and thus to come under the administration of British officials in southern Africa. Montshiwa initially refused to agree to this administration, preferring a direct relationship with the British Crown to any diluted relationships with a proxy settler government, and he petitioned both Victoria herself and colonial officials in opposition to the plan. In 1895, the chiefs Kgama, Sebele, and Bathoen visited London on a diplomatic mission that garnered some support among the British public and achieved a degree of success in persuading the British to continue with direct rule of their lands, but at the same time, Montshiwa and some of the leaders who had remained in Africa were deceived and coerced into agreeing to annexation.[8]

---

6. See Molema, *Montshiwa 1815–1896*, 191–92; A. Sillery, *The Bechuanaland Protectorate* (Oxford: Oxford University Press, 1952), 48; and I. Schapera, *A Handbook of Tswana Law and Custom* (London: Frank Cass, 1970), 195–213. A wider discussion of the Tshidi Rolong in the nineteenth century can be found in Jean Comaroff, *Body of Power, Spirit of Resistance: The Culture and History of a South African People* (Chicago: University of Chicago Press, 1985).

7. Sillery, 173–74.

8. Molema, *Montshiwa 1815–1896*, 188–89; Sillery, 69–71. See also the wider context of African diplomatic missions to London at this time in Neil Parsons, "Southern African Royalty and Delegates Visit Queen Victoria, 1882–95," in *Mistress of Everything: Queen Victoria in Indigenous Worlds*, ed. Sarah Carter and Maria Nugent, 166–83 (Manchester: Manchester University Press, 2016), 166–83.

Plaatje's first experience of formal diplomacy with the British might have occurred at this time; he is said to have spoken against annexation in 1895.[9] Starting in 1901, he began to assume a more significant position in the local affairs of the Rolong in Mafeking, taking on a role as an adviser and mediator between the local chief and the representatives of the colonial government and emerging as an important go-between, even though he was of wider Rolong (and not specifically Tshidi Rolong) descent.[10] In the Tshidi Rolong community in Mafeking, the *kgotla* (chiefly court) was central to all decision making and the chief and his council remained the first point of contact for any community decisions, but traditional African diplomatic processes focused on maintaining good relationships within a community and allowing multiple voices to have a say in conflict resolution.[11] The chief was likewise able to appoint or consult advisers as he saw fit, including an *induna*, or principal assistant.[12] These assistants were usually commoners who possessed particular skills that were useful to the chief and the kgotla. Plaatje was deeply involved in this world of tribal politics and diplomacy, drawing up petitions to officials, testifying in formal settings, participating in delegations, and using his role as a newspaper editor to push for Native land

---

9. Seetsele Modiri Molema, *Lover of His People: A Biography of Sol Plaatje*, trans. and ed. by D. S. Matjila and Karen Haire, 27 (Johannesburg: Wits University Press, 2012).

10. Willan, *Sol Plaatje*, 94–95.

11. Willan, *Sol Plaatje*, 62; Adejo Armstrong, "Traditional African Diplomacy and Conflict Resolution," *Journal of Cultural Studies* 6, no. 1 (2004): 134–49; Schapera, 75–83. For wider studies of African diplomacy in the nineteenth century, see Graham W. Irwin, "Precolonial African Diplomacy: The Example of Asante," *The International Journal of African Historical Studies* 8, no. 1 (1975): 81–96; A. A. Boahen, "Traditional African Diplomacy and Diplomatic Techniques," *International Congress of Africanists, 3rd Session, December 9–19, 1973, Addis Ababa, Ethiopia*; Robert S. Smith, *Warfare and Diplomacy in Pre-Colonial West Africa*, 2nd rev. ed. (London: James Currey, 1989); Re Sumo Attuquayefio Jr., "The Antecedents of Contemporary African Diplomacy: A Theoretical Study of Intertribal and International Relations in Traditional Africa" (PhD thesis, American University, Washington, DC, 1969); and Joseph K. Adjaye, *Diplomacy and Diplomats in Nineteenth Century Asante* (Lanham, MD: University Press of America, 1984). For insights into the continuing importance of older diplomatic practices in modern African life, see Patience M. Sone, "Relevance of Traditional Methods of Conflict Resolution in the Justice Systems in Africa," *Africa Insight* 46, no. 3 (2016): 51–66.

12. Schapera, 75–77.

rights.¹³ In particular, like the other Indigenous diplomats this book considers, Plaatje represented an emerging generation of leaders and communicators who were seen as especially skilled in understanding both the English language and European and settler discourses, which had a profound effect on the written components of African diplomacy.¹⁴ As his contemporary Seetsele Modiri Molema pointed out, "Plaatje could decipher government legislation written in complex English—he could unmask the hidden intentions lurking beneath the surface of the words."¹⁵ While his skills as a writer and communicator linked him to a modern African elite, Plaatje remained deeply committed to the traditional forms of Rolong leadership and community.¹⁶ As time passed, he came to be seen, not only as a spokesperson for the Tshidi Rolong, but also as a leader with a wider constituency among Black South Africans, especially once he became general secretary of the SANNC after it formed in 1912 to advocate for Black rights in the new political context of the 1909 Union of South Africa.¹⁷

Plaatje, along with the rest of the SANNC leadership, was horrified by the specifics of the proposed Natives' Land Bill in 1913, which he believed laid the groundwork for racial segregation and deprived Africans of existing land and tenancy rights. He requested that the British high commissioner withhold assent for the bill, but his request was refused and the bill was passed into law. Plaatje witnessed firsthand some of its immediate effects, which he wrote about in his newspaper articles and

---

13. See, for example, his testimony to the South African Native Affairs Commission: "Evidence of S. T. Plaatje," *South African Native Affairs Commission, Minutes of Evidence* (Sept. 15, 1904), 4:264–70; and Willan, *Sol Plaatje*, 114–18.

14. See the discussion of the Asante "English chancery" in Adjaye, 160–219, and especially his comment about the growing literary sophistication of African diplomacy in English in the late nineteenth century (210).

15. Molema, *Lover of His People*, 62.

16. Ndana, "Of 'Disinclined Trains and Clever Actors to be Admired and Not Followed': Sol Plaatje, William Shakespeare and the Dilemma of the African Intellectual 1894–1920s," *Marang: Journal of Language and Literature* 18 (2008): 161–70; 164. As André Odendaal has pointed out, understanding Plaatje's work requires an understanding of the African networks of which he was both part and product; see Odendaal, "'Native Lives' behind Native Life: Intellectual and Political Influences on the ANC and Democratic South Africa," in *Sol Plaatje's Native Life in South Africa: Past and Present*, ed. Janet Remmington, Brian Willan, and Bhekizizwe Peterson, 155–46; 121 (Johannesburg: Wits University Press, 2016).

17. Willan, *Sol Plaatje*, 118–19, 124–25.

testified to before the Natives Land Commission.[18] The only possible hope of overturning the new act lay with the British government, which could theoretically overrule the legislation. In February 1914, the SANNC met in Kimberley to finalize arrangements for a delegation to England. Few if any of the SANNC leaders believed that the delegation would be successful, since the British had already indicated that they considered the South African government free to behave as it chose without imperial interference.[19] But the delegation regarded a formal appeal to the British Crown as appropriate, given not only the long-standing diplomatic connections between Britain and South Africa and between Britain and the Indigenous African nations, but also the forms of traditional African diplomacy; as Plaatje later wrote in *Native Life in South Africa*, when the South African governor-general asked the delegation not to travel to England, "the deputation replied that, even in native politics there was always an appeal from the action of an induna to the native chief and from the latter to the ruler; that it was straining the loyalty of the black millions of South Africa to tell them that there was no appeal to His Majesty the King against the oppressive laws of a parliament in which they had no representatives" (186).[20]

At an official level, this approach entirely failed. Lord Harcourt, the colonial secretary, met with the delegation but refused to support their cause, and the debate on the matter in the British House of Commons did not produce any gains for the SANNC.[21] The delegates' campaign of pamphlets, meetings, lectures, and letters, which was largely led by Plaatje, was somewhat more successful; as the newspaper report just quoted suggests, there was quite a lot of public sympathy for the African cause and

---

18. Plaatje's testimony can be found in William Henry Beaumont, *Report of the Natives Land Commission, UG22—'16* (Cape Town: South African Government Printers, 1916), 2:92–94.

19. Willan, *Sol Plaatje*, 161–67.

20. Plaatje also received authorization from the Rolong to act on their behalf while in England, not simply on behalf of the wider SANNC organization; see Marcelle Jacobson, ed., *The Silas T. Molema and Solomon T. Plaatje Papers* (Johannesburg: University of the Witwatersrand, 1978), 39. It was common for settler officials to attempt to thwart African attempts to negotiate directly with the British; see the similar response to an Asante delegation in the late nineteenth century in Adjaye, 146–47.

21. The correspondence between British and South African officials and between the Colonial Office and the SAANC can be found in the National Archives (UK), CO/551/64, CO/551/67, CO 879/114/2, and CO 529/1.

some disquiet about the British abandonment of their former subjects.[22] But this sympathy was part of a pattern of the same well-meaning inertia that greeted Brant and Copway in Europe and greeted Boudinot in parts of the northeastern United States; as Plaatje wrote in a private letter, "I am beginning to understand now why native deputations . . . always start so well and then end up in smoke immediately afterwards."[23] The SANNC decided that it was appropriate to suspend their campaign at the outbreak of World War I, although Plaatje, alone among the London delegates, stayed in England throughout the war to continue his advocacy, speaking to over 300 meetings and working the narrative of wartime loyalty to the British into the final version of *Native Life in South Africa*.[24]

Plaatje had always believed that while the British government was unlikely to support their cause, the mobilization of British public feeling might still provoke some action. Speaking to the Kimberley branch of the African People's Association in the months leading up to their departure, he cast "sympathy" as a key ingredient in the case that the SANNC wished to make:

> In the midst of all these difficulties, the only sympathy received by our people from the government is the paternal advice that they must not appeal to England. We have been to Parliament and also to the Governor-General before the Act was passed, and got no sympathy. Since the Act came into force, we have been to the ministry with desperate appeals for help under the harsh provisions of that remarkable Act, and got no sympathy. So we turn our eyes to England as a last resort.[25]

---

22. Willan, *Sol Plaatje*, 201. Examples of the sympathetic coverage can be found in the Solomon T. Plaatje Papers at the School of Oriental and African Studies, University of London; for example, Anon., "Biography: Mr. Plaatje's Career," *African Times and Orient Review*, January 1917, 17–18; S. T. Plaatje Papers, School of Oriental and African Studies, University of London, MS 375495/4.

23. Solomon Plaatje, letter to Mrs. Colenso, August 31, 1914, cited in Willan, *Sol Plaatje*, 182.

24. Willan, *Sol Plaatje*, 203.

25. Sol Plaatje, *Sol Plaatje: Selected Writings*, ed. Brian Willan, 168 (Johannesburg: Witwatersrand University Press, 1996). The SAANC also made this point to the Anti-Slavery and Aborigines Protection Society, writing to request the society's help in the hope that "British public opinion may be brought to bear in the matter and upon the Government" (Bodleian Library Special Collections. South African Society MSS. Brit. Emp. S.22 G203, 22).

The repetition of the term "sympathy" here reminds us that Plaatje was at work crafting an appeal based on both political and ethical foundations but cast in the language of sentimental literature.[26] Plaatje's familiarity with English literature was acquired through his own reading as well as his time at the mission school. Friends recalled seeing works by Milton, Shakespeare, Byron, Shelley, Keats, Longfellow, and Burns in his personal library.[27] During his time in Kimberley, Plaatje joined the South Africans Improvement Society, a group that valued the English language and English literature as keys to Black advancement and at whose meetings members would recite English texts.[28] For someone who was simultaneously a diplomat and an author, an expert in both the traditions of his own people and the settler canon, this approach might have come naturally. The specific term he chooses to emphasize, however, serves as a reminder that he had considered carefully which part of the English canon to repurpose in his diplomatic efforts. To invoke "sympathy" was to invoke the British literature of the late eighteenth century, and to invoke this literature in the cause of sympathies involving land, exile, and the loss of place-based lifeways led almost effortlessly to Goldsmith and *The Deserted Village*.

Native Life in Auburn

Quotation was a central part of Plaatje's intellectual framework. Contemporaries often mentioned his formidable memory and ability to quote at length, including from rather dry texts such as pieces of legislation, while Brian Willan has alluded to the diplomatic skill of Plaatje's style in English: "He knew exactly the compliments to pay, the names to drop, the tone to adopt."[29] *Native Life in South Africa* manifests these abilities and converts them into a rhetorical strategy that resembles Copway's

---

26. In their reading of Plaatje's interpretation of, and response to, the act, William Beinart and Peter Delius suggest that this literary framing of his concerns might have contributed to what they regard as Plaatje's misrepresentation of some aspects of the new legislation; see Beinart and Delius, "The Historical Context and Legacy of the Natives Land Act of 1913," *Journal of Southern African Studies* 40, no. 4 (2014): 667–88, esp. 673.

27. Molema, *Lover of His People*, 6.

28. Willan, *Sol Plaatje*, 36–37.

29. See for example, Molema, *Lover of His People*, 6; and Willan, *Sol Plaatje*, 147.

approach in *Running Sketches*. The book includes extracts from speeches by South African politicians and from *Hansard*, as well as the entirety of the Natives' Land Act itself.[30] Snippets of newspaper reports about the hardships Africans faced under the act are interspersed with citations from firsthand conversations Plaatje had with his fellow citizens as he traveled and reported on the act's effects. Legal documents and proclamations are quoted in detail, while the longest single piece of quoted text is the entire speech given by Dr. Abdullah Abdurahman at Kimberley on September 29, 1913, at the opening of the tenth annual Conference of the African Peoples' Organization (131–44). Threaded through the entire book are numerous literary and biblical quotations, sometimes in the form of epigraphs and sometimes integrated into Plaatje's prose. This material was so central to Plaatje's vision for the book that when Sir Harry Johnston, the retired colonial administrator whom Plaatje had asked to write an introduction for *Native Life in South Africa*, suggested removing the quotations, Plaatje decided instead to do without Johnston's introduction.[31] As Khwezi Mkhize has written, "Plaatje's citations curated texts and debates for metropolitan audiences that were particular to their colonial space, bringing to life contestations that were taking place at the margins of empire."[32]

Separating the literary material into a different rhetorical category from the more quotidian or legalistic examples of quotation hampers our ability to understand Plaatje's text, as it does that of all the Indigenous diplomats that this book considers. While scholars such as Elleke Boehmer, A. E. Voss, and Jane Stafford have provided rich readings of the role that quotation plays in *Native Life in South Africa*, it is still necessary to think further about the *diplomatic* importance of quotation, rather than its aesthetic and literary importance, and to situate Plaatje within a longer, global tradition of Indigenous diplomats working with British Romantic

---

30. Sol. T. Plaatje, *Native Life in South Africa*, ed. Brian Willan, 51–56 (1916; reprint, New York: Picador, 2007), 51–56. Subsequent references to *Native Life in South Africa* are included in parentheses in the text.

31. Willan, *Sol Plaatje*, 189.

32. Khwezi Mkhize, "African Intellectual History, Black Cosmopolitanism and Native Life in South Africa," in *Sol Plaatje's Native Life in South Africa: Past and Present*, ed. Janet Remmington, Brian Willan, and Bhekizizwe Peterson, 95–114; 97–98 (Johannesburg: Wits University Press, 2016).

poetry.[33] Plaatje's literary quotations, like all the other examples of quoted text mentioned here, were specifically oriented toward diplomacy, and especially a kind of diplomacy that aimed at the British public rather than simply British officials. It was designed both to convey and to generate a detailed, nuanced understanding of the conditions brought about by the Natives' Land Act and the political context in which the act operated. Most of the quoted material, such as the speeches and legal documents, had been produced in relation to this context and manifested literal connections to unfolding events in South Africa. The literary quotations are clearly at a remove from these other bits of text, in that they were neither written in this specific context nor serve to connect in any literal way to the South African situation. But that distance from a central cluster of bureaucratic and political text should not be overestimated. The Natives' Land Act and the demands of the SANNC delegation in 1914 operate as the gravitational core of the text, pulling all the quoted material into its diplomatic orbit. The literary quotation may be peripheral, but its connection to the central concerns of the text cannot be dismissed. It participated in the multimodal approach to diplomacy that Plaatje wanted to generate and in which he excelled.

In his work on decolonizing diplomacy, Sam Okoth Opondo discusses the ways in which European practices sought to produce a diplomatically legible African "official" with whom to negotiate. This process involved exposing such potential officials to both Christian and European traditions, but also creating practices that "act as a cover for ontological investments within which coloured bodies, other gods and ways of being-with-the-other are excluded from the way we think about diplomacy."[34] On the surface, Plaatje might seem to be just such a legible subject, someone translated into an official whom the British could recognize via his mission education and deployment of biblical and English literary language and forms. But Opondo also points out that recognition of an African

---

33. Elleke Boehmer, *Empire, the National, and the Postcolonial, 1890–1920: Resistance in Action* (Oxford: Oxford University Press, 2005), 126–56; A. E. Voss, "Sol Plaatje, the Eighteenth Century, and South African Cultural Memory," *English in Africa* 21. nos. 1–2 (1994): 59–75; Jane Stafford, *Colonial Literature and the Native Author: Indigeneity and Empire* (Basingstoke: Palgrave, 2016), 61–105.

34. Sam Okoth Opondo, "Decolonizing Diplomacy: Reflections of African Estrangement and Exclusion," in *Sustainable Diplomacies*, ed. Costas M. Constantinou and James Der Derian, 109–27; 119 (Basingstoke: Palgrave, 2010).

diplomat also "presupposes a prior division between the diplomatic and the non-diplomatic," in which only some people or some discourses are rendered appropriate to diplomatic settings, and which contradicts African diplomatic norms.[35] Plaatje's deployment of British literary text actively breaks down and rejects this prior generic division, insisting on the diplomatic value of poetry and its inseparability from broader diplomatic discourse in ways that should remind us of Brant, Boudinot, and Copway. While Plaatje appears to center the needs, values, and forms of his British audience, he does so from the foundation of African diplomatic norms, not British ones.

Plaatje's literary quotations in *Native Life in South Africa* came from a range of sources. There are numerous epigraphs from British authors whom we might consider canonical: Scott, Burns, Cowper, and Tennyson, for example. However, the only extended piece of poetic quotation is the long extract from Goldsmith's *The Deserted Village*. Although all the epigraphs and short quotations should be considered part of the wider diplomatic aims of the volume, this extract from Goldsmith seems much more closely related to the more obviously political extracts, such as those from speeches, legislation, and parliamentary debates, which inhabit the main body of the text. Rather than occupying the epigraphic space at the start of a chapter, which allows a quotation to provide a thematic framework for what follows, Goldsmith's poem is incorporated into the argument of Plaatje's chapter. It does not simply set the tone; rather, it is provided as a kind of evidence, which can be analyzed, drawn on, and mobilized in the case that Plaatje wishes to make. The length at which it is quoted, its placement within the body of a chapter rather than at the start, and the ways in which Plaatje engages with it in his own surrounding prose make Goldsmith's verse much more like the key political texts that Plaatje handles in a similar fashion throughout *Native Life in South Africa* than like one of the epigraphs. In other words, if the political prose extracts are central to Plaatje's diplomatic efforts in this book and the shorter literary quotations are related but peripheral material, the extract from Goldsmith is the hinge between the two.

The chapter in which Goldsmith's poem appears, "The Passing of Cape Ideals," mourns the potential loss of the Cape Colony way of life, which Plaatje had hoped would be extended to the rest of South

---

35. Opondo, 118.

Africa.³⁶ The betrayal of Cape values was a key theme of the book and a particular concern of the SANNC, since there had been no color bar to voting in the Cape.³⁷ As Mkhize points out, for Plaatje, "'The Cape' is . . . not simply a colonial geography but a once-historical ideal that could have been the foundation of South Africa."³⁸ In this sense, the Cape functions in Plaatje's text in a similar fashion to the way Auburn functions in Goldsmith's poem: it is less a cartographical map than what we might call a roadmap, a kind of poetic constitution that could have proved to be the blueprint for a fairer and more just nation. It is not surprising, then, that Plaatje's chosen excerpt is from early in the poem, covering lines 1–86, where Goldsmith's speaker describes the Auburn he knew as a young man (160–61). These lines are entirely suitable for Plaatje's purposes, since they represent Goldsmith's fiercest critique of the evils of enclosure and had been used effectively in the past by antienclosure activists in Britain, including in the Romantic period.³⁹ The quotation has been curated to suit Plaatje's purposes, however, in a manner that echoes Copway's curation of Byron; approximately half the lines in this section of the poem are omitted, and the word "village" is changed to the localized "Province" in the line "These were thy charms, sweet village" (31).⁴⁰ Plaatje also interrupts the quotation to provide a brief piece of commentary of his own.

But while these decisions demonstrate Plaatje's confident repurposing of Goldsmith's words, perhaps the most striking aspect of the insertion of this excerpt is how *little* Plaatje does to localize his example. The impact of his deployment of Goldsmith comes instead from the near-total iden-

---

36. References to Goldsmith's poetry are to Oliver Goldsmith, *Collected Works of Oliver Goldsmith*, vol. 4, ed. Arthur Friedman (Oxford: Clarendon Press, 1966), unless otherwise stated.

37. For discussion of the importance to the SANNC of the Cape franchise, which had no color bar, see Walshe, 24, and Vivian Bickford-Smith, "Revisiting Anglicisation in the Nineteenth-Century Cape Colony," *Journal of Imperial and Commonwealth History* 31, no. 2 (2003): 82–95.

38. Mkhize, 101.

39. See for example the pseudonymous pamphlet *Examinator's Letters, or A Mirror for British Monopolists and Irish Financiers* (n.p., 1786), which used key lines from Goldsmith's poem as its epigraph.

40. In this way, Plaatje uses a process that Isabel Hofmeyr has traced in African adaptations of *The Pilgrim's Progress*; see Hofmeyr, *The Portable Bunyan: A Transnational History of* The Pilgrim's Progress (Princeton: Princeton University Press, 2004), esp. 234–36.

tification he makes between Auburn and the Cape. All Auburn's virtues are here transplanted to Africa. Details so specific that they have led to carefully mapped correspondences between Auburn and Goldsmith's native Lissoy in Ireland in scholarship that insists on an autobiographical reading, and that also clearly mark the setting as a European one, are presented as authentic details of native life in the Cape, such as:

> The shelter'd cot, the cultivated farm,
> The never failing brook, the busy mill,
> The decent church that topt the neighbouring hill
> The hawthorn bush with seats beneath the shade. (10–13).[41]

The collapse of Cape life, meanwhile, is presented in exactly the same terms as the collapse of Auburn life:

> And trembling, shrinking from the spoiler's hand,
> Far, far away, thy children leave the land.
> Ill fares the land, to hastening ills a prey,
> Where wealth accumulates and men decay. (49–52)

The sense of analogous situations suits Plaatje's diplomatic aims here. The universality of Goldsmith's message is stressed in this deployment, which connects injustices abroad with injustices at home for British readers and uses their own literature as a precedent. As A. E. Voss has suggested in regard to the stripping of Native land rights, Plaatje's intention was "partly to condemn this procedure out of the mouths of its promoters, and partly to give authority and emotional power to an alternative, universal moral and social code by whose standards the procedure should be condemned."[42]

In some senses, this means that Plaatje offers a radical reinterpretation of the poem. The good life that Auburn represents is not only, in Plaatje's rendering, universal, but can actually be found in precisely the places Goldsmith suggested it could not. When Goldsmith's archetypal family

---

[41]. In a general sense, the lines do evoke some aspects of Plaatje's early family life, although not the living conditions of many of those around him; see Willan, *Sol Plaatje*, 14. Friedman's introduction to the poem outlines the history of identifying the poem's details with Lissoy; see Goldsmith, 4:273–74.

[42]. Voss, 68.

of emigrants prepared to leave Auburn, they "took a long farewell, and wished in vain / For seats like these beyond the western main" (367–68). In Goldsmith's eyes, Auburn and villages like it could not be found or even built by the new colonists in the Americas, or indeed in Africa. Plaatje proposes the opposing view: that the Indigenous residents of the colonies already saw their homeland in the idyllic terms of an Auburn.

In this respect, Plaatje disputes a point that Goldsmith made in another poem, *The Traveller* (1764), about the universal sentiment of attachment to one's home, no matter how unappealing such homes might seem to outsiders. Goldsmith's lines, a critique of thoughtless patriotism and part of a wider pattern of anti-Black and anti-African thinking that is clear in his journalism, draw attention to what the poet sees as the foolishness of regarding one's own land as ideal:

> The shudd'ring tenant of the frigid zone
> Boldly proclaims that happiest spot his own,
> Extols the treasures of his stormy seas,
> And his long nights of revelry and ease;
> The naked Negro, panting at the line,
> Boasts of his golden sands and palmy wine,
> Basks in the glare, or stems the tepid wave,
> And thanks his Gods for all the good they gave.
> Such is the patriot's boast, where'er we roam,
> His first best country ever is at home. (65–74)[43]

Although not engaging directly with this poem or passage, Plaatje's interpretation of the Cape implicitly takes sentiments like those expressed by the "shudd'ring tenant of the frigid zone" and the "naked Negro, panting at the line," as entirely reasonable. Stripped of Goldsmith's Eurocentrism and racism, these places are accepted as the beloved homelands of their peoples. Goldsmith rejects the universal sentiment of patriotism and attachment to home, but Plaatje does not. His Cape is like Goldsmith's Auburn, not because the details actually match despite how carefully he includes them, but because the sentiments that underpin the details match.

---

43. "The Traveller" also features in *Native Life in South Africa*; see the reference in the speech by Dr. A. Abdurahman that Plaatje includes in *Native Life*, 131–39. For the inherent racism of Goldsmith's wider thought, see James Watt, "Goldsmith's Cosmopolitanism," *Eighteenth-Century Life* 30, no. 1 (2006): 56–75; 68–69.

In fact, the absence of realism only underlines the force of the analogy; the potential incongruity of the hawthorn bush in the Cape reinforces the fact that Goldsmith's poem is potentially about both specific experiences and universal emotions.

Where Plaatje does draw distinctions between Auburn and Africa is on the question of the severity of the losses that were experienced. He signals this break from Goldsmith by inserting a brief piece of commentary of his own. Immediately after quoting the famous lines, "Ill fares the land, to hastening ills a prey, / Where wealth accumulates and men decay" (51–52), Plaatje offers this comment and extension of the quotation:

> The Cape native can thoroughly endorse these sentiments of Oliver Goldsmith, which, however, compared with his own present lot, are mild in the extreme; for it could not have been amid scenes of this description, and with an outlook half as bad as ours, that the same author further sings:
>
> A time there was e'er [sic] England's grief began,
> When every rood of ground maintain'd its man;
> But times are alter'd: Trade's unfeeling train
> Usurp the land and dispossess the swain.
> Those gentle hours that plenty bade to bloom,
> Those calm desires that ask'd but little room,
> Liv'd in each look and brighten'd all the green,
> These far departing seek a kinder shore,
> And rural mirth and manners are no more.
> In all my wand'rings round this world of care,
> In all my griefs—and God has giv'n my share—
> I still had hopes my latest hours to crown,
> Amidst these humble bowers to lay me down. [57–86][44]

Plaatje's Auburn is an Auburn intensified, its injustices magnified by the racial discrimination of the Natives' Land Act. Having established the idea that Auburn and the Cape might be considered to mirror one another, Plaatje then suggests to his British readers that scenes in contemporary South Africa actually dwarf the misery that Goldsmith described, with

---

44. The lines are reproduced here as they appear in Plaatje's text rather than in Goldsmith's original poem; Plaatje has omitted several lines from the original text.

perhaps the complementary assumption that the pleasures lost were superior to Auburn's pleasures too. It is important, in order to achieve this multifaceted reading of the poem, that Plaatje both does and does not alter what Goldsmith says. Plaatje's British readers are being presented with both a radical universalism and a potentially confronting sense of the way in which the crises of colonialism have in fact escalated and intensified as they radiated out from land experiments in eighteenth-century Britain.

Plaatje's decision to quote at length from Goldsmith reinforces the centrality of Romantic poetry and its themes, in particular, to Indigenous diplomacy throughout the nineteenth and early twentieth centuries. It needs to be read, however, less as a deferential gesture to the English canon and more as a recognition of a preexisting but unintentional Africanness in Goldsmith's lines. In D. S. Matjila and Karen Haire's reading, which is aimed, as their book's title suggests, at "bringing Plaatje home," it is Setswana thought that is central to his corpus. Their broad description of African attitudes to land, for example, demands some reconsideration of what we consider to be "Romantic" about Plaatje's work:

> Africans revere and admire the land. They perceive it as admirable beauty with all its concomitant blemishes. Poets, politicians, shepherds, and intellectuals alike share this view. Nature, in a reciprocal relationship with man, is a nourisher of the soul. The awe, wonder, and inner elation that is felt by the poet, is outwardly reflected in the lyricism, music, tone, and mood of his poetry. Trees, grass, and flowers are experienced as agents of calm, comfort, peace, and relaxation. . . . Given the view of equality and partnership with nature in traditional African society, it is not surprising that listening to the language of the birds, the animals, the insects, the trees, and the rivers is both natural and central to human existence.[45]

To the ear of a Romanticist, this description might sound like both Goldsmith's conception of land and that of wider British Romanticism. But Matjila and Haire interpret this land-based aspect of Plaatje's writing

---

45. D. S. Matjila and Karen Haire, *Bringing Plaatje Back Home—Ga E Phetsolele Nageng: 'Re-Storying' the African and Batswana Sensibilities in His Oeuvre* (Trenton, NJ: Africa World Press, 2015), 86–87.

as emblematic of his "Setswana and African sensibilities."[46] This framing helps underline the need to stop thinking of Indigenous quotation in a unidirectional way, even if sympathetically, and start seeing the underlying power of Romanticism for Indigenous diplomats as genuinely consistent with, and perhaps chronologically subsequent to, their own epistemologies.

But while *The Deserted Village* seems to make perfect sense as a text to excerpt in this moment, the choice of Goldsmith as a focal point is, in some ways, surprising, coming from a writer and thinker who was so heavily invested in the works of Shakespeare. On his return to South Africa in 1917, Plaatje produced translations of *Julius Caesar, The Merchant of Venice, Othello, Much Ado about Nothing*, and *The Comedy of Errors* into his native language of Setswana. He was especially drawn to *The Merchant of Venice*, and one of his notebooks contains a brief reworking of the character of Shylock under the African name Mochuana.[47] In 1916, the same year *Native Life in South Africa* appeared, he contributed a short bilingual essay to the collection *A Book of Homage to Shakespeare*, in which he outlined a theory of cultural compatibility between Shakespeare and African thought and highlighted moments when he had used Shakespearean quotations in his own writing.[48] There is certainly a Shakespearean influence on *Native Life in South Africa*: an epigraph from *The Merchant of Venice* opens one chapter (116), and passing reference is made to *King Lear* elsewhere (126).

Why, then, was Shakespeare not the central literary reference point for *Native Life in South Africa*? For all Plaatje's affection for Shakespeare's work, the themes of British Romanticism were simply far more relevant to his diplomatic efforts. He was not quoting English literature in order

---

46. Matjila and Haire, 50.

47. Solomon T. Plaatje, "With Apologies to Shakespeare's 'Merchant of Venice,'" *English in Africa* 3, no. 2 (1976): 7.

48. Solomon Plaatje, "A South African's Homage," in *A Book of Homage to Shakespeare*, ed. Israel Gollancz, 336–39 (Oxford: Oxford University Press, 1916). For a broader discussion of the role of Shakespeare in Plaatje's writing life, see David Schalkwyk and Lerothodi Lapula, "Solomon Plaatje, William Shakespeare, and the Translations of Culture," *Pretexts* 9, no. 1 (2000): 9–26; Deborah Seddon, "Shakespeare's Orality: Solomon Plaatje's Setswana Translations," *English Studies in Africa* 47. no. 2 (2004): 77–95; David Johnson, *Shakespeare and South Africa* (Oxford: Oxford University Press, 1996), 74–110; and Brian Willan, "'A South African's Homage' at One Hundred: Revisiting Sol Plaatje's Contribution to the Book of Homage to Shakespeare (1916)," *Shakespeare in Southern Africa* 28 (2016): 1–19.

to seem cultured or intellectually credible. Rather, he was making use of Romanticism's particular meditations on land, sympathy, and imperialism in order to motivate British sentiment as well as to locate the Africans' plight within a global history that stretched back to at least Goldsmith's time. Mkhize notes that "what is important about *Native Life* is that it is a text animated by spaces where the colonial, the national, and the imperial are interlinked. It offers an expanded and complex cartography through which to consider a form of black intellectual work that is deeply sensitive to (yet able to work in tension with) the idea of nation."[49] This expanded cartography is also, I would suggest, an expanded chronology, one that is able to take in eighteenth-century Auburn as well as twentieth-century Durban. The political forces against which Goldsmith raged in *The Deserted Village* were the same global and economic forces that had led to the Natives' Land Act, and the emotional reaction that Goldsmith hoped to provoke in readers considering eighteenth-century enclosures, displacements, and mistreatments is the same reaction Plaatje hoped to provoke in regard to twentieth-century South Africa.[50]

The potential confluence of Goldsmith's ideas with Plaatje's can be sensed in other parts of the book, beyond the chapter on the Cape ideals, in which Plaatje's own prose reflects some of the language or preoccupations of *The Deserted Village*, in rather the same way in which Copway makes use of a Byronic rhetoric in his writings, and that Boudinot and other contributors to the *Cherokee Phoenix* appear to be in conversation with Hemans's ideas. When he describes traveling around South Africa to observe the effects of the Natives' Land Act on Africans, Plaatje notes that he felt a terrible grief that reminds him of his father's death, before remarking: "but then we lived in a happy South Africa that was full pleasant [sic] anticipations, and now—what changes for the worse have we undergone!" (68). The sentiment echoes the line that ends Goldsmith's opening description of the Auburn he remembers from his youth: "These were thy charms—But all these charms are fled" (34). A similar effect occurs when Plaatje talks about the South African parliament's desire "to

---

49. Mkhize, 108.

50. John Montague makes the point that it is the "pattern of economic greed" that is the real target of Goldsmith's verse; see Montague, "The Sentimental Prophecy: A Study of *The Deserted Village*," in *The Art of Oliver Goldsmith*, ed. Andrew Swarbrick, 90–106; 102 (London: Vision, 1984).

hound us out of our ancestral homes" (68), an idea that chimes with Goldsmith's description of villagers exiled from their "native walks" (364) by British land policies and the greed of landowners. Plaatje does not need Goldsmith's poem in order to express such thoughts about the Natives' Land Act, but the connections between his ideas and Goldsmith's might suggest why *The Deserted Village* came to occupy such a prominent place in *Native Life in South Africa*.

Plaatje joins a long list of writers internationally who saw the potential of Goldsmith's poem to further their own political and diplomatic aims. As Vincent Newey has suggested, the apparatus of Goldsmith's poem "is prospective as well as retrospective," offering, not just a romantic vision of an idealized past, but also a blueprint for the future.[51] The poem does not simply mourn what is lost; it agitates for a radical change in historical trajectory. Newey points out that the political assumptions underpinning *The Deserted Village* have, by the end of the poem, "been theorized, wrought into a manifesto, set out for others to take up."[52] In other words, the poem operates as a kind of diplomatic text, organized as a versified political demand, which can then circulate for discussion. The history of the poem's transatlantic reception demonstrates this diplomatic dimension. It was taken as a reference point in wider debates about enclosure, luxury, and depopulation and, as it was gradually adopted by an increasingly radical readership, it was deployed in texts from poems to economic treatises.[53]

While Plaatje's adaptation of Goldsmith might seem to distort its original purpose, there is a considerable overlap in the two authors'

---

51. Vincent Newey, "Goldsmith's 'Pensive Plain': Re-viewing *The Deserted Village*," in *Early Romantics: Perspectives in British Poetry from Pope to Wordsworth*, edited by Thomas M. Woodman, 93–116; 97 (Basingstoke: Macmillan, 1998). See also Suvir Kaul's reading of the poem as mourning the declining power of the English, as global economic forces shifted influence to colonies like the Cape, in Kaul, *Poems of Nation, Anthems of Empire: English Verse in the Long Eighteenth Century* (Charlottesville: University Press of Virginia, 2000), 117–21.

52. Newey, 107.

53. Alfred Lutz, "The Politics of Reception: The Case of Goldsmith's 'The Deserted Village,'" *Studies in Philology* 95, no. 2 (1998): 174–96; 178–80. See also Matthew Clarke, "The 'Luxury of Woe': The Deserted Village and the Politics of Publication," *European Romantic Review* 26, no. 2 (2015): 165–83; and John Barrell, *The Dark Side of the Landscape: The Rural Poor in English Painting 1730–1840* (Cambridge: Cambridge University Press, 1980), 87–88.

apparent aims. John Montague reads *The Deserted Village* as a carefully constructed oscillation between sentimental imagery and political reality:

> Goldsmith's technique in *The Deserted Village* is to carry his thesis by the emotional effect of his skilful alternation between images of original innocence and malignant destruction; the relatively few didactic passages are made as simple as possible. It is not that his argument is unimportant—it is rather so important to him, so much a part of his total vision, that he is prepared to use all the poetic means in his power to invade the reader on its behalf. This is why we cannot, like Alice, read *The Deserted Village* just for its pictures, because its pictures are part of a calculated attack upon our sympathies.[54]

Plaatje's alternations pivot on a different axis, crossing genres rather than simply chronologies, but the effect is similar. The lines of poetry do not trump the vast array of other, less literary material in *Native Life in South Africa*, but nor do they stand apart from that material. As readers, we cannot simply extract the poetry, but nor should we gloss over it in search of the "real" political argument. The notion that the sentimental effect of poetry might yield real political results is one that Plaatje might have borrowed, in part, from Goldsmith himself. Just as Plaatje's work can be read as a "portable protest book," Goldsmith's can be read as a portable protest poem.

Phonetics, Proverbs, Petitions, Poems

It is not simply individual texts that acquire this sense of portability in Indigenous diplomacy, however. Ideas, of course, are portable too, moving across genres in ways that do not fit binaries of the literary and the diplomatic. One of the remarkable things about Plaatje's work during his time in England is the extraordinary variety of genres in which he chose to express himself. A significant portion of his time was spent producing what might appear to be very different sorts of texts to *Native Life*

---

54. Montague, 96. Alfred Lutz makes a related point about the ways Goldsmith suggests that the ruling elite have failed to protect social harmony; see Lutz, "'The Deserted Village' and the Politics of Genre," *Modern Language Quarterly* 55, no. 2 (1994): 149–68; 166.

in South Africa, but they all offer us an insight into the intertextuality that both governed his literary career and shaped a text like *Native Life*. They also offer insight into the ways in which he might have imagined effective diplomacy and communication to operate. Between May 1915 and September 1916, Plaatje worked with Daniel Jones, a lecturer in the Phonetics Department at University College London, on a study of Setswana phonetics, as well as compiling a collection of Setswana proverbs for publication. In his preface to *A Sechuana Reader*, Plaatje described the experience of hearing Jones read phonetically: "Since my first introduction to phonetics it has been my pleasure on many occasions to sit and listen to Mr. Jones reading aloud (from phonetic texts) long and difficult Sechuana passages, of which he did not know the meaning, with a purity of sound and tone more perfect than I have ever heard from Englishmen in Africa who did know the meaning of the words they were uttering."[55]

Plaatje's parallel projects suggest some additional ways of reading the quotations in *Native Life in South Africa*, and especially the passage from *The Deserted Village*. His work with Daniel Jones was designed to help willing learners repeat sounds that they did not necessarily understand, in order to generate meaningful language. It assumed that a first step to the recovery of real understanding was the mimicking of what that understanding might sound like. One way of reading the parallels between these volumes might be to assume that Plaatje himself is the phonetic reader of English, parroting the lines of English poetry in an attempt to create meaning for his audience of English speakers. But Plaatje's sophisticated understanding of English literature and language suggests something entirely different, in which *Native Life in South Africa* moves the process of uncomprehending mimicry into surprising territory. In many ways, it is the British readers of the text who are using poetic language without understanding and who need to be guided toward a correct articulation of their own language and literature. In his use of quotation from English literary sources, Plaatje implies that his English readers do, in fact, lack comprehension of the words of their own poets. They make the noises, but they do not understand what those noises truly imply. Plaatje repeats the poetic words and urges his readers' simultaneous repetition of them

---

55. Daniel Jones and Solomon Tshekisho Plaatje, *A Sechuana Reader* (London: University of London Press, 1916), ix. See Boehmer, 143, for a discussion of the centrality of Plaatje's work with Jones to his thinking at this time. "Sechuana" is an older spelling of the word that is now more usually spelled "Setswana."

in order to motivate a realignment of language, meaning, and action. This insight can be applied to any of the quoted literary texts, such as the numerous epigraphs, but it is really the extended extract from *The Deserted Village* that demands the mobilization of existing British cultural understandings of land, sympathy, and dispossession in the service of action that is both supportive of Africans and consistent with the British values encoded in much-loved literary works.

Another seemingly disconnected publication from this intensely productive period of Plaatje's life also helps to contextualize the role of quotation and cross-cultural sympathy in *Native Life in South Africa*. In the same year that *Native Life* appeared, Plaatje published *Sechuana Proverbs with Literal Translations and Their European Equivalents*. The collection, which Plaatje appears to have assembled from memory, was organized into three columns, with each entry featuring a Setswana proverb followed by a literal translation into English and then an equivalent European proverb. While some of the European proverbs that are supplied are, indeed, proverbial (such as "forgive and forget"), others came from literary authors, including Tennyson and Pope.[56] Plaatje clearly regarded English literature as, in some cases, inherently proverbial, and thus able to be repurposed as shared cultural knowledge rather than specific intellectual property. This repurposing had the same kind of diplomatic impulse that shaped *Native Life in South Africa*, in the sense that it aims at generating cross-cultural understanding and sympathy for (in this instance) a language threatened by colonization. In his preface, Plaatje pointed out that the proverbs illustrated "the similarity between all pastoral nations," but also gestured to the peril in which the Indigenous people of his land found themselves and their culture: "The object of this book," he wrote, "is to save from oblivion, as far as this can still be done, the proverbial expressions" of his people.[57] Language, lore, and land were all under threat in South Africa, and Plaatje's trip to England and the publications he produced there were intimately connected in a diplomatic mission to preserve them.

The connections between all these elements can be summed up in one of the Setswana proverbs Plaatje included in this collection: "always build a fence around the King's word."[58] As Jane Starfield has pointed

---

56. Solomon T. Plaatje, *Sechuana Proverbs with Literal Translations and their European Equivalents* (London: Kegan Paul, 1916). See, for example, pp. 22, 28, 60, and 74.
57. Plaatje, *Sechuana Proverbs*, 1.
58. Plaatje, *Sechuana Proverbs*, 33.

out, this proverb links leadership, language, and land in vital ways, reconstructing political discourse as a kind of metaphorical territory that must be defended.[59] The proverb also provides a productive way to think about Plaatje's deployment of Goldsmith's verse. It depicts the broad notion of "enclosure" as a potentially positive and protective move, designed to defend land, language, and leadership in the face of encroaching forces. It also, I think, offers a useful reflection on quotation as a practice. In the proverb's formulation, it is not simply the promise or "word" of the king that needs protecting, but also the exact language in which that promise is contained. The word of the king is sacrosanct and needs to be preserved from dilution or manipulation, but it also needs to be tended, rather like an enclosed plot of land. Starfield connects this proverb to Plaatje's loyal service to the Rolong rulers, as well as his broader adherence to African structures of chieftainship and his desire to see these structures respected. In representing the SANNC and the Rolong in Britain, Plaatje was participating in this proverbial fence building, faithfully delivering the chiefs' words to their British interlocutors. But what might it mean to think about Britain's chiefs and their words in similar terms? Plaatje returns over and over again to the promises made by Queen Victoria, her successors, and officials in Britain and their proxies in Africa, paying close attention to the language that encodes those promises.[60] *Native Life in South Africa* implies that the British have not built a fence around their kings' words, allowing those words instead to fade conveniently from the collective memory. Toward the end of the book, Plaatje strategically praises the early British imperialists in Africa, "who all told us that they spoke in the name of Queen Victoria and on behalf of her heirs and successors. What has suddenly become of the Briton's word—his bond—that solemn obligations of such Imperialists should cease to count?" (362). His deployment of poetry operates in a similar fashion, suggesting that the wisdom and authority of lines like Goldsmith's have become neglected and overgrown. Quotation can provide some of the protection and the

---

59. Jane Starfield, "The Lore and the Proverbs: Sol Plaatje as Historian," African Studies Seminar Paper No. 299 (University of Witwatersrand, Johannesburg, South Africa, 1991), 18.

60. For a discussion of the role of Victoria in African political relationships with Britain, see Hilary Sapire, "'We Have Seen the Son of Heaven / We Have Seen the Son of Our Queen': African Encounters with Prince Alfred on His Royal Tour, 1860," in *Mistress of Everything: Queen Victoria in Indigenous Worlds*, ed. Sarah Carter and Maria Nugent (Manchester: Manchester University Press, 2016), 25–53.

tendance for these particular regal words, paring back the rhetorical weeds that surround them to allow their full moral force to be observed.

Phonetics and proverbs provide some ways of approaching Plaatje's work in 1916, and of reimagining his diplomatic evocation of Goldsmith's verse. But there is one further, very significant, genre in which Plaatje was also simultaneously working at this time. In an exhilarating reading of *Native Life in South Africa*, Bhekizizwe Peterson suggests that the book should, itself, be read as a petition. Without this framing of the book, Peterson argues, "it can become easy to lose sight of its function and to confuse or conflate its formal tensions and contradictions as being synonymous with the political and ideological limitations of colonial subjects who decide to use it as a political strategy."[61] As Peterson shows, petitions inherently manifest a sense of long-standing bonds and obligations between the petitioner and the addressee. The addressee has the power to grant the petition, but the petitioner invokes that power in order to claim the rights inherent in the preexisting relationship. For colonized petitioners, Peterson argues, "The petition, in its European configuration, is a form of inherited technology with paradoxical possibilities: it is both the manifestation and testing of the colonially derived instruments of governance."[62] Quotation, I would argue, participates in this same paradox by simultaneously claiming and outsourcing the documents on which a relationship is built. Like petitioning itself, quotation by Indigenous diplomats takes up the texts of the powerful in order to demand some redress on that power's own terms and in its own genres and vocabularies.

The petitioning context is vital because Plaatje was not simply a metaphorical petitioner. Building on his previous experience drafting a petition to the British Crown on Montshiwa's behalf in 1903, Plaatje contributed to the petitions and pamphlets the SANNC issued during

---

61. Bhekizizwe Peterson, "Sol Plaatje's Native Life in South Africa: Melancholy Narratives, Petitioning Selves and the Ethics of Suffering," *Journal of Commonwealth Literature* 43, no. 1 (2008): 79–95; 84. For a wider discussion of the importance of petitions for Indigenous communities worldwide, see Alan Lester and Zoë Laidlaw, "Indigenous Sites and Mobilities: Connected Struggles in the Long Nineteenth Century," in *Indigenous Communities and Settler Colonialism: Land Holding, Loss and Survival in an Interconnected World*, ed. Zoë Laidlaw and Alan Lester, 1–23; 13–14 (Basingstoke: Palgrave, 2015); and Ravi De Costa, "Identity, Authority, and the Moral Worlds of Indigenous Petitions," *Comparative Studies in Society and History* 48, no. 3 (2006): 669–98.

62. Peterson, 85.

their battle against the Natives' Land Act.[63] He was the author of *An Appeal to the Members of the Imperial Parliament and Public of Great Britain* and a formal petition to George V.[64] These texts, which included multiple instances of quotation of official documents, speeches, prior petitions, and correspondence, took the position that the Natives' Land Act was a violation of both legal and moral relationships between the British and Africans, and that their effect would be to bring British values and conduct into disrepute.[65] In every case, they were full of quoted material from earlier discussions and documents. But the rhetorical strategy by which the texts made these points differed significantly. The *Appeal* based its case in reason and rational argument, outlining in detail the events that had brought the delegation to England, quoting sections of the Natives' Land Act, and outlining specific cases of the act's effects, before ending with the remark that the petitioners were "confident that these documents, together with the foregoing statement, establish the reasonableness of our appeal, and the urgent necessity of some public action on the part of the Parliament and people of the United Kingdom."[66] However, the petition to the king, while including quotations from relevant documents, adopted a very different tone. Addressing George V as "their father and protector" and making similarly devoted declarations of loyalty to Queen Victoria, the petitioners this time invoked emotional language to express both the diplomatic relationships between Britons and Africans and the wishes of their people.[67] The effect was to create a petition of feeling, one grounded in an emotional case for justice. To some extent, this emotional connection, and the moral consistency that it demanded of the British, was recognized by contemporary readers. As one newspaper noted of the 1914 SANNC delegation, their approach, led by Plaatje's rhetoric,

---

63. Montshiwa's petition can be found in CO 529/1, South Africa, Secretary of State's Tour 1902–1903, 17803. Willan confirms that Plaatje, in his role as an adviser to Montshiwa, is the author of this document (*Sol Plaatje*, 114).

64. Willan, *Sol Plaatje*, 179.

65. See for example "Native Protest," a document produced by the 1914 delegates, which liberally quotes from a range of material to make its points (Bodleian Library Special Collections, South African Society MSS. Brit. Emp. S.22 G203, 72–78).

66. South African Native National Congress, *An Appeal to the Members of the Imperial Parliament and Public of Great Britain, From Protest to Challenge*, ed. Sheridan Johns III (Chicago: Hoover Institution Press, 1972), 130–33; 133.

67. National Archives (UK), CO 879/114/2, no. 1012/143, 226.

stretched the form of the petition into much wider moral, philosophical, and cultural territory: "They appeal to the English people for justice, they bring a pathetic trust in our love for fair dealing and humane brotherhood. They believe we only need to know our duty for us to brush aside all technicalities and get it done. Such trust is more than a petition; it is a judgment that tests our national character and sincerity."[68]

The language of Romantic poetry, and of Goldsmith's poem in particular, lurks in the background of some of these documents; at one point, for example, the king's petitioners note that they are "the denizens of this land, the former owners of this land, whose all in all is in this land."[69] In approaching George V in this way, Plaatje might also have been drawing on the recent history of imperial petitions by the Rolong: in 1895, Montshiwa had addressed Queen Victoria in a petition that called on existing international agreements and asked for British protection for their lands in Bechuanaland. The language of this petition also resonates with the language of Goldsmith's poem, and with Romanticism's values more generally. In *The Deserted Village,* Goldsmith had asked what was to be done for people deprived of their land:

> Where then, ah, where shall poverty reside,
> To scape the pressure of contiguous pride;
> If to some common's fenceless limits strayed,
> He drives his flock to pick the scanty blade,
> Those fenceless fields the sons of wealth divide,
> And even the bare-worn common is denied. (303–8)[70]

---

68. "The Call of Chivalry," *Sheffield Independent,* July 21, 1914, 4.

69. National Archives (UK), CO 879/114/2, no. 1012/143, 226.

70. This approach of drawing together Rolong concerns with Romantic phrasing was one he would maintain throughout his time in England; in a 1917 pamphlet, *Some of the Legal Disabilities Suffered by the Native Population of the Union of South Africa and Imperial Responsibility*, Plaatje wrote that the Natives' Land Act "has cut off the very roots of native life by depriving us of nature's richest gift—our ancient occupation of breeding cattle and cultivating the soil. . . . Thousands of former farm tenants finding their life-long occupation suddenly made illegal have been forced to sell their cattle for what they would fetch, and have drifted into the cities where, among strange surroundings and incomprehensible restrictions, their lot has become unbearable. Others, after trekking round with their emaciated stock in search of a place to graze them and losing many head by starvation on the trek, have . . . perished through privations or succumbed to malarial fever or other climatic diseases in strange regions." See Plaatje, *Some of the*

This question echoes through Montshiwa's petition too, in which he wrote: "Our Land there is a good land, our fathers lived in it and are buried in it, and we keep all our cattle in it. What will we do if you give our land away?"[71]

Goldsmith's repeated term "fenceless" in this section of the poem gestures to the commons and the shared land that enclosure had claimed. Plaatje did not want an exclusionary fence around the land, any more than Goldsmith did, but he did want a fence around Montshiwa's word, around Victoria's word, around George V's word, and, indeed, around Goldsmith's word—around the literary representation of what he took to be British values. By fencing those terms within poems, proverbs, petitions, and proclamations, Plaatje hoped, as all the diplomats discussed in this book similarly hoped, to draw his interlocutors' eyes to their own culture, their own words, and their own promises and to encourage them to tend them well.

Part of the difficulty in conveying this point to his readers, however, was that Goldsmith's imagery was malleable enough to be used in arguments that undermined Plaatje's interpretation of the Natives' Land Act. Some of this undermining came from a somewhat surprising source. The Anti-Slavery and Aborigines Protection Society, which both John Brant and George Copway had addressed and met with during their respective visits to England, did not provide the solidarity that Plaatje and his compatriots were expecting when they reached out for support.[72] Its organizing secretary, John Harris, was in favor of segregation, believing it to be a benevolent way for African interests to be maintained, and thus did not object to this aspect of the Natives' Land Act. Harris's writings about the Natives' Land Act make use of the same Auburn imagery that Plaatje was citing, imagining the proposed tribal areas as places where "contented populations enjoyed the free play of every legitimate tribal institution, flocks and herds, pasture and crops, music and song, everywhere

---

Legal Disabilities Suffered by the Native Population of the Union of South Africa and Imperial Responsibility (London: St. Clements Press, 1917), 5.

71. Molema, *Montshiwa*, 181.

72. The correspondence about and with the SAANC can be found in the Anti-Slavery and Aborigines Protection Society Papers, Bodleian Library Special Collections. South African Society MSS. Brit. Emp. S.22 G201–G204.

abounding under the control of tribal chiefs."[73] Goldsmith's conservatism could serve multiple ends, and thus the immediate context of authorship, ideology, and intertextuality shaped what an evocation of Auburn might signify and achieve.

The same point might be made about Romanticism more generally; it contained, and continues to contain, both radical and conservative energies. Plaatje ended his book with a soaring appeal to the standard Romantic tropes of nature, justice, and a new, radical dawn:

> But now that the country is throwing off its winter cloak and dressing itself in its green, gorgeous array; now that King Day shines in all his glory through the mist by day, and the moon and stars appear in their brilliancy in the evenings; now that, as if in harmony with the artistic rendering of Easter anthems by your choirs, the thrush and the blackbird twitter forth the disappearance of the foggy winter with its snow, sleet and wet; now that the flocks of fleecy sheep, which for the past four months have been in hiding and conspicuous by their absence, come forward again and spread triumphantly over the green as if in celebration of the dawn of the new spring; now that the violet and the daffodil, the marguerite and the hyacinth, the snowdrop and the bluebell, glorious in appearance, also announce, each in its own way, the advent of sunny spring, we are encouraged to hope that, "when peace again reigns over Europe," when white men cease warring against white men, when the warriors put away the torpedoes and the bayonets and take up less dangerous implements, you will in the interest of your flag, for the safety of your coloured subjects, the glory of your Empire, and the purity of your religion, grapple with this dark blot on the Imperial emblem, the South African anomaly that compromises the justice of British rule and seems almost to belie the beauty, the sublimity and the sincerity of Christianity. (338)

---

73. Cited in Brian Willan, "The Anti-Slavery and Aborigines' Protection Society and the South African Natives' Land Act of 1913," *Journal of African History* 20, no. 1 (1979): 83–102; 94.

However, the final lines of the book reveal the fragility of this radical Romantic vision. Plaatje asks his British reader, "Shall we appeal to you in vain? I HOPE NOT" (338). Even in shared language, shared tropes, shared poetry, there was always the possibility that settler-imperial readers would not, in the end, defend the values that their canonical poets so publicly championed, even when the hypocrisy of that position was held up in front of them. Plaatje, as David Schalkwyk has suggested, "appears to put too much faith in the word," a word around which no secure fence had ever been built.[74]

---

74. David Schalkwyk, "Portrait and Proxy: Representing Plaatje and Plaatje Represented," *scrutiny2* 4, no. 2 (1999): 14–29; 27.

Chapter 5

Petitions and Repetitions

Rēweti Kōhere and the Ashes of Byron and Macaulay

Readers of the October 1926 issue of the Māori-language monthly *Te Toa Takitini* might have been struck by two very similar snippets of verse printed in close proximity in one of the articles.[1] The poetry was supplied, in English and in a Māori translation, by the journalist and intellectual Rēweti Kōhere, a frequent contributor to the periodical. The first set of lines comes from the opening section of Byron's *The Giaour:*

> Snatch from the ashes of your sires
> The embers of their former fires;
> And he who in the strife expires
> Will add to theirs a name of fear
> That tyranny shall quake to hear. (116–20)[2]

---

1. It is my practice to use the correct modern diacritical marks for Māori words in my own prose but to omit them when quoting if they were omitted in the original source. Hence, in my own prose, for example, I use "Māori" rather than "Maori."

2. I have given the lines here as they are presented in *Te Toa Takitini*, which altered the comma that usually ends line 120 in order to suggest a self-contained quote. See Rēweti T. Kōhere, "He Kupu Tohunga," *Te Toa Takitini*, October 1926, 479–82; 480. For an authorized text of the poem, see Lord Byron, *The Complete Poetical Works*, ed. Jerome J. McGann, 3:39–82 (Oxford: Clarendon Press, 1981). Kōhere's Māori version reads:

> Kapohia mai i nga pungarehu o koutou matua
> Nga ngarehu o ratou ahi o nga ra ka huri;
> A ko ia e hinga i te riri
> E hono atu ki o ratou he ingoa e wehingia
> E tu wiri ai te tangata kino.

The second set of lines was from Thomas Babington Macaulay's *Horatius*:

> To every man upon this earth
> Death cometh soon or late.
> And how can man die better
> Than facing fearful odds,
> For the ashes of his fathers,
> And the temples of his gods? (stanza XXVII, 3–8)[3]

It was not unusual to see English poetry published in this particular Māori periodical. Regular readers of *Te Toa Takitini* would have been familiar with Kōhere's series of essays, "He Kupu Tohunga" ("Wise Sayings"), which was designed to introduce English literature to Māori readers. Educated in English at the prestigious Māori boys' school Te Aute College, throughout his career Kōhere produced writings that were peppered with quotations from his favorite writers, including Burns and Shakespeare, which he almost always presented in both English and Māori. The range of his quotations is impressive; Kōhere rarely repeated himself, and instead produced new illustrative examples of apt English verse depending on the topic and argument of the essay in question. The exceptions to this pattern are the lines quoted here. Kōhere returned to Byron's and, much more frequently, Macaulay's lines in the course of a long and bitter negotiation with the New Zealand government over his traditional lands. While Macaulay might seem to be the embodiment of Victorian, rather than Romantic, values and writings, I would like to read Kōhere's intertwining of Macaulay with Byron as a critical reimagining

---

3. I have given the lines here as they are presented in *Te Toa Takitini*, which replaced the comma at the end of line 8 with a question mark in order to suggest a self-contained quote and did not capitalize "Gods." See Rēweti T. Kōhere, "He Kupu Tohunga," 481. For an authorized version of the text, see Thomas Babington Macaulay, *The Life and Works of Lord Macaulay* (London: Longmans, Green and Co., 1897), 8:466–84. Kōhere's Māori version reads:

> Ki ia tangata, ki ia tangata i tenei ao
> He mate ano te mutunga a tona ra,
> A he aha te mate tika atu mo te tangata
> I te whawhai ki nga tino kaha
> Mo nga koiwi o nga matua,
> Mo nga ahurewa o ona atua?

of some of the Romantic ideas contained within a poem like *Horatius*. Just as Plaatje's Romanticism took in a pre-Romantic poem like *The Deserted Village*, Kōhere's Romanticism incorporates post-Romantic verses like Macaulay's 1830s poetry.[4] The borders of Romanticism are pushed out by the diplomatic activities of these writers, for whom the Romantic period was not confined to the conventional dates of 1789–1832, but could extend, in either direction, back to their ancestors and forward to their own moment in time.

The citation of English poetry by the Indigenous intellectuals in this book is always a kind of repetition: a reminder of promises and values to which the other party in a diplomatic negotiation can be held. Kōhere's case, however, extends and deepens the process of repetition, linking texts divided by genre, date, and audience into a single networked text held together across time and space by the constant repetition of the same few lyrical words. Together, these texts form an extended conversation between Kōhere, the people he represents, and the government. This focused repetition mirrors, I would argue, the establishment of a contentious but stable text at the heart of diplomatic relationships between Māori and *Pākehā* (the Māori name for white settlers and their descendants), a text that could be, and is, repeatedly cited, word for word, as these relationships are renegotiated over the centuries in Aotearoa New Zealand: the 1840 Treaty of Waitangi.

"He Iwi Tahi Tatou": The Treaty of Waitangi and Patterns of Diplomacy

Diplomatic relationships between Māori and Europeans were well over a century old by the time Kōhere was writing in the 1920s. Initial contact in the late seventeenth century led to more regular exchanges in the eighteenth century between Māori and European scientists, invaders, and explorers, including James Cook, before developing into extensive trading and commercial relationships in the early nineteenth century. The first New Zealand missionary station was established in 1814, and small

---

4. Byron's poem was published in 1813. Macaulay's poem appeared in his collection *Lays of Ancient Rome* in 1842 but was actually composed sometime between 1834 and 1838, while Macaulay was a government official in India.

settlements of European traders and merchants began to cluster around coastal areas at about the same time. Local and personal connections were gradually replaced by increasingly formal measures to manage relationships between Māori and British settlers and between competing European interests, as Britain passed laws in 1817, 1823, and 1828 that aimed to control lawlessness among the British-settler population. This legislation recognized New Zealand as an independent territory, and Māori were made aware of these documents, especially the 1823 Act, which was translated into Māori.[5]

From the 1820s onward, Māori engaged in many formal diplomatic processes with the British Crown, including trips to England by chiefs such as Waikato and Hongi Hika, who visited Cambridge at a time when Macaulay was also there.[6] Back in Aotearoa New Zealand, Māori produced petitions for protection and engaged in negotiations with the newly appointed official resident, James Busby, who arrived in May 1833. The ceremonies to acknowledge Busby's arrival brought together two diplomatic traditions, one signaled by a seven-gun salute and the reading of an official letter from the king, the other by the protocols of a *pōwhiri* (welcoming ceremony). As Claudia Orange notes, in these carefully choreographed events, "there was more than a suggestion of ambassadorial representation to an independent country."[7] These events also had a significant textual legacy; speeches from the day were printed to confirm what the Crown had said to the chiefs who had gathered to meet Busby. The same mixture of independent sovereign status, formal negotiation, and textual artefact occurred on October 28, 1835, when Busby convened a meeting of northern chiefs to sign a declaration of independence. Designed to forestall French ambitions in Aotearoa New Zealand, to lay the foundation for a Māori-led parliamentary system, and to help Māori manage the growing European intrusion on their lands and resources, the declaration of independence was accepted by the British Colonial Office, whose answer was sent out in a circular letter to the signatory chiefs.[8]

---

5. Claudia Orange, *The Treaty of Waitangi*, 2nd ed. (Wellington, NZ: Bridget Williams Books, 2011), 18–19.

6. Michael Bright, "Macaulay's New Zealander," *The Arnoldian* 10, no. 1 (1982): 8–27; 15.

7. Orange, 22.

8. Orange, 30–31.

This history of negotiation and textual production informed the most significant diplomatic engagement between the British and Māori: the signing of the Treaty of Waitangi on February 6, 1840, which was orchestrated by the newly arrived lieutenant governor of the colony, William Hobson. From the British perspective, a treaty was necessary in order to manage what was seen as the inevitable British colonization of the country and to secure both an orderly transition of authority and some rights and protections for Māori, who were still regarded as the sovereign power in Aotearoa New Zealand. From a Māori perspective, a treaty would help confirm independence, as well as offering protection via the British Crown, and a framework to control European settlement and provide law and order.[9]

The treaty document contained three articles, and copies were produced in both English and Māori. Due to the limitations of the translators, however, the two texts did not say exactly the same thing, a complication that has had major ramifications in New Zealand history. In Article One, Māori ceded "sovereignty" in the English text, but only the more limited *kāwanatanga,* or "governance," in the Māori text. Article Two guaranteed Māori, in the English text, "full exclusive and undisturbed possession of their Lands and Estates Forests Fisheries and other properties" as long as they wished to retain them, whereas the Māori text guaranteed *tino rangatiratanga,* or absolute sovereignty and chieftainship. The least complicated article at a linguistic level was Article Three, which provided Māori with "the Rights and Privileges of British Subjects."[10]

The deliberations began at Busby's house at Waitangi, in the far north of Aotearoa New Zealand, on February 5, 1840. A large number of missionaries, settlers, and local merchants were present alongside the Māori contingent, which was led by local chiefs, some of whom had signed the 1835 Declaration of Independence. The missionary and translator Henry Williams read the Māori text aloud, providing the assembled listeners, as he later recalled, "but one version, explaining clause by clause."[11] But in the speeches that followed, Williams, Busby and others gave oral

---

9. Orange, 41.

10. For the texts of the Treaty of Waitangi, see Orange, 270–72. For a broad overview of the linguistic issues posed by the two texts see Orange, 43–49.

11. Hugh Carleton, *The Life of Henry Williams, Archdeacon of Waimate,* 2 vols. (Auckland, NZ: Upton and Co., 1874–77), 2:14.

explanations of the text that distorted its likely impact, playing down the consequences of ceding sovereignty and exaggerating the nature of the future relationship between Māori and Queen Victoria.[12] The assembled chiefs then debated the treaty for five hours, using the traditional Māori structures of diplomacy, including *whaikōrero* (formal speeches) and the handling of symbolic objects such as a *taiaha* (spear or paddle). Many of the early speakers spoke against the document, and they were encouraged by comments from the assembled Pākehā audience indicating that Williams had not adequately explained the import of the treaty.[13] The meeting ended, however, on a more positive note, as several chiefs with long-standing connections to the missionaries spoke in favor of the proposal. The assembled Māori continued to debate in private on the evening of February 5, consulting with their Pākehā contacts as needed.

These assurances led the assembled chiefs to make the decision to sign the treaty on February 6, despite the fact that the official signing ceremony had been scheduled for the following day. At a hastily assembled gathering, a copy of the treaty in Māori was laid on the table and read once more by Williams. Despite further concerns expressed by Pākehā onlookers such as William Colenso, who was convinced that the Māori leaders did not understand the nature of the text, the chiefs came forward one by one to sign, starting with the young leader Hone Heke.[14] The ceremony itself combined the diplomatic traditions of the two parties, the act of signing a textual agreement accompanied by ongoing speeches that continued throughout the signing process, and an exchange of objects, as Colenso gave each chief blankets and tobacco and the chief Patuone gave Hobson a *mere* (club) to be presented to Queen Victoria. It was also a ceremony marked by a significant verbal repetition; as each chief signed and shook Hobson's hand, it is sometimes said that he repeated the phrase, "*He iwi tahi tatou*" ("We are now one people").

The Treaty of Waitangi was thus complicated by two different, apparently authoritative, texts, and by the conjunction of oral and writ-

---

12. Orange, 52.

13. Orange, 53–55.

14. William Colenso, *The Authentic and Genuine History of the Signing of the Treaty of Waitangi, New Zealand, February 5 and 6 1840: Being a Faithful and Circumstantial, though Brief, Narration of Events which Happened on that Memorable Occasion; with Copies of the Treaty in English and Maori, and of the Three Early Proclamations Respecting the Founding of the Colony* (Wellington, NZ: George Didbury, Government Printer, 1890), 32–33.

ten understandings of the promises that were made.[15] As Claudia Orange has pointed out, the oral deliberations at Waitangi were "of paramount importance, particularly in a Māori tradition in which relationships were customarily sustained and modified through lengthy discussion. Since chiefs at Waitangi did not have the Treaty text before them, the oral record was all the more crucial to understanding."[16] For Māori, the text of the Treaty of Waitangi took its significance from the fact that such documents were known to be important to Europeans; while the textual legacy of the deliberations might not matter as much as the oral record in a Māori framework, the guarantees offered by the Treaty of Waitangi seemed assured by the fact that the Pākehā negotiators had codified them in a form that took priority in a European framework.

The pattern of diplomacy, speech making, debate, signing (or not), and exchange of objects that took place at Waitangi was repeated across the country in the ensuing months. Hobson and his officials took the treaty document to different locations in an attempt to gather as many signatures as possible, although they considered the ceremony at Waitangi to have confirmed the transfer of sovereignty to the British Crown.[17] In each new setting, the same questions were raised and the same answers given. In some cases, local Māori drew on the experiences of earlier debates and showed that they were already well aware of what had taken place at Waitangi; chiefs like Makoare Taonui asked to see the text of the treaty, demonstrating an awareness of the significance of the written words themselves in terms of the promises that were being made.[18] The role of repetition, of referring back to the Treaty of Waitangi as a key diplomatic text in the Māori-Pākehā relationship, was thus established very early on.

The written document's status was of particular significance to the colonial government, which tried to keep the text of the Treaty of Waitangi at the forefront of its relationship with Māori in order to insist on the legality of its jurisdiction. An early issue of the monthly government newspaper, *Te Karere Maori*, carried the Māori text of the treaty, and it

---

15. For the significance of the Treaty of Waitangi in New Zealand print culture, see D. F. McKenzie, *Oral Culture, Literacy and Print in Early New Zealand: The Treaty of Waitangi* (Wellington, NZ: Victoria University Press, 1985).

16. Orange, 61.

17. A map of the different locations for the signings can be found in Orange, 70–71.

18. Orange, 65–66.

was reprinted as new disputes emerged.¹⁹ For Māori, however, the treaty document was just one part of their diplomatic relationship with Pākehā. Many chiefs did not sign and did not consider themselves bound by the document; others referred to the oral record in preference to the text itself. Nonetheless, its significance began to shape encounters between the colonial government and Māori as the century progressed. The Treaty of Waitangi was, at least from the perspective of the settler government, at the heart of the Kohimārama Conference of 1860, to which 200 chiefs were invited. The text was read to the assembled audience by Native Secretary Donald McLean and referred to by some of the chiefs in their speeches, although often in the context of a much broader range of issues.²⁰ Kohimārama was thus one more repetition of the treaty text and its complex significations in the post-1840 period; as Orange notes, "Every time the question [of land] arose in the colony's first twenty years, Pākehā arguments were reiterated and Māori anxieties regenerated."²¹

Escalating tensions concerning land led to a series of wars in the 1860s between Māori and government forces, with the latter supported in some instances by certain Māori groups. The wars culminated in Māori land being confiscated, sometimes from groups that had in fact remained on friendly terms with the colonial government, under legislation that became, and remains, a source of bitterness. One of those affected by the conflict was Mokena Kōhere, Rēweti Kōhere's grandfather. Mokena, who was a chief of the Ngāti Porou people, had attempted to maintain a neutral stance during the early 1860s, in part to avoid the possibility of land losses for his people. Eventually, however, Mokena fought for the government against the Hauhau forces on the east coast of the North Island, in a series of military and diplomatic actions that preserved Ngāti Porou's land from confiscation. Mokena was awarded a sword of honor by Queen Victoria in 1870 and a New Zealand War Medal in 1871, and he became a member of the Legislative Council (the Upper House of the New Zealand Parliament) in 1872. Throughout these years, Mokena

---

19. See for example Orange, 127–28.

20. See *Proceedings of the Kohimarama Conference, Comprising Nos. 13 to 18 of the "Maori Messenger"* (n.p., 1860). Lachy Paterson argues for a broader reading of the Conference than Orange provides, pointing out that for the Māori delegates, Kohimārama was not primarily about the treaty at all; see Paterson, "The Kohimārama Conference of 1860: A Contextual Reading," *Journal of New Zealand Studies* 12 (2011): 29–46.

21. Orange, 96–97.

remained committed to the agreements made in the Treaty of Waitangi, which his own brother had signed.[22]

The 1860s saw an enhancement of the Treaty of Waitangi's significance in public discourse. Throughout the years of armed conflict and confiscation, the government cited the treaty repeatedly as evidence of what it regarded as the true legal and diplomatic relationship between Māori and Pākehā. Thomas Gore Browne, the incumbent governor of the colony, had quoted Article Two of the treaty verbatim in a letter to Māori published in the government newspaper *Te Karere Maori* in March 1861, commenting, "I repeat this assurance to you now."[23] He would quote Article Two verbatim again when demanding the disbanding of Māori forces in the Waikato region two months later.[24] The Native Lands Act 1862, which aimed to take control of, and satisfy settler demands for, Māori land, began with a preamble that also cited the words of Article Two verbatim, but which attempted to alter the treaty's provisions and established the Native Land Court as a body to ascertain Māori land ownership in order to facilitate quicker sales.[25] The text of the Treaty of Waitangi, in both languages, was tabled in the House of Representatives in August 1865.[26] However, as more and more Māori land was confiscated or sold to settlers through the Native Land Court process, the treaty became less and less significant for the government.

The opposite process occurred in Māori responses to the Treaty of Waitangi. Instead of seeing it as just one part of a much wider diplomatic relationship, Māori leaders began to rely more heavily on the treaty text to

---

22. For a more detailed account of Mokena's life, see Rarawa Kohere, "Kohere, Mokena," in *Te Ara: The Encyclopedia of New Zealand* (Wellington: New Zealand Government Ministry for Culture and Heritage, 1990). http://www.teara.govt.nz/en/biographies/1k15/kohere-mokena, and Rēweti T. Kōhere, *The Story of a Maori Chief* (Wellington, NZ: Reed, 1949). See also Richard Boast, *Buying the Land, Selling the Land: Governments and Maori Land in the North Island 1865–1921* (Wellington, NZ: Victoria University Press, 2008), 376–78.

23. Thomas Gore Browne, "Let the Pakeha and the Maori be United," *Te Karere Maori or Maori Messenger* 1, no. 2 (March 15, 1861): 1.

24. Article Two in particular, and the Treaty of Waitangi in general, were also the subject of detailed reports to Parliament in 1861; see "Further Papers Relative to the Taranaki Question," *Appendix to the Journals of the House of Representatives*, session I, E-2 (1861), especially 2–3.

25. This power was extended in the 1865 Native Lands Act, which "effectively severed the threads of Crown protection and nullified the Treaty's second article" (Orange, 169).

26. *New Zealand Parliamentary Debates* (1865): 292–93.

articulate their complaints after the 1860s. During a nine-day conference in February 1879, Māori leaders, mostly from the Ngāti Whātua people, discussed the significance of the Treaty of Waitangi, with the conference organizer, Pāora Tūhaere, reading the entire text to the assembled participants.[27] The terms of the treaty were picked up by subsequent speakers, such as the Ngāpuhi leader Renata Paraire Kawatupu, who quoted the clauses, analyzed their language closely, and closed by saying (in phrases here translated into English), "These words are very good; but in some instances they are disregarded, and the promise is not carried out. I think all those original promises should be fulfilled."[28] Several speakers also insisted on the validity of the oral record of their ancestors, reminding the audience of words spoken about the Treaty of Waitangi in the past: Nopera Te Waitaheke said (here translated into English), "This is a cry over the words left by our parents to us. They were not left to be disregarded. These words are still in existence, though the bodies of those who uttered them have decayed. Do not let us depart from those words, either to the right or to the left."[29] The speeches were interspersed with quotations from other sources too, including the Bible.[30] These processes were repeated in subsequent annual conferences in 1880 and 1881, and then again in the Kotahitanga (unity) movement and parliaments of the 1890s.[31]

The growing significance of the Treaty of Waitangi for Māori was also evident from the thousands of formal petitions sent to Parliament, and sometimes to the British Crown, from 1870 onward.[32] As well as making references to the guarantees contained in the treaty in general terms, the petitioners sometimes drew on the specific language of the text, such as

---

27. *Appendix to the Journals of the House of Representatives*, session II, G-8 (1879): 10.

28. *Appendix to the Journals of the House of Representatives*, 12–13.

29. *Appendix to the Journals of the House of Representatives*, 13.

30. See, for example, Manihera's comments, *Appendix to the Journal of the House of Representatives*, 22.

31. The exact language of the Māori text of the treaty was cited in the deliberations of the Kotahitanga Parliament; see, for example, *Proceedings of the First Kotahitanga Parliament* (June 14, 1892), 12.

32. Orange, 174–75. See, for example, the 1882 petition directly to Queen Victoria, *Appendix to the Journals of the House of Representatives*, session I, A-6 (1883): 1–3; and King Tawhiao's plea to Queen Victoria to "confirm her words given in that treaty" (cited in Orange, 198).

the 1883 petition from members of the Maniapoto, Raukawa, Tūwharetoa, and Whanganui peoples, which commented: "We have carefully watched the tendency of the laws which you have enacted from the beginning up to the present day; they all tend to deprive us of the privileges secured to us by the second and third articles of the Treaty of Waitangi, which confirmed to us the exclusive and undisturbed possession of our lands."[33] Petitioners debated the meaning of the exact words of the treaty in front of the Native Affairs Committee in 1898.[34] Members of Parliament representing the Māori electorates, meanwhile, quoted the articles of the treaty in the House of Representatives.[35] While the written version of the treaty remained less important to Māori than the oral record, the idea of a formal, quotable text that could be mobilized in disagreements with the government became part of the diplomatic discourse of late nineteenth- and early twentieth-century Aotearoa New Zealand. It was this diplomatic tradition that Rēweti Kōhere invoked when he began his campaign for the return of the lands of his grandfather Mokena Kōhere.

As Chadwick Allen has argued, the Treaty of Waitangi can act as

> a "silent second text" against which contemporary Maori works can be read as allegory. But because this silent second text speaks in two distinct, conflicting voices, the resultant allegory always explicitly rehearses the difficulty of reconciling the Treaty's divergent Maori- and English-language versions. However strongly a particular allegory might promote one version, it cannot suppress the other. Even in those works that never allude to treaty documents specifically, tension between competing Maori and Pakeha versions of the "truth" often is

---

33. This petition was composed in Māori and then translated for submission to the House of Representatives; in the original version, the authors use the exact words of the Māori text of Article Two to describe what was confirmed to them in the Treaty of Waitangi. See "Petition of the Maniapoto, Raukawa, Tuwharetoa, and Whanganui Tribes," *Appendix to the Journals of the House of Representatives*, session I, J-01 (1883): 1–4, esp. 1–2.

34. See, for example, "Native Affairs Committee: Report on the Native Lands Settlement and Administration Bill," *Appendix to the Journals of the House of Representatives*, session I, I3a (1898): 7, 19, 35, 40.

35. See for example Hēnare Kaihau's speech in *Nga Korero Paremete* (Wellington: New Zealand Government Printers, 1904), 108.

suggestive of treaty allegory. This effect is only enhanced in bilingual and dual-language texts.[36]

While Allen's framework is designed for the analysis of post–World War II literary writing by Māori, it is nevertheless a useful one for considering an earlier example like Kōhere's integration of English texts into his writing. The mobilization of the two languages and their respective literary canons, ostensibly expressing the same sentiment but also operating in entirely different epistemological frameworks, mirrors the foundational diplomatic moment of the Treaty of Waitangi. To move between English and Māori in this way is always, as Allen suggests, to evoke the treaty and the diplomatic partnership it both emerged from and encoded. "Treaty allegory" is a productive way in which to read what Kōhere strives for when he cites Byron and Macaulay: as a reminder of the Treaty of Waitangi and its complex linguistic and political status and a reanimation of the relationship it envisaged.

"A Marae on Paper": Kōhere and the Forms of Māori Diplomacy

When Rēweti Kōhere brought together the lines from Byron and Macaulay in his 1926 article, he was responding and contributing to two kinds of resonance. The first was the way in which the English texts resonate with each other. The strong verbal echo of "the ashes of your sires" (Byron) and "the ashes of his fathers" (Macaulay) is part of a wider connection between poems that speak of ancestry, bravery, the defense of one's homeland, and the importance of remembering the past. The second resonance was between this cluster of Romantic ideas, as expressed in the poems' figurative language, and Māori conceptions of land and identity. *Whakapapa* (ancestry or genealogy) is central to Māori identity and provides one basis by which ownership of land may be confirmed. The significance of genealogy to identity is conveyed, to some extent, in the word *iwi*, which can mean both "tribe" and "bones." Present-day affiliations are shaped by the metaphorical bones of one's ancestors. Another, related concept, in conversations about land tenure and ancestry is *ahikaaroa* (literally,

---

36. Chadwick Allen, 20.

"long burning fires"), a word indicating that the long-term occupation of land—the occupation by one's ancestors as well as oneself, in other words—constitutes a legitimate indicator of ownership.[37] The poetry of Byron and Macaulay was quintessentially English, but it sounded right in a Māori framework.

Kōhere's 1926 gloss on these lines emphasizes, not their foreign or English quality, but their obvious significance for his Māori readers. In the Māori prose that separates the two poetic quotations in the 1926 article, Kōhere addressed his readers directly: "Waihoki e te iwi whakaohongia nga toto o tatou tipuna, kia mau ki o tatou morehu rangatira, ki nga tikanga rangatira, mo to tatou ngaro rawa ake i te ao ka whakamoea tatou ki 'nga urupa o te hunga e kore nei e mate.'" (Kōhere himself provides no translation of these comments, since he was writing for a Māori-speaking audience, but in English they read: "Also, to you all, awaken to the blood of your ancestors, hold onto the vestiges of our greatness, to the ways of greatness, so that when we become lost in this world we lie proudly as those in 'the graves of those that cannot die.'")[38] Kōhere thus works a further line from Byron's poem—"the graves of those who cannot die" *(The Giaour, 135)*—into his explanation of how Māori readers should use the verse's message. There was clearly something urgent about the words of Byron and Macaulay that Kōhere wished to convey to his readers, something that went beyond a sense of similarity in underpinning cultural concepts. Kōhere's readers were being exhorted, in the present moment, to heed the lesson of these poetic words. In an instance of internal diplomacy, Kōhere speaks to his Māori readers of a collective vision of present-day activity that draws on past knowledge and successes.

For Kōhere, this context was especially topical in 1926. A 1913 ruling by the Native Land Court had vested ownership of the Marangairoa 1D Block of land in a rival claimant group, in contradiction to Rēweti Kōhere's testimony that his grandfather Mokena Kōhere had secured the land for his descendants.[39] There had been a further investigation of the

---

37. For information on ahikaaroa, see Hirini Moko Mead, *Tikanga Māori: Living By Māori Values* (Wellington, NZ: Huia Publishers, 2003), 41–43, 359; and Mason Durie, Te Mana, Te Kāwanatanga: *The Politics of Māori Self-Determination* (Oxford: Oxford University Press, 1998), 115–16.

38. My thanks go to Tai Ahu for this translation.

39. A very detailed history of the struggle over the Marangairoa block, written by a

title in 1919, which resulted in the Native Land Court ruling that the land should be subdivided into twenty freeholdings. Kōhere then began a long campaign of petitioning the government for the return of the land. He authored two petitions in 1920 and a further four in 1922, none of which led to the resolution for which he hoped.[40] By 1926, his persistent efforts at diplomatic engagement led the government to introduce the Native Land Amendment and Native Land Claims Adjustment Bill, which aimed, among other things, to clear up the question of ownership of the Marangairoa 1D Block. The bill was accompanied by the announcement of terms of reference for a royal commission on the confiscation of Māori land.[41]

It was at this point that Kōhere began the process of repeating Byron's and Macaulay's lines. In August 1926, as the Native Land Amendment and Native Land Claims Adjustment Bill was being drafted, Kōhere first quoted Byron's lines from *The Giaour*, in a cover article in *Te Toa Takitini*.[42] The lines were quoted without any commentary or any sense of their significance. Presumably, however, they were meant to be a gloss on the prose part of the cover article, headlined "Niu Tireni me Tona Iwi Maori" (New Zealand and Its Indigenous People), which deals with a speech given by the British M.P. Sir Henry Brittain in Sydney the previous year, during a tour of New Zealand and Australia as leader of the Imperial Press Conference. Kōhere predictably draws out those elements of the speech that focused on New Zealand. But there is one particular comment of Brittain's that he emphasizes: the moment in which Brittain specifically made reference to the Māori people. When he gets to this remark, Kōhere includes a direct quote, in English, from a newspaper report of Brittain's speech: "For the Maori they [the Imperial Press

---

member of the Kōhere family, can be found in Rarawa Kohere, "Tāwakewake: An Historical Case Study and Situational Analysis of Ngāti Ruawaipu Leadership" (PhD thesis, Massey University of New Zealand, Palmerston North, 2005). There is an especially clear and succinct appendix that outlines the history of the litigation (339–42).

40. These petitions can be found in the National Archives of New Zealand, MA1 Boxes 111–13.

41. See the statement by the prime minister and native affairs minister Gordon Coates, which linked the introduction of the bill and the establishment of the royal commission, in *New Zealand Parliamentary Debates* 208 (1925): 773–74. The full title of the commission was the Royal Commission to Inquire into Confiscations of Native Lands and Other Grievances Alleged by Natives.

42. [Rēweti T. Kōhere], "Nui Tireni me Tona Iwi Maori," *Te Toa Takitini*, August 1926, 435.

Conference delegates] conceived the warmest affection. There probably was no more intelligent native race to be found." As legislators worked on the Native Land Amendment and Native Land Claims Adjustment Bill, Kōhere reminded them and his Māori readers, in bursts of English prose and English poetry, that Māori were intelligent, globally connected citizens, and that they had diplomatic ties to both the British and the New Zealand governments.

In the intervening two months between this first citation of Byron and the October 1926 issue of *Te Toa Takitini*, when Kōhere repeated Byron's lines and connected them with Macaulay's poem, Parliament had passed this legislation and announced the terms of reference for the Royal Commission on land confiscations.[43] Late 1926 was thus a period of intense engagement between the government and Māori on the subject of land ownership and its history in Aotearoa New Zealand in general, but also a period of engagement that attended to the Marangairoa 1D Block specifically. The lines from Byron and Macaulay not only underscored Māori sophistication and cosmopolitanism, but also served as a blueprint for, and warning about, how Māori might respond to legislation that interfered with their land rights or to a Royal Commission's invitation to testify on confiscations. The bones of one's ancestors and the fires of ahikaaroa could be invoked and mobilized, not only via Māori law, but also via English poetry.

Kōhere might have hoped that the legislative and administrative developments of 1926 would lead to the resolution of his grievance, but unfortunately, the cycle of repetitive petitioning simply continued. The hearings into the Marangairoa 1D Block in 1927, which were prompted

---

43. The debate on the Native Land Amendment and Native Land Claims Adjustment Bill in the lower and upper houses of Parliament can be found in *New Zealand Parliamentary Debates* 211 (1926): 285–95, 378–79. The section about Marangairoa 1D was not the subject of any comment in these debates, however. For more detail on the Royal Commission, see Bryan Gilling, "Raupatu: the Punitive Confiscation of Maori Land in the 1860s," in *Raupatu: The Confiscation of Maori Land*, ed. Richard Boast and Richard S. Hill, 13–30 (Wellington:Victoria University Press, 2009); and Mark Hickford, "Strands from the Afterlife of Confiscation: Property Rights, Constitutional Histories and the Political Incorporation of Maori, 1920s," in *Raupatu: The Confiscation of Maori Land*, 169–204; Richard S. Hill, *Enthroning "Justice above Might"? The Sim Commission, Tainui and the Crown* (Wellington: New Zealand Department of Justice, 1989). The commission's findings were published as *Confiscated Native Lands and Other Grievances. Report of the Royal Commission to Inquire into Confiscations of Native Lands and Other Grievances Alleged by Natives* (1928).

by the 1926 legislation, did not resolve the issue in his favor. For the rest of his life, Kōhere continued, often cantankerously and in defiance of the wishes of some of his own people, to petition Parliament for redress and to draw on the poetic terms he had established in *Te Toa Takitini* in 1926 as the legal, moral, and emotional grounds for his case.[44]

Kōhere's petitions work within the standard formula for such documents. They outline his people's case and, as the body of evidence builds up through each new inquiry, they cite more and more material from earlier decisions, histories, and commentaries, bringing in the verbatim language of elders, judges, and parliamentarians. Kōhere's petitioning is thus always an exercise in citation, in the repetition of words that he believes constitute the agreement he has with the government about his people's legitimate title to the Marangairoa 1D Block. They come back, again and again, to the central points of ancestry and occupation, conveyed in Kōhere's prose by images of bones and fire. In a 1935 letter to the prime minister, Kōhere lamented the 1913 ruling by the Native Land Court: "We, by it, lost three burial-grounds in one of which my own father rests—if it be rest. . . . In order to keep the matter alive or as a Maori would say, 'To keep the fires burning on the land' we have lodged another petition praying for a further hearing of the Marangairoa 1D case."[45] He would continue to repeat himself on these topics, commenting in a 1947 petition that, despite ongoing disappointments, "we continued petitioning, not with any hope of success, but just to use a Maori phrase, 'to keep our fires burning.'"[46] In some cases, he schooled his correspondents on the significance of these metaphors in terms of land tenure, telling the Minister of Māori Affairs: "The Maori term for occupation is 'ahikaroa' [*sic*], or the 'long burning fire.'"[47] In others, he testified to the significance of the burial sites, arguing that "To hand over tribal burial-grounds, in one of which my own father was buried, is heinous and ghoulish," and

---

44. A detailed summary of the various hearings and decisions around the Marangairoa 1D Block up until the mid-1930s can be found in the April 27, 1936, memorandum in National Archives of New Zealand, MA1 Box 112, Petition No. 286/32.

45. Rēweti T. Kōhere, Letter, February 12, 1935, National Archives of New Zealand, MA1 Box 112.

46. Rēweti T. Kōhere et al., National Archives of New Zealand, MA1 Box 112, Petition No. 97/1947, 3.

47. Rēweti T. Kōhere, Letter, June 29, 1953, National Archives of New Zealand, MA1 Box 113, 1.

asking, "Am I to be harassed and barred from recovering my father's bones? It is unthinkable."[48] Through multiple official documents, Kōhere produces the same ideas: bones, fire, land, and law.

It is telling, then, that one of the cycles of repetition in these documents makes use of Romantic poetry. Throughout his communications with the government, Kōhere returns to the lines of Byron and Macaulay, especially the latter, deploying them as part of an increasingly angry diplomatic discourse. In his 1929 petition, for example, Kōhere asks: "Who would have the heart to find fault with us for fighting and, maybe, for dying, for our heritage and for 'the ashes of our fathers?'"[49] In an official letter of complaint to the under-secretary of the Native Department in 1946, Kōhere commented, "All Courts in the past paid me respect for they recognised I was fighting for 'the ashes of my fathers,' and truth."[50] His deployment of poetry in these instances, and the way in which he marks out the quotation in speech marks, suggests his desire to mobilize official Pākehā sympathy for his cause by linking it to a tradition of heroic action from within the European canon. But the lines from Byron and Macaulay are also connected directly to the *legal* case that Kōhere wishes to mount, which is based on the combination of the presence of burial grounds on the disputed land and what he calls the "fundamental fact of occupation."[51] The ashes of his sires and fathers are quite literally present on the land; so too are the ashes of ahikaaroa, which serve as the principal basis for claiming occupation and thus ownership. The fact that courts in the past had "recognised" this suggests both the sense of formal legal recognition and an underlying human sympathy that poetry can help generate.

The ways in which Māori understandings can be inferred from the English poetry are even more obvious in other engagements between Kōhere and the government. In a 1930 petition, for example, Kōhere wrote: "We are absolutely certain our case has not been dealt with on its merits and we earnestly do not wish to appear to make a threat but it has been

---

48. Rēweti T. Kōhere, "Charge of Bias against Judges J. Harvey and E. M. Beechey," National Archives of New Zealand, MA1 Box 112, 19; and Rēweti T. Kōhere, Letter, June 3, 1950, National Archives of New Zealand, MA1 Box 113, 1.

49. Rēweti T. Kōhere et al., National Archives of New Zealand, MA1 Box 111, Petition No. 98/1929, 4.

50. Rēweti T. Kōhere, "Charge of Bias," 17.

51. Rēweti T. Kōhere et al., National Archives of New Zealand, MA1 Box 111, Petition No. 98/1929, 1.

handed down from time immemorial that for a Maori to die for his land and in defence of 'the ashes of his fathers' is to die a noble death. To expect us to desist is to expect us to play the coward."[52] Here it is a traditional concept, one rooted in Māori history, that is laid out as the basis for the claim, but in order to convey the solemnity and longevity of this concept, Kōhere turns to a quotation that he expects his Pākehā interlocutors to comprehend immediately and to connect with the validity of his argument. Macaulay's words are here cited almost as if they are a *whakataukī* (proverb), the kind of rhetorical device that a Māori speaker might use in a speech or whaikōrero during a diplomatic negotiation or encounter. The two cultures, and their different poetic, rhetorical, and diplomatic norms, are here fused into a single appeal to both sentiment and legality.

One of the last publications of Kōhere's life brought together his battles over the land, his diplomatic relationships with the government, his ancestors, and the importance of particular poems to his understanding of these issues. In *The Story of a Maori Chief* (1949), his biography of Mokena, Kōhere included a chapter titled, "The Native Land Court: A Long Litigation." The chapter begins in this way:

> It has been said that the history of Kautuku (or Marangairoa 1 D) is the history of Mokena Kohere, so it would not be out of place to say something of the case in which I have been a litigant for over 35 years and in which I mean to fight until I recover my people's ancestral home and sacred places.
>
> It is a well-known saying of the Maoris, "He wahine, he whenua, ka ngaro te tangata" ("For women and land men perish"). And everybody is familiar with Macaulay's words:
>
> To every man upon this earth
> Death cometh soon or late;
> And how can man die better
> Than facing fearful odds,
> For the ashes of his fathers,
> And the temples of his gods![53]

---

52. Rēweti T. Kōhere et al., National Archives of New Zealand, MA1 Box 111, Petition No. 87/1930, 1–2.

53. Rēweti T. Kohere, *The Story of a Maori Chief*, 86. He would again make reference to the whakataukī—"For women and land men perish"—in a letter to the minister of

This chapter contains a vast array of cited material: quotes from the judges in the various Native Land Court hearings, from people who knew Mokena, from traditional Māori stories, and from the reports of various experts inquiring into the land tenure at Marangairoa. It might seem unusual for a biography to move into events well beyond the life span of its subject, but for Kōhere, this was the point of the exercise. Mokena's life was entirely bound up with questions of land: how one claimed it through one's ancestors and demonstrated ahikaaroa, and how connections to the land existed without interruption through past, present, and future.

Mokena himself was associated with fire and with land, both by his grandson-biographer and by his people more generally. The *Encyclopedia of New Zealand* entry for Mokena (written by another of his descendants) makes this remark about his reputation and the way it is recorded in Ngāti Porou history:

> A Ngati Porou haka contains the line, "But for Mokena, what then?" It commemorates Mokena's timely intervention to save captured Ngati Porou Hauhau from execution at Te Pito, near East Cape. While it relates to a specific incident, the phrase may equally be applied to Mokena's service to the people throughout his lifetime. Some years after his death it was said: "Mokena Kohere was the chief who enabled tribal fires to be rekindled, both in Waiapu and in Poverty Bay . . . much of the heritage of his people might have been lost, but for Mokena." (ellipsis in the original)[54]

Rēweti Kōhere, meanwhile, refers to his grandfather as a "firebrand" and "a fiery peacemaker."[55] He cites comments made by Mokena and passed on to him by his grandfather's acquaintances, including a remark, made while Mokena hoisted the Union Jack and ensured that Ngāti Porou remained loyal to the government, thus preserving their lands from confiscation: "E hoki ia hapu, ia hapu, ki te tahu i tana ahi, i tana ahi (Let each sub-tribe return home to re-kindle its own fire)."[56]

Māori affairs about the Marangairoa 1D Block; see Rēweti T. Kōhere, Letter, June 29, 1953, National Archives of New Zealand, MA1 Box 113, 1.
54. Rarawa Kohere, "Kohere, Mokena," n.p.
55. Rēweti T. Kohere, *The Story of a Maori Chief*, 37, 45–46.
56. Rēweti T. Kohere, *The Story of a Maori Chief*, 58.

To talk about fire, ancestry, and land was thus not simply to evoke general Māori concepts, although they too were important. Instead, the nexus of fire, ancestry, and land particularly pertained, in Rēweti Kōhere's mind, to Mokena, to the piece of land, now known as the Marangairoa 1D Block, that he had fought to protect, and to the contentious modern history of that land. Mokena was the sire, the father, whose ashes, literal and metaphorical, needed to be remembered and rekindled in the twentieth century. For his grandson Rēweti, he was a real-life model of the imagined or generic figures to whom Byron and Macaulay alluded.

The biography of Mokena was, in fact, another piece of diplomatic text, composed by Kōhere in the hope of engaging further with the government: at one point in the biography he comments "I hope [Native Land Court] Judges Harvey and Beechey will some day read this book."[57] Macaulay's words are included here as part of the evidence, alongside a host of other documents including court reports, judgments, and firsthand testimonies, as part of the history of Kōhere and his people's ongoing diplomacy with the New Zealand government. They are a reminder of things said in petitions, in newspaper articles, and in letters of complaint over decades. But they are also, crucially, a reminder to judges, politicians, and other figures in Pākehā public life that their own culture had encoded the values of land, ancestry, and *mana* (human dignity) in verse, with the metaphor of fire binding those notions together.

The rhetoric and form of Māori diplomacy in the period in which Kōhere was writing is usefully illustrated by these examples. Engaging the attention of the state meant writing in English, either on one's own or via a lawyer, and adopting the terms and forms of the petition as a genre. This circumstance in part reveals the power dynamics at play: the New Zealand settler government controlled the process by which grievances could be heard, and could thus dictate the language and shape in which the grievance could be legitimately expressed. But it also reveals Māori skill at working within the parameters of this diplomatic engagement. All of the possible cultural and historical information that might have been brought to bear on a question of confiscation and reparation is not simply curtailed but also curated; the right evidence is brought into the frame of the negotiation, in the language of one's interlocutors and in a form that they will appreciate and comprehend. This form frequently

---

57. Rēweti T. Kohere, *The Story of a Maori Chief*, 87.

involves citing or repeating past promises in order to establish the evidential base for reparations.

But citation and repetition were also always factors in Māori diplomacy. The negotiations involving the Treaty of Waitangi in February 1840 demonstrated the formal characteristics of this diplomatic tradition, and in particular, the role of whaikōrero (speechmaking) in the deliberations. One important characteristic of whaikōrero is its strategic use of repetition. Speakers repeat chants, songs, proverbs, genealogies, formulaic expressions, and the words of previous speakers, as well as their own ideas. The cited material may be sourced from any moment from the very recent past (such as a previous speaker on the same occasion) to the beginning of creation.[58] As Anne Salmond has noted, there is a dynamic relationship between repetition and originality in an effective whaikōrero:

> The central text of a *whaikōrero* is still highly stylised, but unlike the opening chants it is not completely predictable in wording. The orator cuts his cloth to fit the occasion, but weaves it out of a large set of phrases which are heard over and over again, in different arrangements. These phrases are poetic and mythological, providing a sort of verbal embroidery for the speech. Skilled orators use poetic sayings with an off-hand deftness, and it is these speakers who are most likely to abandon the well-worn repertoire for something more striking and original. They coin poetry of their own, or launch into vivid, witty prose, leaving aside the standard structures altogether.[59]

As well as inhabiting European forms of diplomacy, then, Kōhere's use of Byron and Macaulay simultaneously inhabits the rhetorical world of whaikōrero. He draws together the time scales of the early decades of the nineteenth century, when these English poems were originally composed, and the political and judicial controversies around Māori land in the early decades of the twentieth century. As techniques, the citation of poetry, the repetition of the words of others, and an awareness of the

---

58. Poia Rewi, *Whaikōrero: The World of Māori Oratory* (Auckland, NZ: Auckland University Press, 2010), 19.
59. Anne Salmond, *Hui: A Study of Maori Ceremonial Gatherings*, rev. ed. (New York: Penguin, 2004), 164–65.

very distant and the very recent past were all entirely conventional elements of Māori rhetoric. Byron and Macaulay, in other words, belonged to the Māori world too.

Byron, Macaulay, and the Uses of History

Kōhere's understanding of the potential of his quotations emerges from within the poems' own formulations of history and its uses. The lines of Byron's that he cites come from the opening section of *The Giaour*, in which the speaker laments the fate of Regency-era Greece and its fall from the heights of its history. In the first 167 lines of the poem, Byron's speaker treats Greece as a corpse: "'Tis Greece—but living Greece no more!" (90–91). Many critics refer to this section as a eulogy, but the particular passage from which Kōhere quotes is one motivated more by insurrection than encomium, a tone made clearer if the longer poetic sentence from which he excerpts is considered. Addressing the Greece of 1813, the speaker rehearses some of the major glories of Greek history, and then declares:

> These scenes—their story not unknown—
> Arise, and make again your own;
> Snatch from the ashes of your sires
> The embers of their former fires,
> And he who in the strife expires
> Will add to theirs a name to fear,
> That Tyranny shall quake to hear,
> And leave the sons a hope, a fame,
> They too will rather die than shame;
> For Freedom's battle once begun,
> Bequeathed by bleeding Sire to Son,
> Though baffled oft is ever won. (114–25)

Far from conceding the death of Greece, Byron's speaker is militantly optimistic, determined to provoke a rebellion that draws on the legacies of Greek culture and inspires coming generations to claim a lost political and cultural heritage across Europe.

To use Byron's *Giaour* in an excerpted and hybrid form is to participate in Byron's own practice, in ways that echo Copway's digressive use of a similarly digressive Byron. The original poem foregrounds its fragmentariness and multiple voices. As Yin Yuan has argued, in *The Giaour*, "narrative fragments, voiced from different but always partial perspectives, call each other into question."[60] Byron sets a range of voices, genres, and meaning-making activities alongside each other in a way that destabilizes the story at the heart of the poem. There are at least four (and perhaps five) of these perspectives, and they generate, not only different accounts of the events, but also accounts in different subgenres.[61] The juxtapositions of these elements ask the reader to absorb and evaluate competing accounts of history, and to produce new historical awarenesses from that process. Yuan persuasively suggests of the various stories contained within *The Giaour* that "the limited nature of each of these accounts, and, as a natural if unfortunate corollary, the efforts that each commits toward the suppression of others, allows Byron to foreground not simply the distinction between an event and its discursive presentation, but more significantly, the violence that the elevation of any one of those accounts entails."[62] To put lines from *The Giaour* into conversation with such diverse intertextual elements as a speech by a British member of Parliament, an exhortation to claim back a threatened sovereignty, the terms of reference for a Royal Commission, a piece of legislation, and a sequence of petitions is to reactivate part of the poem's own fragmented nature. It is also to acknowledge the tension between different voices and the hierarchy of voices within a political sphere as central to the poem's argument.

Kōhere's appropriation of *The Giaour* also underlines how overtly political and topical were both the subject and the method of Byron's poem in its moment of publication. Byron's real target, as Marilyn Butler argued, was the attitude of the British public to Greek independence in 1813, a pressing contemporary issue.[63] The poem as a whole, and

---

60. Yin Yuan, "Invasion and Retreat: Representations of the Oriental Other in Byron's *The Giaour*," *Studies in Romanticism* 54, no. 1 (2015): 3–31; 24. See also Ruth Knezevich, "The Empire of the Page: Footnotes in Byron's *The Giaour*," *Essays in Romanticism* 24, no. 1 (2017): 35–52, which makes a different but related point about the way Byron outsources authority.

61. See Yuan, 23, and Jerome J. McGann, *Fiery Dust: Byron's Poetic Development* (Chicago: University of Chicago Press, 1968), 144.

62. Yuan, 24.

63. Marilyn Butler, "The Orientalism of Byron's Giaour," in *Byron and the Limits of Fiction*, ed. Bernard Beatty and Vincent Newey, 78–96; 83–85 (Liverpool: Liverpool University Press, 1988). See also Marjorie Levinson, *The Romantic Fragment Poem: A Critique of a Form* (Chapel Hill: University of North Carolina Press, 1986), 115–28; and Robert Gleckner, *Byron and the Ruins of Paradise* (Baltimore, MD: Johns Hopkins University Press, 1967), 91–138.

certainly the opening lines, were in this sense fundamentally diplomatic; the poem aimed to train British readers to accept Greek sovereignty and to mobilize their sympathies behind that goal. But they were also deeply concerned with colonization, with what, in his reading of *The Giaour*, Nigel Leask has called "a world suppressed under the (modern) sign of imperialism."[64] The radical potential of Byron's words, as a statement against imperialism and an invitation to reactivate a dormant past, is something to which Kōhere wishes his readers, especially the Māori readers of *Te Toa Takitini*, to respond.

Macaulay's volume *Lays of Ancient Rome*, which opens with *Horatius*, had a different purpose in its own historical moment. The poems were composed between 1834 and 1838, while Macaulay was in India, in a period in which his thinking about colonization, Britishness, and the supposed superiority and practical uses of British literature was at its most acute.[65] While the adoption of a classical subject might not seem inherently related to the British Empire, Meredith Martin has pointed out the ways in which the imperial periphery and its subjects were central to the conception of the *Lays* volume, which she reads "as a bridge between late eighteenth- and early nineteenth-century romantic ideas of poetry, imagined primitive communities and fragmentary history, and later revivals of these ideas."[66] In an instantiation of what Martin calls "the ballad-theory of civilization," Macaulay's poems aim at a universal ballad history, woven into the fabric of all societies and thus feeding and shaping a comprehensive identity for the British Empire and its peoples. Martin specifically locates this universality in the same lines from *Horatius* that Kōhere chose to quote: the declaration of the character Horatius about "the ashes of his fathers, / And the temples of his gods," and she notes that the poem "is now in the universal realm—about respecting the valor of any martial enemy, the purity of it, the beauty and simplicity of combat, what is seen as pure, primitive, and perfect about war and songs about war."[67] When we read this universalizing tendency from the

---

64. Nigel Leask, *British Romantic Writers and the East: Anxieties of Empire* (Cambridge: Cambridge University Press, 1992), 30.

65. See Thomas Babington Macaulay, *The Letters of Thomas Babington Macaulay*, 6 vols., ed. Thomas Pinney, 4:66 (Cambridge: Cambridge University Press, 1981).

66. Meredith Martin, "'Imperfectly Civilized': Ballads, Nations, and Histories of Form," *ELH* 82, no. 2 (2015): 345–63; 360.

67. Martin, 357.

perspective of a British author, it is natural to locate it within a wider imperial rhetoric that aims to romanticize a primitive past and eliminate cultural difference; as Catherine Hall has shown, it was these lines from *Horatius*, in particular, that were "repeated by generation after generation of boys schooled in imperial patriotism" both in Britain and in countries like Aotearoa New Zealand.[68] The example of Rēweti Kōhere demonstrates the ways in which such universalizing might be deployed by those targeted by British imperialism to productive ends, however. It is precisely the fact that Macaulay's lines *do* suggest a universal and natural human emotion that makes them suitable for Indigenous diplomacy.

Moreover, Macaulay's project is entirely invested in ideas of repetition. Martin locates in the *Lays* as a whole, and in *Horatius* in particular, a pattern of what she calls "double and triple projections," in which Macaulay yokes together British India, the glory of the British military past, Roman military success and bravery, and, in *Horatius* itself, the invocation of an even more distant past and its martial traditions to which the Roman characters in the poem are being urged to respond by Horatius when he speaks.[69] Macaulay's own historical moment is being reframed by a series of past moments and the values they appear to encode. Kōhere adds an additional historical moment to this matrix, connecting Macaulay's work with Byron's, a rhetorical move that seems unsurprising when the close verbal echo of the two sets of relevant lines is considered, but one that has not been much noticed by literary historians. Kōhere's project thus aligns with Macaulay's aims here, although not in the way Macaulay would have envisaged. He places a series of new projections alongside Macaulay's own ones, adding not only Regency England and revolutionary Greece to the sites in which the values of *Horatius* make sense and can be invoked, but also nineteenth- and twentieth-century Aotearoa New Zealand. Macaulay's project is all too successful, in this sense: it universalizes emotions and values throughout the British world to the point where they not only become the property of citizens whom he discounted, rather in the manner that Goldsmith discounted Black emotional life and patriotism, but are used as a measure of the moral failings of the culture that encoded them in poetry.

Macaulay produced one of the most memorable nineteenth-century images of New Zealand and its inhabitants in his famous formulation

---

68. Catherine Hall, "Macaulay's Nation," *Victorian Studies* 51, no. 3 (2009): 505–23; 518.
69. Martin, 355.

of a fallen London, in which "some traveller from New Zealand shall, in the midst of a vast solitude, take his stand on a broken arch of London Bridge to sketch the ruins of St. Paul's."[70] This image is often read as conjuring up a Pākehā New Zealander, a settler who has returned from the periphery to a fallen center.[71] But in 1840, the year in which Macaulay composed this image, the term "New Zealander" referred, not to all residents of the islands of New Zealand, but rather to Māori as the sovereign peoples of Aotearoa.[72] This sovereignty was a topical question in 1840 New Zealand as well as 1840 Britain, since this was the year of the signing of the Treaty of Waitangi. Macaulay may have been present in the House of Commons on July 7, 1840, when British MPs debated the nature of the new arrangements in the colony. His awareness of a Māori figure of the sort he describes would have emerged from within the diplomatic discourse concerning this new international treaty.[73] Macaulay's Māori was mobile, traversing not only the geographic space between England and Aotearoa New Zealand and the temporal space between the flourishing empire and its inevitable fall, but also the cultural space between Indigenous and European art forms. He was able to articulate his

---

70. Thomas Babington Macaulay, *Critical and Historical Essays, Contributed to the Edinburgh Review*, 5th ed. (London: Longman, Brown, Green, and Longmans, 1848), 3: 209.

71. See, for example, Robert Dingley, "The Ruins of the Future: Macaulay's New Zealander and the Spirit of the Age," in *Histories of the Future: Studies in Fact, Fantasy and Science Fiction*, ed. Alan Sandison and Robert Dingley, 15–33 (Basingstoke: Palgrave, 2000); and David Skilton, "Contemplating the Ruins of London: Macaulay's New Zealander and Others," *Literary London: Interdisciplinary Studies in the Representation of London* 2, no. 2 (2004), http://literarylondon.org/the-literary-london-journal/archive-of-the-literary-london-journal/issue-2-1/contemplating-the-ruins-of-london-macaulays-new-zealander-and-others/. It is interesting that there is an example of another Indigenous person reading Macaulay's New Zealander as probably Māori; in Adam Spry's discussion of an Anishinaabe periodical, he notes an article in which the contributor known as "Wah-Boose" ("Rabbit") comments: "Macauley [sic] says that history has a tendency to repeat itself; in his mind's eye he saw the New Zeelander [sic] gazing from the bridge upon the ruins of London! Pursue the analogy, and might not the future red man gaze upon the ruins of New York and Brooklyn from their great suspension bridge?" See Spry, *Our War Paint Is Writers' Ink: Anishinaabe Literary Transnationalism* (Albany: State University of New York Press, 2018), 40.

72. Alice Te Punga Somerville has pointed this out in her reflections on the 2016 Brexit referendum; see Alice Te Punga Somerville, "A View of Brexit from Elsewhere," June 25, 2016, *Once Were Pacific*, http://oncewerepacific.blogspot.com/2016/06/a-view-of-brexit-from-elsewhere.html.

73. This connection is made in Bright, 14.

thinking about past, present, and future, via the idea of a mobile Māori, a character called into being in the British imagination by the recent diplomatic activity at Waitangi. But in Kōhere's appropriation of the lines from *Horatius* and *The Giaour*, it is Macaulay and Byron who are figured as mobile and exotic, with their texts reaching Aotearoa New Zealand and undergoing various translations, appropriations, and reinterpretations. Kōhere repurposes their verse as a site to reimagine time scales, histories, languages, and geographies, just as Macaulay himself had done when he placed a "New Zealander" at the center of a reimagined metropolis.

The citations of Byron and Macaulay in Kōhere's writings have the potential to create quite different effects for different audiences. To an Anglophone Pākehā reader, these lines are conventional and their authors canonical. The verses read as a familiar, perhaps even predictable, poetic flourish, but they are delivered in entirely unexpected forums and contexts: Māori periodicals, petitions, and formal letters to the government. To a Māori reader, the lines are operating in an almost diametrically opposed fashion, especially on the first occasion when Kōhere uses them. They are new and unfamiliar, drawn from outside the conventional storehouse of verse, but the deployment of poetry itself is not unexpected, nor is the possibility that the speaker or author will introduce a striking literary example to illustrate their point. The citation of someone else's words marks the moment at which Kōhere seems, paradoxically, most original, as he deviates from both the Māori language and the conventional whakataukī (proverbs) of Māori poetry and oratory.

But if there is an electrifying effect when Kōhere first uses these lines, there is a different kind of energy harnessed when they are repeated across many years, many texts, and many genres. The lines of poetry take root in the rhetorical space of Māori diplomacy, and while they remain a feature of Kōhere's personal expression, they have simultaneously been offered as a contribution to the collective pool of poetic resources. They are beginning a potential journey toward becoming commonplace. To a Māori reader, they are more familiar with each iteration, helping to connect, via poetry, the contexts of Māori sovereignty, Pākehā government, and Aotearoa New Zealand history. To the Anglophone Pākehā reader, however, they are perhaps becoming less familiar with each repetition. The fact of their tentative socialization within the various Māori-authored texts in which they appear unsettles the sense in which the lines can strictly be considered English poetry, as they come to seem connected to debates in the Māori world. Robert Te Kotahi Mahuta writes about whaikōrero as collaborative endeavors between the orator and their audience, noting that there is a skill in listening to whaikōrero effectively that is partly shaped by the mixture of repetition and originality. As Mahuta comments, skilled listeners are not paying equal attention to every element; instead, "all they need to have attention for is the new or novel theme and the reference to contemporary affairs."[74] To different readers, for different reasons, and on different occasions, Kōhere's citation of *The Giaour* and *Horatius* would have seemed new or novel, a moment to tune in and pay attention.

As twenty-first-century readers, what do we learn by tuning in to Kōhere? His juxtaposition of Byron and Macaulay is unusual; few readers have considered them alongside one another, despite the prominent verbal echo of the ashes in these two poems. But it draws out some ideas that challenge scholarly thinking. Daniel P. Watkins reads Byron's opening lines to Greece as demonstrating a frustration that "that the past and present somehow have become disconnected" and containing "an ideology of lost greatness, that is, a value system that locates human worth only within a context that no longer exists and cannot be recovered."[75] But the section of *The Giaour* that Kōhere quotes aligns Byron's poem with the ostensibly optimistic tone of Macaulay; history, via poetry, is perpetually available as a resource for common reflection and action. Kōhere's reading suggests a fundamental continuity between past and present; when he quotes and then glosses Byron's lines in October 1926, he suggests that Māori behavior in the present can, and should, mirror the behavior of their ancestors. It is in fact Byron's "ashes" that are still burning, able to be reactivated in the way that the Māori concept of ahikaaroa operates. Macaulay's "ashes" are dead, representing instead the solemnity of the urupā, or burial ground, and the importance of tending the literal ashes of one's ancestors. Both concepts are significant, providing separate but related ways to speak, in English, both to Māori and Pākehā audiences alike. And both suggest the ways in which history, land, law, fire, bones, and poetry are part of a shared diplomatic tradition in Aotearoa New Zealand.

---

74. Robert Te Kotahi Mahuta, "Whaikoorero: A Study of Formal Maori Speech" (PhD thesis, University of Auckland, Auckland, New Zealand, 1974, 7. See also Salmond, 165.

75. Daniel P. Watkins, "Social Relations in Byron's *The Giaour*," *ELH* 52, no. 4 (1985): 873–92; 876.

It is this complex hybrid model of diplomacy that can be seen in Kōhere's use of Byron and Macaulay. As with all the examples in this book, the choice of English-language texts, especially poems by canonical authors, reveals a profound engagement with the norms and frames of reference of potential Anglophone interlocutors. It presents the case for a resurgent Māori identity from within a European tradition and aesthetic. Poetry here is construed as promise. Byron's attitude to Greek independence and sovereignty is taken as emblematic of a Pākehā undertaking to support the aspirations of subjugated peoples, while Macaulay's construction of a history informed by one's ancestors is taken to signal a Pākehā understanding of historical continuity and genealogy as central to modern identities. The poetry participates in a process that New Zealand social anthropologist Raymond Firth described in an article published at almost exactly the same moment that Kōhere quoted Byron and Macaulay alongside one another. Firth's 1926 articles on "Proverbs in Native Life" argued that the citation and repetition of proverbs in Māori rhetoric served as "an enforcement of social conduct," in which "the precise words" operated as "a means of praise, reproach, and stimulation."[76] In the case of Kōhere's use of English poetry, it is actually Pākehā social conduct that is being enforced. Both sets of lines make sense within Māori epistemology, but citing them in the original English serves as a reminder to both Pākehā and Māori interlocutors that it is also European tradition that claims to value these aspirations.

The poetry thus acts as a compelling diplomatic text to mediate between two peoples and as an example of Allen's notion of the "Treaty allegory." Pākehā audiences are perhaps chastened by the reminder that their own literature has spoken authoritatively about cultural sovereignty; Māori audiences are perhaps emboldened by being armed with the language and forms in which Pākehā sympathies and understandings can be harnessed, in lines that closely echo their own intellectual grounds for identity and the transfer of knowledge. Like the formal constraints of the petition, the poetry can be read as both limiting Māori expression to the language and rhetoric of the colonizers, and as opening up a space in which cross-cultural diplomacy can occur.

---

76. Raymond Firth, "Proverbs in Native Life, with Special Reference to those of the Maori, II (Continued)," *Folklore* 37, no. 3 (September 1926): 245–70; 259, 261, 264.

Michael Belgrave has described courts and commissions of inquiry in Aotearoa New Zealand as "points of friction" in which Indigenous and settler narratives are rehearsed and realigned.[77] Friction connotes conflict, of course, but also a means by which power and dynamism might be released, by which fires might be generated. This generative potential is significant in the face of the typical intentions of a court or commission of inquiry into Indigenous land in the settler colonies, including Aotearoa New Zealand. There are not many nouns that naturally take the verb "to extinguish" in English, but "fire" and "native title" certainly do. The literary symbolism and legal ramifications of history's ashes could not be clearer for Indigenous peoples.

---

77. Michael Belgrave, *Historical Frictions: Maori Claims & Reinvented Histories* (Auckland: Auckland University Press, 2005), 3.

Conclusion

Coming to Terms with Romantic Poetry

The chronology of this book has, I hope, allowed us to track the way Romantic poetry was repurposed differently as the British colonial project moved from North America to Africa and the Pacific. John Brant was able to confront British Romantic literature in its own moment and place of production. Elias Boudinot, the editor of the *Cherokee Phoenix*, republished Hemans's poems almost as soon as they appeared; he was responding to her poetry in real time, and he had the potential to shape American responses to her work within the framing of the Cherokees' diplomatic imperatives. George Copway's life overlapped with Byron's, and although the poet was dead by the time *Running Sketches* appeared, Copway was speaking to an audience in early 1850s Europe and the United States that had been profoundly shaped by Byron's thought (in some cases, he was addressing people who had even known Byron personally). Kōhere and Plaatje were dealing with quite a different scenario: the memory of British Romanticism in both the southern settler colonies and the imperial center. This gradual and inevitable move away from Romanticism's own period changes the nature of its potential as a diplomatic tool; it drifts from being work-in-progress that could be altered, made more honest, or mobilized in its own moment to a corpus that increasingly implied a lost set of settler-imperial values that might be reengaged. Throughout these changing eras, locales, and identities of Indigenous leaders, however, one thing remained the same: the exact words of British Romantic poetry were assumed to have some potential diplomatic power.

In that sense, the title of this chapter is meant to be taken literally. As this book shows, Indigenous diplomats believed that Romantic poetry could be used to come to "terms" with settler-imperial governments and publics, whether the terms of a treaty, a negotiated relationship, or an act of intervention or restitution. But my chapter title also speaks to the twenty-first-century implications of Romanticism, especially for those of us who live and work in the settler colonies. How are we to come to terms with Romanticism's legacies today? How does Romantic literature continue to have an impact on Indigenous writers, intellectuals, and diplomats? And what uses might contemporary Indigenous figures have for British Romantic poetry?

The Flowers that Grow in the "Daffodil Gap"

In literary criticism, the poem that has come to symbolize colonial education is, of course, a Romantic poem: William Wordsworth's "I Wandered Lonely as a Cloud," which is colloquially referred to as "Daffodils." Helen Tiffin famously connected this poem to a wider complex of colonial power relations when she commented in a footnote that "the gap between the lived colonial or post-colonial experience and the imported/imposed world of the Anglo-written has often been referred to by Commonwealth post-colonial writers and critics as 'the daffodil gap.'"[1] In her own reading of the works of Erna Brodber and Jamaica Kincaid, Tiffin made a convincing case for the disempowering potential of Wordsworth's poem and all that it symbolizes. Forced to learn, internalize, and recite a poem that dealt with a natural phenomenon unknown to them, colonized peoples, in this interpretation, were compelled to substitute for lived experiences and landscapes a wholly alien world, one in which they could not operate comfortably. The daffodil gap metaphor has been taken up in much postcolonial criticism in the twenty-five years since Tiffin articulated this point, providing a scholarly shorthand for a global phenomenon.

But recent scholarship has challenged some of the ideas that Tiffin advanced. Katherine Bergren's superb study *The Global Wordsworth: Romanticism Out of Place* rethinks the significance of Wordsworth's poetry generally, and "Daffodils" in particular, as a way of considering the mobility

---

1. Helen Tiffin, "Cold Hearts and (Foreign) Tongues: Recitation and the Reclamation of the Female Body in the Works of Erna Brodber and Jamaica Kincaid," *Callaloo* 16, no. 4 (1993): 909–21; 920n.

of Romanticism. In doing so, Bergren considers what effect the term "the daffodil gap" has had on our understanding of these ideas and offers a different reading of the ways in which colonized writers make use of Wordsworth:

> The dynamics of the "daffodil gap" are altered by the repurposings of Wordsworth that his poetry inspires or provokes. No longer a one-way exercise of colonial power, the gap becomes a space whose circulating currents, while never flowing free from the relations of domination and subordination that link Britain to its colonies, nevertheless travel to and fro "with the respirations of the tide," as Wordsworth puts it in *The Excursion*. If Wordsworth provokes readers beyond Britain to write him into new existences, these writers provoke readers of Wordsworth to listen to him differently, as if he were engaged in an ongoing conversation with writers who interpolated him.[2]

Like Bergren, I am interested in both the utility and the limitations of Tiffin's idea, and I want to use the term "gap" in the phrase the "daffodil gap" to think through some concluding points. While I comprehend why Tiffin chose to frame the idea this way, as she wished to highlight a real injustice in colonial curricula and pedagogies, the term she expressed imagines a world of separations rather than one of relations. It imagines a world in which people are, neither literally nor figuratively, linking arms. It assumes that the frame of reference for recitation is a schoolroom, in which the Indigenous presence is already presumed to be a child or an infantilized adult. But to take this as a starting point is to assume, even if sympathetically, that sovereignty has already been ceded, that Indigenous peoples are already somehow wards of the settler state, and that Indigenous readers are unable to determine their own uses of English-language text, and literary text in particular. What if we were to assume a frame of reference for recitation that was, metaphorically, a treaty ground, or a legislature, or an international congress? How might the disempowerment that is assumed in the space of the schoolroom be transformed, even if the words and points of reference remained the

---

2. Katherine Bergren, *The Global Wordsworth: Romanticism Out of Place* (Lewisburg, PA: Bucknell University Press, 2018), 40.

same? What if we stopped talking gaps and started talking tangents, as Vine Deloria does in his imagining of the contact points between Indigenous and settler expression?[3] What if, in other words, we thought of quotation as diplomacy?

In order to center diplomacy (both for us as a critical practice, and also for the original Indigenous deployers of Romantic poetry that this book has examined), you have to believe that you are a partner in a negotiation. The power to act diplomatically comes from faith in one's own sovereignty, regardless of one's actual power, and in the inherent worth and dignity that diplomatic relations assume the parties accord each other. One reason why the daffodil gap thesis has taken hold is because it arises out of a particular historical moment in which Indigenous and colonized peoples had far less power to act diplomatically than they had possessed in the nineteenth and early twentieth centuries. Tiffin's examples come from the mid-twentieth-century Caribbean and her articulation of the daffodil gap represents an accurate inference, on one level, from the erasure of colonized peoples' sovereignty globally in that moment, although Bergren's reading of some of the same material provides an alternative and very convincing analysis. However, it would not be accurate to read that same erasure back into the long nineteenth century. Brant, Boudinot, Copway, Plaatje, and Kōhere were members of sovereign peoples whose rights were guaranteed under the terms of treaties and wider domestic and international laws. More significantly still, they conducted themselves in that knowledge, alarmed by the challenges to their sovereignty but in no doubt that it existed and still hopeful that it might be properly recognized and upheld.

However, understanding the underpinning diplomatic reasons for quotation and the mobilization of Romantic poetry in this earlier era also means that it is inaccurate to assume a complete erasure of sovereignty in the twentieth- or twenty-first-century instances of this process as well. The daffodil gap thesis is a politically engaged and sympathetic one, but it does start from the assumption of a lack of power and an absence of sovereignty. It does not frame itself in diplomatic terms because it cannot imagine quotation and recitation as located within a conversation between political equals. Maybe that is simply a pragmatic and honest interpretation of a scene in which a colonized child in a colonial classroom is asked to

---

3. Vine Deloria Jr., *We Talk, You Listen: New Tribes, New Turf* (New York: Macmillan, 1970), 12.

recite Wordsworth. But that child—like my child, with whom I opened this book—is still in possession of sovereignty, still living under the terms of treaties and international law that guarantee their and their people's rights, whether the colonizers and the teacher in the classroom like it or not. We can be frank about coercive power relations that attempt to deny that sovereignty, without, in our critical practice, also putting sovereignty to one side ourselves. And we can do that even in that archetypal case of the Indigenous child's engagement with "Daffodils."

With that in mind, I want to turn to some examples of Indigenous engagement with "Daffodils" that are not covered in Tiffin's or Bergren's accounts. Throughout her body of work, the Sāmoan writer Sia Figiel has returned to Wordsworth's poem as a point of reference, but not one of deference. In an autobiographical 2016 essay, "Pua and Daffodils: Weaving the Ula in Postcolonial Oceania," Figiel includes an epigraph from the first quatrain of "Daffodils" alongside one from a Sāmoan children's song (in Sāmoan and English), and quotes from Toni Morrison and the scholar Epeli Hau'ofa.[4] She describes learning to recite Wordsworth's poem while in school in Sāmoa, and she shares her frustration at being asked to engage with a poem about a flower she had never seen (an experience that she has integrated into her fictional work as well and one that is held in common with other writers who were compelled to learn Wordsworth's lyric).[5] She points out the ways in which those experiences informed the writer she became:

> The Samoan creation myth as told to us by Aunty Kupukala situates Samoa as the sacred centre of the universe. The idea also that each man, woman and child carried their sacred centre with them meant for me that England, a far away place where daffodils grew in its meadows, could not possibly be "the centre." At least to Samoans or Pacific peoples.[6]

---

4. Sia Figiel, "Pua and Daffodils: Weaving the Ula in Postcolonial Oceania," *Journal of New Zealand and Pacific Studies* 4, no. 1 (2016): 5–17; 5–6.

5. Figiel, "Pua and Daffodils," 7, 12. See also the scene concerned with learning the poem in her novel *Where We Once Belonged* (Honolulu: Pasifika Press, 1996), 167–68; the description in *To a young artist in contemplation: Poetry & Prose* (Laucala, Fiji: University of the South Pacific, Department of Language and Literature, Pacific Writing Forum, 1998), 94; and the allusion in *They Who Do Not Grieve* (New York: Vintage, 1999), 172.

6. Figiel, "Pua and Daffodils," 14.

When Figiel then discusses winning a 1997 Commonwealth Writer's Prize, she comments, "To think it all started with daffodils. A flower that made me feel ignorant and defeated."[7] These comments appear to align with the idea of the daffodil gap and the almost laughable unsuitability of Wordsworth's poem for Indigenous and colonized readers and authors. But Figiel's responses to Wordsworth are not simply dismissive; as the quote above suggests, she does not push aside but rather works expertly with Wordsworth's poem as part of a process of recentering Sāmoan and Pasifika sovereignty in her creative work.

While some of that deployment uses Wordsworth's lines as a reference point, such as the discussion in "Pua and Daffodils" or the brilliant prose poem "I Don't Know What a Daffodil Is," quotation is also a significant factor in Figiel's use of "Daffodils." In her collection *To a Young Artist in Contemplation: Poetry & Prose*, Figiel quotes from Wordsworth's poem twice. One of her poems is blunter, reflecting the wider point about her experience of learning the poem as a child. In "The Daffodils (the other version)," Figiel takes the opening stanza of Wordsworth's poem as the opening stanza of her own, and then concludes her piece with the lines, "I wandered and wondered / Wondered and wondered / What the fuck is a daffodil?" (5–7).[8] This deployment of Wordsworth's verse seems straightforward enough, as a counterpoint to the thought processes of the young speaker. But there are two layers of subtlety to this poem, and its place within the wider volume, that reveal some of the diplomatic work that Figiel is undertaking.

The first is that "The Daffodils (the other version)" is on the facing page to the poem "My friend Mr. Ambassador."[9] In part, the latter poem reflects wryly on some of the politics of Pacific diplomacy and positions that diplomatic sphere alongside but distinct from a poetic sphere, for example in these lines:

> Rain
> falls on the former
> ambassador's car
> outside parliament building

---

7. Figiel, "Pua and Daffodils," 15.
8. Figiel, *To a Young Artist in Contemplation*, 40.
9. Figiel, *To a Young Artist in Contemplation*, 41–42.

> while committees negotiate
> and renegotiate the price of
> *imported taro*
> rain falls on
> keeps falling
> on the ambassador's car
> each raindrop
> a poem
> (he does not hear) (15–27; italics in the original)

The poem ends with the lines "Ambassadors are very friendly people / Unlike poets / Ambassadors are very friendly" (59–61). In the opposition between the ambassador and the poet in these lines, two different kinds of diplomats are being evoked, one friendly but ineffectual, bureaucratic, and unaware of the poetic potential around him, and one incisive and observant, creatively situating diplomacy within and among poems and poetry. Turning back to the previous poem, "The Daffodils (the other version)," the reader cannot help but notice how the imported taro seems to connect to the imported flower, and also to the similarly imported education system that regarded that flower, that poem, as so central.

A second kind of subtlety is revealed in the phrase "the other version" in Figiel's title. She possibly identifies the poem this way because, earlier in the collection, she has already mobilized quotations from Wordsworth to produce a lengthy and astute interrogation of his verse. In "The daffodils—from a native's perspective," Figiel weaves lines of Wordsworth's poem, and indeed Blake's "The Tyger," into her own:

> Apologies Mr.
> Wordsworth
> But I too wandered
> Lonely as
> A cloud
> When I first heard your
> Little poem
> Form three
> Literature class
> That floats on high
> O'er vales
> And hills

> She made us me
> Morize you
> Along with tiger!
> Tiger!
> Burning bright!
> In the forest of your other
> 19th century
> Roman
> Tic friends
> When all at once
> She'd pull my ear
> Each time
> I stared
> At the auke bush
> Next to the mango tree
> Outside
> But in the end I
> Became quite the expert
> On your host of golden daffodils beside the lake beneath
> The trees fluttering and dancing
> Under the pulu tree (1–33)[10]

Figiel goes on to amplify the decidedly Sāmoan setting of her speaker's childhood, but every so often she returns to Wordsworth's language:

> Whenever
> I lie
> On my mat
> Oft
> In pensive mood
> Trying to find some bliss
> Of solitude
> Now
> And then
> Without the dogs
> The roosters
> The aiga (58–69)

---

10. Figiel, *To a Young Artist in Contemplation*, 30–33.

As the speaker suggests, she enjoyed the poem "Not knowing what / Was fluttering / What / Was dancing" (46–49), but nevertheless considered the flowers and the poem that depicted them to be "*Your* precious daffodils / *My* precious / Daffodils" (38–40; emphasis in the original). These are sentiments she addresses directly to the poet himself, reworking language from his poem and assuming that if she is meant to appreciate his poetic rendering of everyday life and experience of nature in the Lake District, he will likewise appreciate her reflections on her life in Sāmoa. The final lines articulate the challenge of this position, however, with their repetition of the question:

Do
You
Know
What
I
Mean
Mr.
Words
Worth?
Do
You
Know
What
I
Mean? (83–97)

This repetition suggests that the Wordsworth she addresses is very unlikely to understand the poem, just as she, as a reader, had struggled to understand his poem. The playful confidence of these lines is obvious, and even more evident when Figiel reads it aloud.[11] But the poem does more than simply write back to the empire. It creates, in those final lines, a sense of genuine negotiation by opening up the space in which "Mr. Wordsworth" can respond, not simply to Figiel's poetry, but to his own, and to the legacies and writing that it has generated, in much the same way that John Brant addressed Thomas Campbell, albeit posthumously in

---

11. At the time of writing, there is a video available of Figiel reading the poem posted December 16, 2012: https://www.youtube.com/watch?v=nrOFD6Z9BCQ.

the case of Figiel's work. Her poem takes Wordsworth's words, offers up an equivalent from within Figiel's work and life, and then asks whether some kind of rapprochement or mutual understanding can be reached. In other words, it uses "Daffodils" diplomatically, as a tool to be deployed in a conversation about Indigenous-settler relations that assumes a position of Indigenous intellectual and rhetorical sovereignty.

"Daffodils" was not just a touchstone in Sāmoa, of course. Its influence can be felt throughout the Pacific. The Tongan scholar, poet, and educator Konai Helu-Thaman, for example, has written about her engagement with Wordsworth's poem too:

> As a school student, I never fully appreciated the significance of Wordsworth's *Daffodils* until, many years later, I visited London for the first time and went with some friends to Kew Gardens. There, in front of my very own eyes, was "a sea [*sic*] of golden daffodils." I quietly said the poem to myself, a different poem this time because I moved closer to imagining what the poet must have felt when he wrote the poem. I remembered this occasion when I was asked to write a poem to be used in the launching of our university's project on adult literacy. My poem was called *Heilala*. . . . In order to fully appreciate this poem one would need to know what *heilala* is, and understand its significance to Tongan culture. As a flower with a cultural status and mythology, it provides the cultural context in which the poem is fashioned. Reading it without understanding this context would be to miss a significant part of the meaning of the poem, as I had done when I memorised *Daffodils*.[12]

Helu-Thaman is not simply rehearsing the daffodil gap experience here. Rather, she uses Wordsworth's verses, overlaid with her own experience of learning to recite his poem without an understanding of the flower at its heart, to generate a new work that will perform a similar function from within Tongan life and epistemology. She offers recitation, here undertaken quietly in sight of the daffodils, as a way of reframing understandings of

---

12. Konai Helu-Thaman, "Of Daffodils and Heilala: Understanding Cultural Contexts in Pacific Literature," Invited Address, Multi-Ethnic Literature Society of America (MELUS) Conference, Honolulu, April 18–20, 1997, http://www.directions.usp.ac.fj/collect/direct/index/assoc/D770128.dir/doc.pdf, 7–9; italics in the original.

verse and connecting cultural experiences. Most significantly, she draws the attention of her non-Tongan audience to both the disconcerting experience of her prior engagement with Wordsworth and their own equivalent disorientation and ignorance in the face of her *Heilala,* yet she manifests, in her unfolding understanding of Wordsworth's poem, its possibility as a model of learning to share cultural frames of reference. If there is a gap at the beginning of her process, it has been filled by the end with the *heilala* that grows in the space that quotation opens up.

My point here is not to rehabilitate Wordsworth's poem or its place in a devastatingly monocultural colonial curriculum, nor to suggest that a writer like, say, Figiel in any way requires Wordsworth in order to flourish. But maybe those of us who are Figiel's *palagi* (white) readers do require him; we require, in other words, the touchstone that "Wordsworth" and "Daffodils" represent in order to understand Figiel and others' points about how powerful a force Romantic poetry can be. Many readers would say that the flowers themselves are incidental to the meaning of the poem; what matters is not which flowers, or which natural phenomenon, Wordsworth refers to, but rather the universal human experience of nature, memory, and their effect on our interior lives. But is that a universalism that we have actually practiced in colonial pedagogies? Isn't the history of this poem in colonized countries marked by an insistence that it cannot be replaced by local examples, Indigenous authors, or native flora? And if such a replacement was to occur, would settler audiences feel confident in their understandings of, say, Helu-Thaman's *Heilala* or would we, as she suggests, not be able to grasp the significance of the plant at the center of the verse?

The failed promise of universal humanism in Wordsworth's poem is similar to the failed promises of all the Romantic poems this book considers. The values that they purport to uphold are not, in themselves, unworthy ones. They could have been the biliteral basis for a bilateral relationship, serving as the cultural documents that underpinned equal, equitable, treaty-based states. No wonder Indigenous intellectuals found them promising and promissory.

Diplomacy Is Not a Metaphor

The move this chapter makes into literary reworkings of Wordsworth by Pasifika women could suggest a change of focus, in which the term *diplomacy* is being used a little more figuratively than in earlier chapters. In a sense that might be true: Figiel and Helu-Thaman are not diplomats in the way that, say, Brant or Plaatje was. But I want to turn to one final example that might smooth over this apparent transition. In 2015, the poet Selina Tusitala Marsh, who is of Tuvaluan and Sāmoan descent and who served as Aotearoa New Zealand's poet laureate from 2017 to 2019, was commissioned to write a poem on the theme of "unity," which she then recited at Westminster Abbey in 2016 on Commonwealth Observance Day, in the presence of Queen Elizabeth II. This process could legitimately stand as what we might call cultural diplomacy. In a sense, that was precisely the ambassadorial role in which Marsh was cast when she stood at Westminster Abbey to recite "Unity," a poem which simultaneously and bizarrely, according to the instructions she received, "could not be political" and "had to address the theme of unity among the fifty-three member countries of the Commonwealth."[13] It would suit my purposes beautifully, if, in the presence of the Queen, Prince Philip, and the Commonwealth heads of state who attended, Marsh had explicitly riffed on "Daffodils," but she did not.

That's not quite the end of the story, however. Marsh was also invited to give the 2016 New Zealand Book Council lecture, in which she told the story of composing and delivering "Unity" in London and recited her poem in full. But first, in the opening sections of the talk, she presented the credentials of her name—Tusitala, "teller of tales"—and her literary education in a second-hand bookshop, in which, as she puts it:

> I wandered lonely through the shelves
> Junk crammed in corners and in nooks
> When all at once I saw a crowd,
> A host of Little Golden Books
> Beneath the flamingos, beneath the eaves
> Packed and stacked upon their sheaves[14]

Marsh shares the concerns about Wordsworth's poem expressed by Figiel and Helu-Thaman, writing of the colonial canon in the same Book Council lecture:

---

13. Selina Tusitala Marsh, *Tala Tusi: The Teller Is the Tale* (Wellington: New Zealand Book Council, 2016), 34.
14. Marsh, 19.

This canon still forms the core of an overwhelmingly Eurocentric education curriculum taught throughout the Pacific. Of course there's a place for the memorisation of Wordsworth's "Daffodils." . . . [But] when you're in Tonga or Sāmoa memorising Wordsworth and don't even know what a daffodil looks like, then, Houston—or rather Ha'apai—we have a problem.[15]

Like Helu-Thaman and Figiel, Marsh is able to inhabit the language of Wordsworth's poem, quote bits of it back to an audience largely composed of settler interlocutors, but also make it something entirely new. The spark that Figiel and Marsh, in particular, generate from Wordsworth's words is based on their extraordinary ability to both use and transcend them, to capture their particular cadences and forms while turning them to a critique of colonial education. You need to know the poem well in order to do this; moreover, your *audience* needs to know it well, too. Both poet and interlocutor need to acknowledge the daffodil gap and also be willing to link arms across it.

When you then encounter "Unity" later in the course of Marsh's New Zealand Book Council lecture and the story of her reciting the poem at Westminster Abbey in front of the Commonwealth heads of state, you have thus already been primed to think of Wordsworth's "Daffodils" as a kind of ironic intertext, something that Marsh herself has internalized and has at her disposal, but has moved well beyond. Marsh reinforces this impression by stressing that one of her intentions in the poem was to deal with both climate change and the "stubbornly Eurocentric educational curriculum in our 'postcolonial' era," an echo of her previous comment about memorizing Wordsworth.[16] As you read "Unity," then, little bits of Wordsworth start to flash upon your inward eye because of that priming: her "vast constellations" (28) speaking to his "stars that shine / and twinkle on the milky way" (7–8), her carefully spaced and deliberately abstracted "common wealth" (33) calling up the "wealth the shew to me had brought" (18).[17] Little bits of Wordsworth were being diplomatically

---

15. Marsh, 20–21.

16. Marsh, 35.

17. References to "Daffodils" are to the text of "I wandered lonely as a cloud" in William Wordsworth, *The Poems*, vol. 1, ed. John O. Hayden (New Haven, CT: Yale University Press, 1977).

spoken back in a setting that brought together all the politics and poetry of the British Empire.

There is another way in which we need to come to terms with Romanticism, then, and that is the striking failure of its words, and the values those words seem to encode, to guide the behavior of its followers and descendants. It would be hard to imagine a body of English literature better suited to conceptualizing a universal humanism; a respect for land, nature, and our unity with them; an attentiveness to memory and its shaping powers; a reverence for all generations of people, living, dead, and emerging; a commitment to rights and freedoms; and a rejection of imperialism and its associated violence. And yet every time this body of writing was summoned up by Indigenous thinkers, in the service of reconciliation, sympathy, memory, history, genealogy, and land, it was treated by settler-imperial governments and publics as nothing more than fantasy.

It would serve us all better, in that case, to come to terms with Romanticism by handing over the moral and aesthetic power we invest in British Romantic poetry to modern-day diplomats like Marsh. "Unity," despite the organizers' brief to the poet, could not help but be a political poem, given the identity of the author, the nature of the audience, and the setting of the performance. In a spirit that I would like to call Romantic but I think would be more accurately labeled Pacific, Marsh spoke of the catastrophic effects of climate change on countries like her mother's Tuvalu in terms that echo the best sentiments of British Romanticism:

> We're connected by currents of humanity
> alliances, allegiances, histories
> *for the salt in the sea, like the salt in our blood*
> *like the dust of our bones,*
> *our final return to mud.* (5–8; emphasis in the original)

She did not quote any Romantic poetry that day in Westminster Abbey, nor should she have; that approach to diplomacy, which situates Indigenous rights within the frameworks of British Romanticism, has never succeeded. We are not yet at the point where "some traveller from New Zealand shall, in the midst of a vast solitude, take his stand on a broken arch of London Bridge to sketch the ruins of St. Paul's."[18] But when

---

18. Macaulay, *Critical and Historical Essays*, 3: 209.

Selina Tusitala Marsh took her stand in Westminster Abbey, she talked over and past the Romantic authors to demand from British and settler governments a commitment to the just, natural, and unified world those poets too seemed to demand.

Coda

There's a photo I saw for the first time recently. It shows an elderly woman who looks a bit like me, smiling shyly and standing at attention, like a soldier. She's turned in a three-quarter pose, so your eye is focused on the line from her shoulder down her body. And slung over that shoulder, somewhat incongruously for a photograph in the *New Zealand Woman's Weekly* magazine in the 1970s, is a musket. That woman is my great-grandmother, Jessie Wood. And that musket belonged to Hone Heke.

Hone Heke (1807?–1850) was a leading figure in Ngāpuhi, the dominant iwi in the north of Aotearoa New Zealand and a notable diplomat and revolutionary figure. He is best known for cutting down the flagstaff that flew the British flag at Kororāreka, but he was also the first person to sign the Treaty of Waitangi, as noted in chapter 5. In 1848 or 1849, he gave this musket as a token of friendship to my great-great-great-grandfather William Wells, who had emigrated to Aotearoa from Berkshire in England in 1842. When Wells died, the musket passed to his daughter Harriet, and then to her daughter, Jessie. Family history suggests that Harriet welcomed many visitors to her home to see the musket and that my great-grandparents would also occasionally hear a knock at the door of their house in Grey Lynn, Auckland, as "small groups of Ngapuhi would turn up and ask to hold the gun."[1]

In 1972, Jessie made a decision, in consultation with members of our family. The musket, which she and her mother had cared for, was to be given to what was then called Waitangi House, the former residence of James Busby, the official British resident in Aotearoa New Zealand,

---

1. Peter Wood, *The Story of William and Sarah Wells* (Wellington: First Edition, 2010), 49. The full story of the musket is told on pp. 49–62.

at the treaty grounds at Waitangi (a place I discussed in chapter 5). The family appears to have had offers for the item from the Auckland Museum (and perhaps also from wealthy overseas collectors). But Jessie was adamant that it should go to Waitangi. In a conversation recorded by her grandson Peter Wood, she said: "[A relation] used to say: 'Don't you let anyone have that gun.' But what is the good of keeping it here in the room. I'd sooner give it to the museum because they've got more people who would come. It belongs with the Maoris and it was used by Hone Heke and really should go to Waitangi."[2] Hone Heke's musket is, potentially, an important object in Romantic-era diplomacy. There is strong evidence to suggest that it was one of the muskets originally presented to the chiefs Waikato and Hongi Hika (Hone Heke's uncle) by George IV when they visited England in 1820 (a trip on which they might have encountered Thomas Babington Macaulay in Cambridge).[3] If so, this musket is intimately wrapped up in the issues, personalities, and debates that my book has discussed.

I only met Jessie once, when I was a child, just before she died. I can only guess at her motives, based on family stories and the transcript of her conversation with Peter Wood. The transcript makes it clear that prior to 1972, she had been reluctant to part with the gun, even when asked directly by members of Ngāpuhi who came to visit it, and it is not my intention to excuse her or her conduct. But I do like to think that by the time she made the decision to relinquish the musket, she understood something important about Indigenous-settler diplomacy. Diplomacy is reciprocal, relationship-based, and intergenerational. The musket that was given by George IV to Hongi Hika and then to Hone Heke, William Wells, Harriet and Jessie, and finally back to Waitangi has to be passed back and forth in order to keep diplomatic relationships alive. Those relationships are requickened by handling and exchanging objects, by understanding what promises those objects stand for, and

---

2. Charlie Wood and Peter Wood, "Norman and Jessie Wood: 'Great Mates,'" Peter Wood, 2004, 110. The full transcript of the conversation is pp. 106–10.

3. For details of Hongi Hika and Waikato's trip to London, see Dorothy Ulrich Cloher, *Hongi Hika: Warrior Chief* (New York: Viking, 2003), 119–48; and Coll Thrush, *Indigenous London: Native Travelers at the Heart of Empire* (New Haven, CT: Yale University Press, 2016), 144–45. The Hone Heke musket has the same plaque as the one given to Waikato by George IV, and is thus presumably the musket that was originally Hongi Hika's. See Wood and Wood, 115–16.

by being willing to surrender them to the relationship itself. And those relationships extend through the centuries, right down to me.

I also like to think that Jessie understood something important about being a Pākehā settler. We have been entrusted, through diplomatic and treaty processes, with things that are not ours: stories and material objects, but also, and most significantly, natural resources and land. We can and should be good *kaitiaki* (guardians) to those things while we have them. But when the time comes, we need to be prepared to give them back, no matter how much we have come to think of them as our own. It's all diplomacy. It's all a negotiation.

Bibliography

Abram, Susan M. *Forging a Cherokee-American Alliance in the Creek War: From Creation to Betrayal.* Tuscaloosa: University of Alabama Press, 2015.
Adjaye, Joseph K. *Diplomacy and Diplomats in Nineteenth Century Asante.* Lanham, MD: University Press of America, 1984.
Allen, Chadwick. *Blood Narrative: Indigenous Identity in American Indian and Māori Literary and Activist Texts.* Durham, NC: Duke University Press, 2002.
Allen, Paula Gunn. *The Sacred Hoop: Recovering the Feminine in American Indian Traditions.* Boston: Beacon Press, 1986.
Altman, Heidi M., and Thomas N. Belt. "Reading Cherokee History through a Cherokee Lens." *Native South* 1, no. 1 (2008): 90–98.
Anderson, William L., Jane L. Brown, and Anne F. Rogers, eds. *The Payne-Butrick Papers.* 2 vols. Lincoln: University of Nebraska Press, 2010.
Anonymous. "Biography: Mr. Plaatje's Career." *African Times and Orient Review*, January 1917, 17–18. S. T. Plaatje Papers, School of Oriental and African Studies, University of London.
Appiah, Kwame Anthony. *Cosmopolitanism: Ethics in a World of Strangers.* New York: W. W. Norton, 2006.
Armstrong, Adejo. "Traditional African Diplomacy and Conflict Resolution." *Journal of Cultural Studies* 6, no. 1 (2004): 134–49.
Armstrong, Isobel. "The Gush of the Feminine: How Can We Read Women's Poetry of the Romantic Period?" In *Romantic Women Writers: Voices and Countervoices*, edited by Paula R. Feldman and Theresa M. Kelley, 13–32. Lebanon, NH: University Press of New England, 1995.
Attuquayefio, Re Sumo, Jr. "The Antecedents of Contemporary African Diplomacy: A Theoretical Study of Intertribal and International Relations in Traditional Africa." PhD thesis, American University, Washington, DC, 1969.
Barrell, John. *The Dark Side of the Landscape: The Rural Poor in English Painting 1730–1840.* Cambridge: Cambridge University Press, 1980.
Beaton, Roderick. *Byron's War: Romantic Rebellion, Greek Revolution.* Cambridge: Cambridge University Press, 2013.

Beattie, William. *Life and Letters of Thomas Campbell.* 3 vols. London: Moxon, 1849.
Beaumont, William Henry. *Report of the Natives Land Commission.* Vol. 2. Cape Town: South Africa Government Printers, 1916.
Becker, Mary Druke. "Linking Arms: The Structure of Iroquois Intertribal Diplomacy." In *Beyond the Covenant Chain: The Iroquois and Their Neighbors in Indian North America, 1600–1800,* 2nd ed., edited by Daniel K. Richter and James H. Merrell, 29–39. University Park: Penn State University Press, 2003.
Beinart, William, and Peter Delius. "The Historical Context and Legacy of the Natives Land Act of 1913." *Journal of Southern African Studies* 40, no. 4 (2014): 667–88.
Belgrave, Michael. *Historical Frictions: Māori Claims & Reinvented Histories.* Auckland, NZ: Auckland University Press, 2005.
Bellfy, Phil. *Three Fires Unity: The Anishnaabeg of the Lake Huron Borderland.* Lincoln: University of Nebraska Press, 2011.
Bellin, Joshua David. *The Demon of the Continent: Indians and the Shaping of American Literature.* University Park: Penn State University Press, 2001.
Belmessous, Saliha, ed. *Empire by Treaty: Negotiating European Expansion, 1600–1900.* Oxford: Oxford University Press, 2014.
Belmessous, Saliha. "The Problem of Indigenous Claim-Making in Colonial History." In *Native Claims: Indigenous Law against Empire, 1500–1920,* edited by Saliha Belmessous, 3–16. Oxford: Oxford University Press, 2011.
Bender, Margaret. *Signs of Cherokee Culture: Sequoyah's Syllabary in Eastern Cherokee Life.* Chapel Hill: University of North Carolina Press, 2002.
Benn, Carl. *The Iroquois in the War of 1812.* Toronto: University of Toronto Press, 1998.
Bennett, Paula Bernat, ed. *Nineteenth-Century American Women Poets: An Anthology.* Oxford: Blackwell, 1998.
Bergren, Katherine. *The Global Wordsworth: Romanticism Out of Place.* Lewisburg, PA: Bucknell University Press, 2018.
Berlant, Lauren. *The Female Complaint: The Unfinished Business of Sentimentality in American Culture.* Durham, NC: Duke University Press, 2008.
Berutti, Ronald A. "The Cherokee Cases: The Fight to Save the Supreme Court and the Cherokee Indians." *American Indian Law Review* 17, no. 1 (1992): 291–308.
Bickford-Smith, Vivian. "Revisiting Anglicisation in the Nineteenth-Century Cape Colony." *Journal of Imperial and Commonwealth History* 31, no. 2 (2003): 82–95.
Boahen, A. A. "Traditional African Diplomacy and Diplomatic Techniques." International Congress of Africanists, 3rd session, Addis Ababa, Ethiopia, 1973.
Boast, Richard. *Buying the Land, Selling the Land: Governments and Māori Land in the North Island 1865–1921.* Wellington, NZ: Victoria University Press, 2008.
Boehmer, Elleke. *Empire, the National, and the Postcolonial, 1890–1920: Resistance in Action.* Oxford: Oxford University Press, 2005.

Borrows, John. *Recovering Canada: The Resurgence of Indigenous Law*. Toronto: University of Toronto Press, 2002.

———. "Wampum at Niagara: The Royal Proclamation, Canadian Legal History, and Self-Government." In *Aboriginal and Treaty Rights in Canada: Essays on Law, Equality, and Respect for Difference*, edited by Michael Asch, 155–72. Vancouver: University of British Columbia Press, 1997.

Boudinot, Elias. Editorial. *Cherokee Phoenix*, July 9, 1828, 2.

———. Editorial. *Cherokee Phoenix*, January 28, 1829, 2.

———. Editorial. *Cherokee Phoenix, and Indians' Advocate*, June 17, 1829, 2.

———. "A New Treaty." *Cherokee Phoenix*, July 9, 1828, 2.

———. "Prospectus." *Cherokee Phoenix*, February 28, 1828, 3.

———. "Summary." *Cherokee Phoenix, and Indians' Advocate*, March 25, 1829, 3.

Boulware, Tyler. *Deconstructing the Cherokee Nation: Town, Region, and Nation among Eighteenth-Century Cherokees*. Gainesville: University of Florida Press, 2011.

Brant, John, and Robert Johnson Kerr. Letter to Lord Bathurst. January 31, 1822. Colonial Office Records, National Archives, United Kingdom, CO 42/369.

———. Letter to Lord Bathurst. February 27, 1822. Colonial Office Records, National Archives, United Kingdom, CO 42/369.

———. Letter to Lord Bathurst. March 4, 1822. Colonial Office Records, National Archives, United Kingdom, CO 42/369.

Bright, Michael. "Macaulay's New Zealander." *Arnoldian* 10, no. 1 (1982): 8–27.

"British and Foreign Seamen's Friend Society and Bethel Union." *Morning Post*, October 23–25, 1821.

Brooks, Lisa. *The Common Pot: The Recovery of Native Space in the Northeast*. Minneapolis: University of Minnesota Press, 2008.

———. "Writing and Lasting: Native Northeastern Literary History." In *The Oxford Handbook of Indigenous American Literature*, edited by James H. Cox and Daniel Heath Justice, 536–58. Oxford: Oxford University Press, 2014.

Browne, Thomas Gore. "Let the Pakeha and the Maori Be United." *Te Karere Maori or Maori Messenger* 1, no. 2 (1861): 1.

Brumble, H. David, III. *American Indian Autobiography*. Berkeley: University of California Press, 1988.

Brunson, Alfred. *A Western Pioneer*. 2 vols. New York: Arno Press, 1975.

Burke, Joseph C. "The Cherokee Cases: A Study in Law, Politics, and Morality." *Stanford Law Review* 21, no. 3 (1969): 500–531.

Burton, Antoinette, and Isabel Hofmeyr. "The Spine of Empire? Books and the Making of an Imperial Commons." In *Ten Books That Shaped the British Empire: Creating an Imperial Commons*, edited by Antoinette Burton and Isabel Hofmeyr, 1–28. Durham, NC: Duke University Press, 2014.

Butler, Marilyn. "The Orientalism of Byron's *Giaour*." In *Byron and the Limits of Fiction*, edited by Bernard Beatty and Vincent Newey, 78–96. Liverpool: Liverpool University Press, 1988.

Buzard, James. "The Uses of Romanticism: Byron and the Victorian Continental Tour." *Victorian Studies* 35, no. 1 (1991): 29–49.
Byron, Lord. *The Complete Poetical Works*. Edited by Jerome J. McGann. 7 vols. Oxford: Clarendon Press, 1980–1993.
Caison, Gina. *Red States: Indigeneity, Settler Colonialism, and Southern Studies*. Athens: University of Georgia Press, 2018.
"The Call of Chivalry." *Sheffield Independent*, July 21, 1914, 4.
Calloway, Colin G. *Pen and Ink Witchcraft: Treaties and Treaty Making in American Indian History*. Oxford: Oxford University Press, 2013.
Campbell, Robert. "Memorial to the Honourable the President and Members of the Senate of the State of Georgia." *Cherokee Phoenix, and Indians' Advocate*, April 29, 1829, 1–2.
Campbell, Thomas. "Gertrude of Wyoming." In *The Poetical Works of Thomas Campbell*, 57–94, 340–54. London: Frederick Warne, 1874.
———. "Letter to the Mohawk Chief Ahyonwaeghs, Commonly Called John Brant, Esq. of the Grand River, Upper Canada, from Thomas Campbell." *New Monthly Magazine and Literary Journal* (American Ed.) 3, no. 1 (January 1822): 97–101.
Campbell, William J. *Speculators in Empire: Iroquoia and the 1768 Treaty of Fort Stanwix*. Norman: University of Oklahoma Press, 2012.
Campisi, Jack. "National Policy, States' Rights, and Indian Sovereignty: The Case of the New York Iroquois." In *Extending the Rafters: Interdisciplinary Approaches to Iroquoian Studies*, edited by Michael K. Foster, Jack Campisi, and Marianne Mithun, 95–108. Albany: State University of New York Press, 1984.
Carleton, Hugh. *The Life of Henry Williams, Archdeacon of Waimate*. 2 vols. Auckland, NZ: Upton, 1874.
Carney, Virginia Moore. *Eastern Band Cherokee Women: Cultural Persistence in Their Letters and Speeches*. Knoxville: University of Tennessee Press, 2005.
Chambers, Ian. "The Empire Visits the Metropolis: The Red Atlantic, Spatial Habitus and the Cherokee." *Atlantic Studies* 12, no. 1 (2015): 67–89.
Champagne, Duane. *American Indian Societies: Strategies and Conditions of Political and Cultural Survival*. Cambridge, MA: Cultural Survival, 1989.
———. *Social Order and Political Change: Constitutional Governments among the Cherokee, the Choctaw, the Chickasaw and the Creek*. Stanford, CA: Stanford University Press, 1992.
Chander, Manu Samriti. *Brown Romantics: Poetry and Nationalism in the Global Nineteenth Century*. Lewisburg, PA: Bucknell University Press, 2017.
Circular Addressed to Benevolent Ladies of the United States. Boston: n.p., 1829.
"Circulation of the Scripture." *Morning Post*, October 9, 1821, 3.
Clarke, Matthew. "The 'Luxury of Woe': *The Deserted Village* and the Politics of Publication." *European Romantic Review* 26, no. 2 (2015): 165–83.

Cleland, Charles E. "Preliminary Report of the Ethnohistorical Basis of the Hunting, Fishing, and Gathering Rights of the Mille Lacs Chippewa." In *Fish in the Lakes, Wild Rice, and Game in Abundance: Testimony on Behalf of Mille Lacs Ojibwe Hunting and Fishing Rights*, edited by James M. McClurken, 1–140. East Lansing: Michigan State University Press, 2000.

Clifton, James A. "Wisconsin Death March: Explaining the Extremes in Old Northwest Indian Removal." *Transactions of the Wisconsin Academy of Sciences, Arts and Letters* 75 (1987): 1–40.

Cloher, Dorothy Ulrich. *Hongi Hika: Warrior Chief.* New York: Viking, 2003.

Colenso, William. *The Authentic and Genuine History of the Signing of the Treaty of Waitangi, New Zealand, February 5 and 6 1840: Being a Faithful and Circumstantial, though Brief, Narration of Events which Happened on that Memorable Occasion; with Copies of the Treaty in English and Maori, and of the Three Early Proclamations Respecting the Founding of the Colony.* Wellington, NZ: George Didbury, Government Printer, 1890.

Comaroff, Jean. *Body of Power, Spirit of Resistance: The Culture and History of a South African People.* Chicago: University of Chicago Press, 1985.

"Confiscated Native Lands and Other Grievances. Report of the Royal Commission to Inquire into Confiscations of Native Lands and Other Grievances Alleged by Natives." *Appendix to the Journals of the House of Representatives*, session 1 (1928): G-07.

Conley, Robert J. *The Cherokee Nation: A History.* Albuquerque: University of New Mexico Press, 2005.

Copway, George. *Life, Letters and Speeches: George Copway (Kahgegabowh).* Edited by A. Lavonne Brown Ruoff and Donald B. Smith. Lincoln: University of Nebraska Press, 1997.

———. *Running Sketches of Men and Places, in England, France, Germany, Belgium, and Scotland.* New York: J. C. Riker, 1851.

———. *The Traditional History and Characteristic Sketches of the Ojibway Nation.* Boston: Benjamin B. Mussey, 1851.

Corntassel, Jeff, Chaw-win-is, and T'lakwadzi. "Indigenous Storytelling, Truth-telling, and Community Approaches to Reconciliation." *English Studies in Canada* 35, no. 1 (2009): 137–59.

Cottingham, Myra. "Felicia Hemans's Dead and Dying Bodies." *Women's Writing* 8, no. 2 (2001): 275–94.

Cover, Robert M. "Foreword: *Nomos* and Narrative." *Harvard Law Review* 97, no. 1 (1983): 4–68.

Cumfer, Cynthia. *Separate Peoples, One Land: The Minds of Cherokees, Blacks, and Whites on the Tennessee Frontier.* Chapel Hill: University of North Carolina Press, 2007.

Curti, Merle. *The Learned Blacksmith: The Letters and Journals of Elihu Burritt.* New York: Wilson Erickson, 1937.

Curtis, Paul M. "Byron and the Politics of Editing." *Palgrave Advances in Byron Studies*, edited by Jane Stabler, 60–80. Basingstoke: Palgrave, 2007.
Cushman, Ellen. *The Cherokee Syllabary: Writing the People's Perseverance*. Norman: University of Oklahoma Press, 2011.
Dean, Janet. *Unconventional Politics: Nineteenth-Century Women Writers and U.S. Indian Policy*. Amherst: University of Massachusetts Press, 2016.
De Costa, Ravi. "Identity, Authority, and the Moral Worlds of Indigenous Petitions." *Comparative Studies in Society and History* 48, no. 3 (2006): 669–98.
Deloria, Vine, Jr. *We Talk, You Listen: New Tribes, New Turf*. New York: Macmillan, 1970.
DeVries, Laura. *Conflict in Caledonia: Aboriginal Land Rights and the Rule of Law*. Vancouver: University of British Columbia Press, 2011.
"Diary of Survey of the Indian Surrender in the District of Niagara. Surveyed by order of John Brant, Esquire, Superintendent of the Six Nations Indians." Archives of Ontario, York University, North York, Ontario, 1831, MS 924, RG1-59.
Dingley, Robert. "The Ruins of the Future: Macaulay's New Zealander and the Spirit of the Age." In *Histories of the Future: Studies in Fact, Fantasy and Science Fiction*, edited by Alan Sandison and Robert Dingley, 15–33. Basingstoke: Palgrave, 2000.
Donaldson, Laura E. "'But We Are Your Mothers, You Are Our Sons': Gender, Sovereignty, and the Nation in Early Cherokee Women's Writing." In *Indigenous Women and Feminism: Politics, Activism, Culture*, edited by Cheryl Suzack, Shari M. Huhndorf, Jeanne Perreault, and Jean Barman, 43–55. Vancouver: University of British Columbia Press, 2010.
Druke, Mary A. "Iroquois Treaties: Common Forms, Varying Interpretations." In *The History and Culture of Iroquois Diplomacy: An Interdisciplinary Guide to the Treaties of the Six Nations and Their League*, edited by Francis Jennings, William N. Fenton, Mary A. Druke, and David R. Miller, 85–98. Syracuse, NY: Syracuse University Press, 1985.
Durie, Mason. *Te Mana, Te Kāwanatanga: The Politics of Māori Self-Determination*. Oxford: Oxford University Press, 1998.
Eaton, Rachel Caroline. *John Ross and the Cherokee Indians*. New York: AMS Press, 1921.
Edmonds, Penelope. *Settler Colonialism and (Re)conciliation: Frontier Violence, Affective Performances, and Imaginative Refoundings*. Basingstoke: Palgrave, 2016.
[Edwards, John Passmore?]. "Frankfort Peace Congress." In *The Public Good; Devoted to the Advocacy of Great Principles, the Advancement of Useful Institutions, and the Elevation of Man*. Vol. 1. London: Charles Gilpin, 1850.
Elbourne, Elizabeth. "Broken Alliance: Debating Six Nations' Land Claims in 1822." *Cultural and Social History* 9, no. 4 (2012): 497–525.
Elfenbein, Andrew. *Byron and the Victorians*. Cambridge: Cambridge University Press, 1995.

"Evidence of S. T. Plaatje." *South African Native Affairs Commission, Minutes of Evidence* 4 (September 15, 1904): 264–70.

Fanon, Frantz. *Black Skin, White Masks.* Translated by Charles Lam Markmann. New York: Grove Press, 1967.

———. *The Wretched of the Earth.* Translated by Constance Farrington. New York: Grove Press, 1963.

Feldman, Paula R. "The Poet and the Profits: Felicia Hemans and the Literary Marketplace." In *Women's Poetry, Late Romantic to Late Victorian: Gender and Genre, 1830–1900*, edited by Isobel Armstrong and Virginia Blain, 71–101. Basingstoke: Palgrave, 1999.

Fenton, William N. *The Great Law and the Longhouse: A Political History of the Iroquois Confederacy.* Norman: University of Oklahoma Press, 1998.

———. "Structure, Continuity, and Change in the Process of Iroquois Treaty Making." In *The History and Culture of Iroquois Diplomacy: An Interdisciplinary Guide to the Treaties of the Six Nations and Their League*, edited by Francis Jennings, William N. Fenton, Mary A. Druke, and David R. Miller, 3–36. Syracause, NY: Syracuse University Press, 1985.

Festa, Lynn. *Sentimental Figures of Empire in Eighteenth-Century Britain and France.* Baltimore, MD: Johns Hopkins University Press, 2006.

Figiel, Sia. "Pua and Daffodils: Weaving the *Ula* in Postcolonial Oceania." *Journal of New Zealand and Pacific Studies* 4, no. 1 (2016): 5–17.

———. *They Who Do Not Grieve.* New York: Vintage, 1999.

———. *To a Young Artist in Contemplation: Poetry & Prose.* Suva, Fiji: University of the South Pacific, 1998.

Firth, Raymond. "Proverbs in Native Life, with Special Reference to those of the Maori, II (Continued)." *Folklore* 37, no. 3 (September 1926): 245–70.

Flint, Kate. *The Transatlantic Indian, 1776–1930.* Princeton, NJ: Princeton University Press, 2009.

Foster, Michael K. "On Who Spoke First at Iroquois-White Councils: An Exercise in the Method of Upstreaming." In *Extending the Rafters: Interdisciplinary Approaches to Iroquoian Studies*, edited by Michael K. Foster, Jack Campisi, and Marianne Mithun, 183–207. Albany: State University of New York Press, 1984.

Foxgate Developments Inc. v. Doe et al. 2020 ONSC 6529 (CanLII). http://canlii.ca/t/jb9rh.

Friedman, Arthur. "Introduction to *The Deserted Village*." In *Collected Works of Oliver Goldsmith*. Vol. 4, edited by Arthur Friedman, 273–74. Oxford: Clarendon Press, 1966.

Fulford, Tim. *Romantic Indians: Native Americans, British Literature, and Transatlantic Culture 1756–1830.* Oxford: Oxford University Press, 2006.

Fullagar, Kate. "Envoys of Interest: A Cherokee, a Ra'iatean, and the Eighteenth-Century British Empire." In *Facing Empire: Indigenous Experiences in a Revolutionary Age*, edited by Kate Fullagar and Michael A. McDonnell, 239–55. Baltimore, MD: Johns Hopkins University Press, 2018.

"Further Papers Relative to the Taranaki Question." *Appendix to the Journal of the House of Representatives*, session 1 (1861): E–2.

Gaul, Theresa Strouth. "Editing as Indian Performance: Elias Boudinot, Poetry, and the *Cherokee Phoenix*." In *Native Acts: Indian Performance, 1603–1832*, edited by Joshua David Bellin and Laura L. Miekle, 281–307. Lincoln: University of Nebraska Press, 2011.

Gaul, Theresa Strouth, ed. *To Marry an Indian: The Marriage of Harriett Gold and Elias Boudinot in Letters, 1823–1839*. Chapel Hill: University of North Carolina Press, 2005.

George-Kanentiio, Doug. "Atonement among the Haudenosaunee." *Indigenous Policy Journal* (Fall 2009). https://ipjournal.wordpress.com/2009/12/16/atonement-among-the-haudenosaunee/.

Gibson, Chief John Arthur. *Concerning the League: The Iroquois League Tradition as Dictated in Onondaga*. Algonquin and Iroquoian Linguistics, Memoir 9 (Syracuse, NY: Syracuse University Press, 1992).

Gilling, Bryan. "Raupatu: the Punitive Confiscation of Maori Land in the 1860s." In *Raupatu: The Confiscation of Maori Land*, edited by Richard Boast and Richard S. Hill, 13–30. Wellington, NZ: Victoria University Press, 2009.

Gleckner, Robert. *Byron and the Ruins of Paradise*. Baltimore, MD: Johns Hopkins University Press, 1967.

Goldsmith, Oliver. *Collected Works of Oliver Goldsmith*. Vol. 4. Edited by Arthur Friedman. Oxford: Clarendon Press, 1966.

Goslee, Nancy Moore. "Hemans 'Red Indians': Reading Stereotypes." In *Romanticism, Race, and Imperial Culture, 1780–1834*, edited by Alan Richardson and Sonia Hofkosh, 237–61. Bloomington: Indiana University Press, 1996.

Gourlay, Robert. *General Introduction to Statistical Account of Upper Canada, Compiled with a View of a Grand System of Emigration, in Connexion with a Reform of the Poor Laws*. London: Simpkin and Marshall, 1822.

Graymont, Barbara. *The Iroquois in the American Revolution*. Syracuse, NY: Syracuse University Press, 1972.

Green, Sarah. "An Icon of the Ignoble Savage: The Content and Consequence of Thomas Campbell's Representation of Joseph Brant as a 'Monster' in 'Gertrude of Wyoming.'" PhD thesis, University of Western Ontario, Ontario, Canada, 1995.

Gubele, Rose. "Unlearning the Pictures in Pur Heads: Teaching the *Cherokee Phoenix*, Boudinot, and Cherokee History." In *Survivance, Sovereignty, and Story: Teaching American Indian Rhetorics*, edited by Lisa King, Rose Gubele, and Joyce Rain Anderson, 96–115. Boulder: University Press of Colorado, 2015.

Haake, Claudia B. "Civilization, Law, and Customary Diplomacy: Arguments against Removal in Cherokee and Seneca Letters to the Federal Government." *NAIS: Journal of the Native American and Indigenous Studies Association* 4, no. 2 (2017): 31–51.

Hale, Horatio, ed. *The Iroquois Book of Rites*. 1883. Reprint. New York: AMS Press, 1969.
Hall, Catherine. "Macaulay's Nation." *Victorian Studies* 51, no. 3 (2009): 505–23.
Hall, Francis. *Travels in Canada, and the United States, in 1816 and 1817*. London: Longman, Hurst, Rees, Orme, and Brown, 1818.
H[all], J[ames]. "A Reminiscence." *Knickerbocker* 6 (1835): 13–14.
Hansen, Julia. "Viewless Scenes: Vividness and Nineteenth-Century Ideals of Reading in and through *Gertrude of Wyoming*." *ELH* 84, no. 4 (2017): 943–77.
Harmon, Alexandra, ed. *The Power of Promises: Rethinking Indian Treaties in the Pacific Northwest*. Seattle: University of Washington Press, 2008.
Harring, Sidney L. *White Man's Law: Native People in Nineteenth-Century Canadian Jurisprudence*. Toronto: University of Toronto Press, 1998.
Hatley, Tom. *The Dividing Paths: Cherokees and South Carolinians through the Era of Revolution*. Oxford: Oxford University Press, 1995.
Hawkins, Benjamin, Andrew Pickens, Joseph Martin, and Lachlan McIntosh. "Letter to Richard Henry Lee, President of the Congress, 2 December 1785." *American State Papers: Documents, Legislative and Executive, of the Congress of the United States, Indian Affairs*. Vol. 1, edited by Walter Lowrie and Matthew St. Clair Clarke, 40–43. Washington, DC: Gales and Seaton, 1832.
Helu-Thaman, Konai. "Of Daffodils and *Heilala*: Understanding Cultural Contexts in Pacific Literature." Multi-Ethnic Literature Society of America (MELUS) Conference, April 18–20, Honolulu, Hawaii, 1997.
Hemans, Felicia. "A Parting Song." *Cherokee Phoenix*, October 1, 1828, 4.
———. "Dreams of Heaven." *Cherokee Phoenix, and Indians' Advocate*, November 19, 1831, 4.
———. "Evening Song of the Tyrolese Peasants." *Cherokee Phoenix*, July 9, 1828, 4.
———. "The Indian with His Dead Child." *Cherokee Phoenix, and Indians' Advocate*, July 8, 1829, 4.
———. "Lines to an Orphan." *Cherokee Phoenix, and Indians' Advocate*, December 3, 1829, 4.
———. "The Meeting of the Ships." *Cherokee Phoenix, and Indians' Advocate*, March 18, 1829, 4.
———. "Nature's Farewell." *Cherokee Phoenix*, September 17, 1828, 4.
———. "The Ruined House." *Cherokee Phoenix, and Indians' Advocate*, September 9, 1829, 4.
———. "Song." *Cherokee Phoenix*, August 6, 1828, 4.
———. "The Sunbeam." *Cherokee Phoenix, and Indians' Advocate*, February 18, 1829, 4.
———. "The Treasures of the Sea." *Cherokee Phoenix*, January 28, 1829, 4.
———. "The Two Homes." *Cherokee Phoenix, and Indians' Advocate*, June 17, 1829, 4.
———. "The Voice of the Waves." *Cherokee Phoenix, and Indians' Advocate*, January 13, 1830, 4.

———. "Woman and Fame." *Cherokee Phoenix, and Indians' Advocate*, March 25, 1829, 4.

———. "The Wounded Eagle." *Cherokee Phoenix*, May 6, 1828, 4.

Henderson, Archibald. "The Treaty of Long Island at Holston, July, 1777." *North Carolina Historical Review* 8, no. 1 (1931): 55–116.

Hershberger, Mary. "Mobilizing Women, Anticipating Abolition: The Struggle against Indian Removal in the 1830s." *Journal of American History* 86, no. 1 (1999): 15–40.

Hessell, Nikki. *Romantic Literature and the Colonised World: Lessons from Indigenous Translations*. Basingstoke: Palgrave, 2018.

———. "The Task of Indigenous Translators." *The East Is a Podcast*, episode 15, December 14, 2018. https://eastisapodcast.libsyn.com/the-tasks-of-indigenous-translators-w-nikki-hessel.

Hickford, Mark. "Strands from the Afterlife of Confiscation: Property Rights, Constitutional Histories and the Political Incorporation of Maori, 1920s." In *Raupatu: The Confiscation of Maori Land*, edited by Richard Boast and Richard S. Hill, 169–204. Wellington, NZ: Victoria University Press, 2009.

Hill, Chief G. Ava. *Six Nations Council: United Nations Fourteenth Session of the Permanent Forum on Indigenous Issues*. Six Nations Council, April 2015. http://www.sixnations.ca/UnitedNationsApril2015PresentationChiefHill.pdf.

Hill, Richard S. *Enthroning "Justice above Might"? The Sim Commission, Tainui and the Crown*. Washington, DC: U.S. Department of Justice, 1989.

Hill, Susan M. *The Clay We Are Made Of: Haudenosaunee Land Tenure on the Grand River*. Winnipeg: University of Manitoba Press, 2017.

Hofmeyr, Isabel. *The Portable Bunyan: A Transnational History of* The Pilgrim's Progress. Princeton, NJ: Princeton University Press, 2004.

Holt, Keri. "'We, Too, the People': Rewriting Resistance in the Cherokee Nation." In *Mapping Region in Early American Writing*, edited by Edward Watts, Keri Holt, and John Funchion, 199–225. Athens: University of Georgia Press, 2015.

Howey, Meghan C. L. "'The Question Which Has Puzzled, and Still Puzzles': How American Indian Authors Challenged Dominant Discourse about Native American Origins in the Nineteenth Century." *American Indian Quarterly* 34, no. 3 (2010): 435–74.

Hudson, Angela Pulley. "'Forked Justice': Elias Boudinot, the US Constitution, and Cherokee Removal." In *American Indian Rhetorics of Survivance: Word Medicine, Word Magic*, edited by Ernest Stromberg, 50–65. Pittsburgh: University of Pittsburgh Press, 2006.

[Hughes, Harriet]. *Memoir of the Life and Writings of Mrs. Hemans. By Her Sister*. Philadelphia: Lea and Blanchard, 1840.

Hutchings, Kevin. "'The Nobleness of the Hunter's Deed': British Romanticism, Christianity and Ojibwa Culture in George Copway's *Recollections of a Forest Life*." In *Native Americans and Anglo-American Culture, 1750–1850*, edited by Tim Fulford and Kevin Hutchings, 217–40. Cambridge: Cambridge University Press, 2009.

———. *Romantic Ecologies and Colonial Cultures in the British-Atlantic World 1770–1850*. Montreal: McGill-Queen's University Press, 2009.

Irwin, Graham W. "Precolonial African Diplomacy: The Example of Asante." *International Journal of African Historical Studies* 8, no. 1 (1975): 81–96.

Jacobson, Marcelle, ed. *The Silas T. Molema and Solomon T. Plaatje Papers*. Johannesburg: University of the Witwatersrand, 1978.

Jameson, Anna. *Winter Studies and Summer Rambles in Canada*. 3 vols. London: Saunders and Otley, 1838.

Johns, Sheridan, III, ed. "South African Native National Congress." In *An Appeal to the Members of the Imperial Parliament and Public of Great Britain, from Protest to Challenge*, 130–33. Stanford, CA: Hoover Institution Press, 1972.

Johnson, David. *Shakespeare and South Africa*. Oxford University Press, 1996.

Johnston, Basil. *Ojibway Ceremonies*. Toronto: McClelland and Stewart, 1982.

Johnston, Charles M., ed. *The Valley of the Six Nations: A Collection of Documents on the Indian Lands of the Grand River*. Toronto: Champlain Society, 1964.

Jones, Daniel, and Solomon Tshekisho Plaatje. *A Sechuana Reader*. London: University of London Press, 1916.

Justice, Daniel Heath. *Our Fire Survives the Storm: A Cherokee Literary History*. Minneapolis: University of Minnesota Press, 2006.

———. *Why Indigenous Literatures Matter*. Waterloo: Wilfrid Laurier University Press, 2018.

Kappler, Charles Joseph, ed. *Indian Affairs: Laws and Treaties*. Vol. 5. Washington, DC: U.S. Department of the Interior, 1941.

———. "Treaty with the Cherokee, 1785." In *Indian Affairs: Laws and Treaties*. Volume 2: *Treaties*, 8–11. Washington, DC: U.S. Government Printing Office, 1904.

Kaul, Suvir. *Poems of Nation, Anthems of Empire: English Verse in the Long Eighteenth Century*. Charlottesville: University Press of Virginia, 2000.

Ke-Che-Ha-Gah-Me-Qua. *Sketch of the Life of Captain Joseph Brant, Thayendanagea*. Montreal: John Dougall, 1873.

Kelderman, Frank. *Authorized Agents: Publication and Diplomacy in the Era of Indian Removal*. Albany: State University of New York Press, 2019.

Kelly, Gary. "Death and the Matron: Felicia Hemans, Romantic Death, and the Founding of the Modern Liberal State." In *Felicia Hemans: Reimagining Poetry in the Nineteenth Century*, edited by Nanora Sweet and Julie Melnyk, 196–211. Basingstoke: Palgrave, 2001.

Kelsay, Isabel Thompson. *Joseph Brant 1743–1807: Man of Two Worlds*. Syracuse, NY: Syracuse University Press, 1984.

Kim, Benjamin. *Wordsworth, Hemans, and Politics, 1800–1830: Romantic Crises*. Lewisburg, PA: Bucknell University Press, 2013.

King, Lisa, Rose Gubele, and Joyce Rain Anderson. "Introduction: Careful with the Stories We Tell: Naming Survivance, Sovereignty, and Story." In *Survivance, Sovereignty, and Story: Teaching American Indian Rhetorics*, edited by Lisa King, Rose Gubele, and Joyce Rain Anderson, 3–16. Boulder: University of Press of Colorado, 2015.

Knezevich, Ruth. "The Empire of the Page: Footnotes in Byron's *The Giaour*." *Essays in Romanticism* 24, no. 1 (2017): 35–52.

Kohere, Rarawa. "Kohere, Mokena." Te Ara: The Encyclopedia of New Zealand. Wellington: New Zealand Government Ministry for Culture and Heritage, 1990. http://www.teara.govt.nz/en/biographies/1k15/kohere-mokena.

———. "Tāwakewake: An Historical Case Study and Situational Analysis of Ngāti Ruawaipu Leadership." PhD thesis, Massey University, Wellington, New Zealand, 2005.

Kohere, Rēweti T. "Charge of Bias against Judges J. Harvey and E. M. Beechey." National Archives of New Zealand, MA1, Box 112, Wellington, New Zealand.

———. "He Kupu Tohunga." *Te Toa Takitini*, October 1926, 479–82.

———. Letter, February 12, 1935. National Archives of New Zealand, MA1, Box 112, Wellington, New Zealand.

———. Letter, June 3, 1950. National Archives of New Zealand, MA1, Box 113, Wellington, New Zealand.

———. Letter, June 29, 1953. National Archives of New Zealand, MA1, Box 113, Wellington, New Zealand.

[Kohere, Rēweti T.] "Nui Tireni me Tona Iwi Maori." *Te Toa Takitini*, August 1926, 435.

———. *The Story of a Maori Chief*. Wellington, NZ: Reed, 1949.

Kōhere Rēweti T., et al. Petition no. 97, 1947. National Archives of New Zealand, MA1, Box 112, Wellington, New Zealand.

———. Petition no. 98, 1929. National Archives of New Zealand, MA1, Box 111, Wellington, New Zealand.

———. Petition no. 87, 1930. National Archives of New Zealand, MA1, Box 111, Wellington, New Zealand.

Kohl, Johann Georg. *Kitchi-Gami: Life among the Lake Superior Ojibway*. 1860. Reprint. Nepean, Ontario: Borealis Books, 1985.

Konkle, Maureen. *Writing Indian Nations: Native Intellectuals and the Politics of Historiography, 1827–1863*. Chapel Hill: University of North Carolina Press, 2004.

Krupat, Arnold. *Ethnocriticism: Ethnography, History, Literature*. Berkeley: University of California Press, 1992.

Kugel, Rebecca. *To Be the Main Leaders of Our People: A History of Minnesota Ojibwe Politics, 1825–1898*. East Lansing: Michigan State University Press, 2012.

Lancaster, Barry. "Goh-Soh-Gwa-Go, The Indian Commander at Wyoming." *Allegheny Mail*, July 10, 1849.

Land Rights: A Global Solution. Ontario: Six Nations Lands and Resources Department, 2015.

Leask, Nigel. *British Romantic Writers and the East: Anxieties of Empire*. Cambridge: Cambridge University Press, 1992.

Lester, Alan, and Zoë Laidlaw. "Indigenous Sites and Mobilities: Connected Struggles in the Long Nineteenth Century." In *Indigenous Communities and Settler Colonialism: Land Holding, Loss and Survival in an Interconnected World*, 1–23. Basingstoke: Palgrave, 2015.

"Letter to the Delegation of the State of Connecticut, from an Association of Ladies." *Cherokee Phoenix, and Indians' Advocate*, March 12, 1831, 3.

Levinson, Marjorie. *The Romantic Fragment Poem: A Critique of a Form*. Chapel Hill: University of North Carolina Press, 1986.

Lootens, Tricia. "Hemans and Her American Heirs: Nineteenth-Century Women's Poetry and National Identity." In *Women's Poetry, Late Romantic to Late Victorian: Gender and Genre, 1830–1900*, edited by Isobel Armstrong and Virginia Blain, 243–60. Basingstoke: Macmillan, 1999.

———. "Hemans and Home: Victorianism, Feminine 'Internal Enemies,' and the Domestication of National Identity." *PMLA* 109, no. 2 (1994): 238–53.

Lopenzina, Drew. *Red Ink: Native Americans Picking Up the Pen in the Colonial Period*. Albany: State University of New York Press, 2012.

Lutz, Alfred. "'The Deserted Village' and the Politics of Genre." *Modern Language Quarterly* 55, no. 2 (1994): 149–68.

———. "The Politics of Reception: The Case of Goldsmith's 'The Deserted Village.'" *Studies in Philology* 95, no. 2 (1998): 174–96.

Lydon, Jane. *Imperial Emotions: The Politics of Empathy across the British Empire*. Cambridge: Cambridge University Press, 2019.

Lyons, Scott Richard. "Migrations to Modernity: The Many Voices of George Copway's *Running Sketches of Men and Places, in England, France, Germany, Belgium, and Scotland*." In *The World, the Text, and the Indian: Global Dimensions of American Literature*, 143–82. Albany: State University of New York Press, 2017.

———. "Rhetorical Sovereignty: What Do American Indians Want From Writing?" *College Composition and Communication* 53, no. 3 (2000): 447–68.

———. *X-Marks: Native Signatures of Assent*. Minneapolis: University of Minnesota Press, 2010.

Lytle, Clifford M. "The Supreme Country, Tribal Sovereignty, and Continuing Problems of State Encroachment into Indian Country." *American Indian Law Review* 8, no. 1 (1980): 65–77.

Macaulay, Thomas Babington. *Critical and Historical Essays, Contributed to the Edinburgh Review*. 5th ed. Vol. 3. London: Longman, Brown, Green, and Longmans, 1848.

———. *The Letters of Thomas Babington Macaulay*. Edited by Thomas Pinney. Cambridge: Cambridge University Press, 1981. 6 vols.

———. *The Life and Works of Lord Macaulay*. Vol. 8. London: Longmans, Green, 1897.

Mahuta, Robert Te Kotahi. "Whaikoorero: A Study of Formal Maori Speech." PhD. diss., University of Auckland, New Zealand, 1974.

Mar, Tracey Banivanua. "Imperial Literacy and Indigenous Rights: Tracing Transoceanic Circuits of a Modern Discourse." *Aboriginal History* 37 (2013): 1–28.

Marsh, Selina Tusitala. *Tala Tusi: The Teller Is The Tale a New Zealand Book Council Lecture*. Wellington: New Zealand Book Council, 2016.

Martin, Meredith. "'Imperfectly Civilized': Ballads, Nations, and Histories of Form." *ELH* 82, no. 2 (2015): 345–63.

Martini, Elspeth. "Shawundais and the Methodist Mission to Native North America." In *Facing Empire: Indigenous Experiences in a Revolutionary Age*, edited by Kate Fullagar and Michael A. McDonnell, 303–30. Baltimore, MD: Johns Hopkins University Press, 2018.

Mason, Emma. *Women Poets of the Nineteenth Century*. Blackburn, U.K.: Northcote, 2006.

Matjila, D. S., and Karen Haire. *Bringing Plaatje Back Home—Ga E Phetsolele Nageng: 'Re-Storying' the African and Batswana Sensibilities in His Oeuvre*. Trenton, NJ: Africa World Press, 2015.

McCarthy, Theresa. *In Divided Unity: Haudenosaunee Reclamation at Grand River*. Tucson: University of Arizona Press, 2016.

McCoy, Joseph J. *The Frontier Maid. A Poem*. Wilkes-Barre, PA: Butler and Maffet, 1819.

McGann, Jerome J. "The Composition, Revision, and Meaning of Childe Harold's Pilgrimage III." *Bulletin of the New York Public Library* 71, no. 7 (1967): 415–30.

———. *Fiery Dust: Byron's Poetic Development*. Chicago: University of Chicago Press, 1968.

McKenzie, D. F. *Oral Culture, Literacy and Print in Early New Zealand: The Treaty of Waitangi*. Wellington, NZ: Victoria University Press, 1985.

McLoughlin, William G. *After the Trail of Tears: The Cherokees' Struggle for Sovereignty, 1839–1880*. Chapel Hill: University of North Carolina Press, 1993.

———. *Cherokee Renascence in the New Republic*. Princeton, NJ: Princeton University Press, 1986.

McNally, Michael D. *Ojibwe Singers: Hymns, Grief, and a Native Culture in Motion*. Oxford: Oxford University Press, 2000.

Mead, Hirini Moko. *Tikanga Māori: Living By Māori Values*. Wellington, NZ: Huia Publishers, 2003.

Mellor, Anne K. *Romanticism and Gender*. New York: Routledge, 1993.

"Memorial of John Ross, Richard Taylor, [E]dward Gunter, and William S. Coody, Representatives of the Cherokee Nation of Indians." *Cherokee Phoenix, and Indians' Advocate*, June 17, 1829, 1.

"Memorial of the Ladies of Steubenville, Ohio, against the Forcible Removal of the Indians Without the Limits of the United States." *United States Documents Serial*, vol. 200, doc. 209, February 15, 1830.
M'Henry, James. *The Betrothed of Wyoming: An Historical Tale.* Philadelphia: n.p., 1830.
Miles, Tiya. "'Circular Reasoning': Recentering Cherokee Women in the Antiremoval Campaigns." *American Quarterly* 61, no. 2 (2009): 221–43.
Miller, Cary. *Ogimaag: Anishinaabeg Leadership, 1760–1845.* Lincoln: University of Nebraska Press, 2010.
"Minutes of the Indian Council held on Burlington Heights 24 April 1815." Murray Papers. Adv.MSS.46.6.5, National Library of Scotland, Edinburgh, United Kingdom.
"Miscellaneous Epitome." *Norwich Chronicle and Norwich Gazette*, October 13, 1821, 2.
Mkhize, Khwezi. "African Intellectual History, Black Cosmopolitanism and *Native Life in South Africa*." In *Sol Plaatje's "Native Life in South Africa": Past and Present*, edited by Janet Remmington, Brian Willan, and Bhekizizwe Peterson, 95–114. Johannesburg: Wits University Press, 2016.
Mole, Tom. "Spurgeon, Byron, and the Contingencies of Mediation." *Romanticism and Victorianism on the Net* 57–58 (2010 [pub. 2012]).
Molema, Seetsele Modiri. *Lover of His People: A Biography of Sol Plaatje.* Translated by D. S. Matjila and Karen Haire. Johannesburg: Wits University Press, 2012.
———. *Montshiwa 1815–1896: Barolong Chief and Patriot.* Cape Town: Struik, 1966.
Montague, John. "The Sentimental Prophecy: A Study of *The Deserted Village*." In *The Art of Oliver Goldsmith*, edited by Andrew Swarbrick, 90–106. London: Vision, 1984.
Montiero, Lorrie, ed. "Family Stories from the Trail of Tears." Little Rock, AR: American Native Press Archives and Sequoyah Research Center, 1937. https://ualrexhibits.org/tribalwriters/artifacts/Family-Stories-Trail-of-Tears.html.
Monture, Rick. *Teionkwakhashion Tsi Niionkwariho:ten: We Share Our Matters: Two Centuries of Writing and Resistance at Six Nations of the Grand River.* Winnipeg: University of Manitoba Press, 2014.
Mooney, James. *Myths of the Cherokee.* Washington, DC: U.S. Government Printing Office, 1902.
Morgan, Cecilia. "Kahgegagahbowh's (George Copway's) Transatlantic Performance." *Cultural and Social History* 9, no. 4 (2012): 527–48.
———. "Site of Dispossession, Site of Persistence: The Haudenosaunee (Six Nations) at the Grand River Territories in the Nineteenth and Twentieth Centuries." In *Indigenous Communities and Settler Colonialism: Land Holding, Loss and Survival in an Interconnected World*, edited by Zoë Laidlaw and Alan Lester, 194–213. Basingstoke: Palgrave, 2015.
Ndana, Ndana. "Of 'Disinclined Trains and Clever Actors to Be Admired and Not Followed': Sol Plaatje, William Shakespeare and the Dilemma of the

African Intellectual 1894–1920s." *Marang: Journal of Language and Literature* 18 (2008): 161–70.

Nelson, Joshua B. *Progressive Traditions: Identity in Cherokee Literature and Culture.* Norman: University of Oklahoma Press, 2014.

New England Company Minute Book. November 8, 1816–May 11, 1830. MS7920/2, London Metropolitan Archives, London, United Kingdom.

Newey, Vincent. "Goldsmith's 'Pensive Plain': Re-viewing *The Deserted Village*." In *Early Romantics: Perspectives in British Poetry from Pope to Wordsworth*, edited by Thomas M. Woodman, 93–116. Basingstoke: Macmillan, 1998.

Nga Korero Paremete. Washington, DC: U.S. Government Printing Office, 1904.

Nichols, John D., ed. *Statement Made By the Indians: A Bilingual Petition of the Chippewas of Lake Superior, 1864.* London: University of Western Ontario, 1988.

Nichols, John D. "The Translation of Key Phrases in the Treaties of 1837 and 1855." In *Fish in the Lakes, Wild Rice, and Game in Abundance: Testimony on Behalf of Mille Lacs Ojibwe Hunting and Fishing Rights*, edited by James M. McClurken, 514–24. East Lansing: Michigan State University Press, 2000.

Norgren, Jill. *The Cherokee Cases: The Confrontation of Law and Politics.* New York: McGraw-Hill, 1996.

Odendaal, André. "'Native Lives' behind *Native Life*: Intellectual and Political Influences on the ANC and Democratic South Africa." In *Sol Plaatje's Native Life in South Africa: Past and Present*, edited by Janet Remmington, Brian Willan, and Bhekizizwe Peterson, 115–46. Johannesburg: Wits University Press, 2016.

O'Leary, John. "'Unlocking the Fountains of the Heart'—Settler Verse and the Politics of Sympathy." *Postcolonial Studies* 13, no. 1 (2010): 55–70.

Opondo, Sam Okoth. "Decolonizing Diplomacy: Reflections of African Estrangement and Exclusion." In *Sustainable Diplomacies*, edited by Costas M. Constantinou and James Der Derian, 109–27. Basingstoke: Palgrave, 2010.

Orange, Claudia. *The Treaty of Waitangi*. 2nd ed. Wellington, NZ: Bridget Williams Books, 2011.

Parisi, Laura, and Jeff Corntassel. "A 'Revolution within a Revolution': Indigenous Women's Diplomacies." In *Indigenous Diplomacies*, edited by J. Marshall Beier, 79–95. Basingstoke: Palgrave, 2009.

Parsons, Neil. "Southern African Royalty and Delegates Visit Queen Victoria, 1882–95." In *Mistress of Everything: Queen Victoria in Indigenous Worlds*, edited by Sarah Carter and Maria Nugent, 166–83. Manchester: Manchester University Press, 2016.

Paterson, Lachy. "The Kohimārama Conference of 1860: A Contextual Reading." *Journal of New Zealand Studies* 12 (2011): 29–46.

Paxton, James W. *Joseph Brant and His World: 18th Century Mohawk Warrior and Statesman.* Toronto: James Lorimer, 2008.

"Penn, William" [Jeremiah Evarts]. "Cherokee Treaty Rights, from *The New York American*, 15 September 1829." *Journal of Cherokee Studies* 4, no. 2 (1979): 71–74.

Penner, Robert. "The Ojibwe Renaissance: Transnational Evangelicalism and the Making of an Algonquian Intelligentsia, 1812–1867." *American Review of Canadian Studies* 45, no. 1 (2015): 71–92.

Perdue, Theda, ed. *Cherokee Editor: The Writings of Elias Boudinot.* Knoxville: University of Tennessee Press, 1983.

Perdue, Theda. *Cherokee Women: Gender and Culture Change, 1700–1835.* Lincoln: University of Nebraska Press, 1998.

———. "Cherokee Women and the Trail of Tears." In *Native Women's History in Eastern North America before 1900: A Guide to Research and Writing*, edited by Rebecca Kugel and Lucy Eldersveld Murphy, 277–302. Lincoln: University of Nebraska Press, 2007.

Perdue, Theda, and Michael H. Green. *The Cherokee Nation and the Trail of Tears.* New York: Viking, 2007.

Peterson, Bhekizizwe. "Sol Plaatje's *Native Life in South Africa:* Melancholy Narratives, Petitioning Selves and the Ethics of Suffering." *Journal of Commonwealth Literature* 43, no. 1 (2008): 79–95.

Peyer, Bernd. "A Nineteenth-Century Ojibwa Conquers Germany." In *Germans and Indians: Fantasies, Encounters, Projections*, edited by Colin G. Calloway, Gerd Gemünden, and Susanne Zantop, 141–64. Lincoln: University of Nebraska Press, 2002.

———. *The Tutor'd Mind: Indian Missionary-Writers in Antebellum America.* Amherst: University of Massachusetts Press, 1997.

Pinch, Adela. *Strange Fits of Passion: Epistemologies of Emotion, Hume to Austen.* Stanford, CA: Stanford University Press, 1996.

Plaatje, Solomon T. *Native Life in South Africa.* Edited by Brian Willan. 1916. Reprint. New York: Picador, 2007.

———. *Sechuana Proverbs with Literal Translations and Their European Equivalents.* London: Kegan Paul, 1916.

———. *Some of the Legal Disabilities Suffered by the Native Population of the Union of South Africa and Imperial Responsibility.* London: St. Clements Press, 1917.

———. "A South African's Homage." In *A Book of Homage to Shakespeare*, edited by Israel Gollancz, 336–39. Oxford: Oxford University Press, 1916.

———. "With Apologies to Shakespeare's 'Merchant of Venice.'" *English in Africa* 3, no. 2 (1976): 7.

Portnoy, Alisse. *Their Right to Speak: Women's Activism in the Indian and Slave Debates* Cambridge, MA: Harvard University Press, 2005.

Proceedings of the First Kotahitanga Parliament. June 14, 1892.

"Proceedings of the Kohimarama Conference, Comprising Nos. 13 to 18 of the 'Maori Messenger.'" *New Zealand Electronic Text Collection: Te Pūhikotuhi o Aotearoa.* Auckland: Kohimarama Conference, 1860.

Redding, Cyrus. *Literary Reminiscences and Memoirs of Thomas Campbell.* 2 vols. London: Charles J. Skeet, 1860.

Reder, Deanna. "Âcimisowin as Theoretical Practice: Autobiography as Indigenous Intellectual Tradition in Canada." PhD thesis, University of British Columbia, Vancouver, Canada, 2007.

Redix, Erik M. *The Murder of Joe White: Ojibwe Leadership and Colonialism in Wisconsin.* East Lansing: Michigan State University Press, 2014.

Remmington, Janet. "Going Places: *Native Life in South Africa* and the Politics of Mobility." In *Sol Plaatje's* Native Life in South Africa: *Past and Present*, edited by Janet Remmington, Brian Willan, and Bhekizizwe Peterson, 54–80. Johannesburg: Wits University Press, 2016.

Report of the Proceedings of the Third General Peace Congress, Held in Frankfort, on the 22nd, 23rd, and 24th of August, 1850. London: Charles Gilpin, 1851.

Reville, F. Douglas. *History of the County of Brant.* Brantford, Ontario: Hurley Printing Company, 1920.

Rewi, Poia. *Whaikōrero: The World of Māori Oratory.* Auckland, NZ: Auckland University Press, 2010.

Rex, Cathy. "Survivance and Fluidity: George Copway's *The Life, History, and Travels of Kah-ge-ga-gah-bowh.*" *Studies in American Indian Literatures* 18, no. 2 (2006): 1–33.

Richardson, Robbie. *The Savage and the Modern Self: North American Indians in Eighteenth-Century British Literature and Culture.* Toronto: University of Toronto Press, 2018.

Richter, Daniel K. *The Ordeal of the Longhouse: The Peoples of the Iroquois League in the Era of European Colonization.* Chapel Hill: University of North Carolina Press, 1992.

Rothstein, David. "Forming the Chivalric Subject: Felicia Hemans and the Cultural Uses of History, Memory, and Nostalgia." *Victorian Literature and Culture* 27, no. 1 (1999): 49–68.

Round, Phillip H. *Removable Type: Histories of the Book in Indian Country, 1663–1880.* Chapel Hill: University of North Carolina Press, 2010.

Rudy, Jason R. "Hemans' Passion." *Studies in Romanticism* 45, no. 4 (2006): 543–62.

———. *Imagined Homelands: British Poetry in the Colonies.* Baltimore, MD: Johns Hopkins University Press, 2017.

Ruoff, A. LaVonne Brown. "The Literary and Methodist Contexts of George Copway's *Life, Letters and Speeches.*" In *Life, Letters & Speeches: George Copway (Kahgegagahbowh)*, edited by A. LaVonne Brown Ruoff and Donald B. Smith, 1–21. Lincoln: University of Nebraska Press, 1997.

Ryan, Susan M. *The Grammar of Good Intentions: Race and the Antebellum Culture of Benevolence.* Ithaca, NY: Cornell University Press, 2003.

Sadosky, Leonard J. *Revolutionary Negotiations: Indians, Empires, and Diplomats in the Founding of America.* Charlottesville: University of Virginia Press, 2009.

Saler, Bethel. *The Settlers' Empire: Colonialism and State Formation in America's Old Northwest.* University Park: Penn State University Press, 2014.

Salmond, Anne. *Hui: A Study of Maori Ceremonial Gatherings*. New York: Penguin, 2004.
Sapire, Hilary. "'We Have Seen the Son of Heaven / We Have Seen the Son of Our Queen:' African Encounters with Prince Alfred on His Royal Tour, 1860." In *Mistress of Everything: Queen Victoria in Indigenous Worlds*, edited by Sarah Carter and Maria Nugent, 25–53. Manchester: Manchester University Press, 2016.
Satz, Ronald N. "Chippewa Treaty Rights: The Reserved Rights of Wisconsin's Chippewa Indians in Historical Perspective." *Transactions of the Wisconsin Academy of Sciences, Arts and Letters* 79, no. 1 (1991).
Schalkwyk, David. "Portrait and Proxy: Representing Plaatje and Plaatje Represented." *Scrutiny2* 4, no. 2 (1999): 14–29.
Schalkwyk, David, and Lerothodi Lapula. "Solomon Plaatje, William Shakespeare, and the Translations of Culture." *Pretexts* 9, no. 1 (2000): 9–26.
Schapera, I. *A Handbook of Tswana Law and Custom*. London: Frank Cass, 1970.
Schenck, Theresa M. *William W. Warren: The Life, Letters, and Times of an Ojibwe Leader*. Lincoln: University of Nebraska Press, 2007.
Scott, Jill, and Alana Fletcher. "Polishing the Chain: Haudenosaunee Peacebuilding and Nation-Specific Frameworks of Redress." In *Arts of Engagement: Taking Aesthetic Action In and Beyond the Truth and Reconciliation Commission of Canada*, edited by Dylan Robinson and Keavy Martin, 157–79. Waterloo: Wilfrid Laurier University Press, 2016.
"The Secretary of War to the Cherokee Delegation." *Cherokee Phoenix, and Indians' Advocate*, June 17, 1829, 1–2.
Seddon, Deborah. "Shakespeare's Orality: Solomon Plaatje's Setswana Translations." *English Studies in Africa* 47, no. 2 (2004): 77–95.
Shannon, Timothy J. *Iroquois Diplomacy on the Early American Frontier*. New York: Penguin, 2008.
Shaw, Philip. *Waterloo and the Romantic Imagination*. Basingstoke: Palgrave, 2002.
Sigourney, Lydia. "The Cherokee Mother." *Cherokee Phoenix, and Indians' Advocate*, March 12, 1831, 3.
———. "Introduction." *The Poetical Works of Felicia Hemans, Complete in One Volume, with a Memoir*, by Mrs. L. H. Sigourney. Boston: Phillips, Sampson, 1853.
———. *Traits of the Aborigines: A Poem*. Cambridge, MA: University Press, 1822.
Sillery, A. *The Bechuanaland Protectorate*. Oxford: Oxford University Press, 1952.
Simcoe, John Graves. *The Correspondence of Lieut. Governor John Graves Simcoe*. 5 vols. North York: Ontario Historical Society, 1923–1931.
Simpson, Audra. *Mohawk Interruptus: Political Life across the Borders of Settler States*. Durham, NC: Duke University Press, 2014.
Simpson, David. *Romanticism and the Question of the Stranger*. Chicago: University of Chicago Press, 2013.

Simpson, Leanne. "Looking after Gdoo-naaganinaa: Precolonial Nishnaabeg Diplomatic and Treaty Relationships." *Wicazo Sa Review* 23, no. 2 (2008): 29–42.

Singer, Kate, and Nanora Sweet. "Introduction—Beyond Domesticity: Felicia Hemans in the Wider World." *Women's Writing* 21, no. 1 (2014): 1–8.

Six Miles Deep: Land Rights of the Six Nations of the Grand River. Six Nations Council, 2015. http://www.sixnations.ca/SixMilesDeepBooklet2015Final.pdf.

Six Nations of the Grand River: Land Rights, Financial Justice, Resolutions. Six Nations Council, 2015. http://www.sixnations.ca/SNLands&ResourcesBooklet2015Final.pdf.

Skilton, David. "Contemplating the Ruins of London: Macaulay's New Zealander and Others." *Literary London: Interdisciplinary Studies in the Representation of London* 2, no. 2 (2004). http://www.literarylondon.org/london-journal/march2004/skilton.html.

Smith, Donald B. "Kahgegagahbowh: Canada's First Literary Celebrity in the United States." In *Life, Letters & Speeches: George Copway (Kahgegagahbowh)*, edited by A. LaVonne Brown Ruoff and Donald B. Smith, 23–60. Lincoln: University of Nebraska Press, 1997.

———. "The Life of George Copway or Kah-ge-ga-gah-bowh (1816–1869)—and a Review of His Writings." *Journal of Canadian Studies* 23, no. 3 (1988): 5–38.

Smith, Robert S. *Warfare and Diplomacy in Pre-Colonial West Africa*. 2nd rev. ed. London: James Currey, 1989.

Smithers, Gregory D. *The Cherokee Diaspora: An Indigenous History of Migration, Resettlement, and Identity*. New Haven, CT: Yale University Press, 2015.

Sone, Patience M. "Relevance of Traditional Methods of Conflict Resolution in the Justice Systems in Africa." *Africa Insight* 46, no. 3 (2016): 51–66.

Spry, Adam. *Our War Paint Is Writers' Ink: Anishinaabe Literary Transnationalism*. Albany: State University of New York Press, 2018.

Stabler, Jane. *Byron, Poetics and History*. Cambridge: Cambridge University Press, 2002.

Stafford, Jane. *Colonial Literature and the Native Author: Indigeneity and Empire*. Basingstoke: Palgrave, 2016.

Starfield, Jane. "The Lore and the Proverbs: Sol Plaatje as Historian." African Studies Seminar Paper No. 299. University of Witwatersrand, Johannesburg, South Africa. 1991.

Stock, Paul. *The Shelley-Byron Circle and the Idea of Europe*. Basingstoke: Palgrave, 2010.

Stone, William L. *Life of Joseph Brant (Thayendanegea)*. 2 vols. Albany, NY: J. Munsell, 1864.

Strachan, James. *A Visit to the Province of Upper Canada, in 1819*. Aberdeen: D. Chalmers for J. Strachan, 1820.

Strachan, John. "Capt. Joseph Brant." *Christian Recorder* 2, no. 1 (1820): n.p.

———. "Life of Capt. Brant." *Christian Recorder* 1, no. 4 (1819): n.p.

Strickland, Rennard. "Address: To Do the Right Thing: Reaffirming Cherokee Traditions of Justice under Law." *American Indian Law Review* 17, no. 1 (1992): 337–46.

———. *Fire and the Spirits: Cherokee Law from Clan to Court*. Norman: University of Oklahoma Press, 1975.

"Sunday and Tuesday's Posts." *Bath Chronicle*, October 18, 1821, 2.

Surtees, Robert. *Indian Land Surrenders in Ontario 1763–1867*. Gatineau: Indian and Northern Affairs Canada, 1984.

———. "The Iroquois in Canada." In *The History and Culture of Iroquois Diplomacy: An Interdisciplinary Guide to the Treaties of the Six Nations and Their League*, edited by Francis Jennings, William N. Fenton, Mary A. Druke, and David R. Miller, 67–98. Syracuse, NY: Syracuse University Press, 1985.

Sweet, Timothy. "Pastoral Landscape with Indians: George Copway and the Political Unconscious of the American Pastoral." *Prospects* 18 (1993): 1–27.

"A Talk from the Head-Men and Warriors of the Cherokee Nation, at a Meeting Held at Ustinaire, the Beloved Town, 20th November 1788, addressed to the Honourable Richard Winn, Esquire, Superintendent of the Southern Department, in answer to a Talk sent by him, dated the 12th October, 1788." *Indian Affairs* 2, no. 1 (1832): 45–46.

Taylor, Alan. *The Divided Ground: Indians, Settlers, and the Northern Borderland of the American Revolution*. New York: Knopf, 2006.

Te Punga Somerville, Alice. "A View of Brexit from Elsewhere." *Once Were Pacific*, June 25, 2016. http://oncewerepacific.blogspot.com/2016/06/a-view-of-brexit-from-elsewhere.html.

Teuton, Christopher B. *Deep Waters: The Textual Continuum in American Indian Literature*. Lincoln: University of Nebraska Press, 2010.

Thrush, Coll. *Indigenous London: Native Travelers at the Heart of Empire*. New Haven, CT: Yale University Press, 2016.

Tiffin, Helen. "Cold Hearts and (Foreign) Tongues: Recitation and the Reclamation of the Female Body in the Works of Erna Brodber and Jamaica Kincaid." *Callaloo* 16, no. 4 (1993): 909–21.

Treuer, Anton. *The Assassination of Hole in the Day*. Nepean, Ontario: Borealis Books, 2011.

Turner, Dale. *This is Not a Peace Pipe: Towards a Critical Indigenous Philosophy*. Toronto: University of Toronto Press, 2006.

Tyrrell, Alexander. "Making the Millennium: The Mid-Nineteenth Century Peace Movement." *Historical Journal* 21, no. 1 (1978): 75–95.

Valaskakis, Gail Guthrie. *Indian Country: Essays on Contemporary Native Culture*. Waterloo: Wilfrid Laurier University Press, 2006.

"Views of the Cherokees in Relation to Further Cessions of Their Lands. Communicated to the Senate, April 16, 1824." In *American State Papers: Documents, Legislative and Executive, of the Congress of the United States, Indian*

Affairs. Vol. 2. Edited by Walter Lowrie and Matthew St. Clair Clarke, 502. Washington, DC: Gales and Seaton, 1832.

Viola, Herman J. *Diplomats in Buckskins: A History of Indian Delegations in Washington City*. Bluffton, SC: Rivlio Books, 1995.

Vizenor, Gerald. *The People Named the Chippewa: Narrative Histories*. Minneapolis: University of Minnesota Press, 1984.

Voss, A. E. "Sol Plaatje, the Eighteenth Century, and South African Cultural Memory." *English in Africa* 21, nos. 1–2 (1994): 59–75.

Walker, Cheryl. *Indian Nation: Native American Literature and Nineteenth Century Nationalisms*. Durham, NC: Duke University Press, 1997.

Walshe, Peter. *The Rise of African Nationalism in South Africa: The African National Congress 1912–1952*. London: Hurst, 1970.

Warren, William W. *History of the Ojibway People*. 2nd ed. Edited by Theresa Schenck. St. Paul: Minnesota Historical Society, 2009.

"Washington and the Cherokees. Continued." *Cherokee Phoenix*, September 17, 1828, 1.

Watkins, Daniel P. "Social Relations in Byron's *The Giaour*." *ELH* 52, no. 4 (1985): 873–92.

Watt, James. "Goldsmith's Cosmopolitanism." *Eighteenth-Century Life* 30, no. 1 (2006): 56–75.

Weaver, Jace. *The Red Atlantic: American Indigenes and the Making of the Modern World, 1000–1927*. Chapel Hill: University of North Carolina Press, 2014.

———. *That the People Might Live: Native American Literatures and Native American Community*. Oxford: Oxford University Press, 1997.

West, John. *A Journal of a Mission to the Indians of the British Provinces, of New Brunswick, and Nova Scotia, and the Mohawks, on the Ouse, or Grand River, Upper Canada*. London: L. B. Seeley, 1827.

White, Bruce M. "The Regional Context of the Removal Order of 1850." In *Fish in the Lakes, Wild Rice, and Game in Abundance: Testimony on Behalf of Mille Lacs Ojibwe Hunting and Fishing Rights*, edited by James M. McClurken, 141–328. East Lansing: Michigan State University Press, 2000.

White, Richard. *The Middle Ground: Indians, Empires, and Republics in the Great Lakes Region, 1650–1815*. 2nd ed. Cambridge: Cambridge University Press, 2011.

Willan, Brian. "The Anti-Slavery and Aborigines' Protection Society and the South African Natives' Land Act of 1913." *Journal of African History* 20, no. 1 (1979): 83–102.

———. "Introduction." *Native Life in South Africa*. New York: Picador, 2007.

———. *Sol Plaatje: South African Nationalist 1876–1932*. London: Heinemann, 1984.

Williams, Kayanesenh Paul. *Kayanerenkó:wa The Great Law of Peace*. Winnipeg: University of Manitoba Press, 2018.

Williams, Robert A., Jr. *Linking Arms Together: American Indian Treaty Visions of Law and Peace, 1600–1800*. New York: Routledge, 1999.

Willig, Timothy D. *Restoring the Chain of Friendship: British Policy and the Indians of the Great Lakes, 1783–1815*. Lincoln: University of Nebraska Press, 2008.

Winegard, Timothy C. "Your Home on Native Land? Conflict and Controversy at Caledonia and the Six Nations of the Grand River." In *Blockades or Breakthroughs? Aboriginal Peoples Confront the Canadian State*, edited by Yale D. Belanger and P. Whitney Lackenbauer, 411–44. Montreal: McGill-Queen's University Press, 2014.

Wisecup, Kelly. "Practicing Sovereignty: Colonial Temporalities, Cherokee Justice, and the 'Socrates' Writings of John Ridge." *Journal of the Native American and Indigenous Studies Association* 4, no. 1 (2017): 30–60.

Witgen, Michael. *An Infinity of Nations: How the Native New World Shaped Early North America*. University Park: Penn State University Press, 2011.

Wolfson, Susan J. "Felicia Hemans and the Revolving Doors of Reception." In *Romanticism and Women Poets: Opening the Doors of Reception*, edited by Harriet Kramer Linkin and Stephen C. Behrendt, 214–41. Lexington: University Press of Kentucky, 1999.

Wood, Charlie, and Peter Wood. "Norman and Jessie Wood: 'Great Mates.'" Peter Wood, n.p.: 2004.

Wood, Peter. *The Story of William and Sarah Wells*. Wellington, NZ: First Edition, 2010.

Wordsworth, William. *The Poems*. Vol. 1. Edited by John O. Hayden. New Haven, CT: Yale University Press, 1977.

Young Beaver. "Indian Emigration." *Cherokee Phoenix*, September 17, 1828, 3.

———. "A Revery." *Cherokee Phoenix*, July 9, 1828, 2.

Yuan, Yin. "Invasion and Retreat: Representations of the Oriental Other in Byron's *The Giaour*." *Studies in Romanticism* 54, no. 1 (2015): 3–31.

Zuck, Rochelle Raineri. *Divided Sovereignties: Race, Nationhood, and Citizenship in Nineteenth-Century America*. Athens: University of Georgia Press, 2016.

Index

Aborigines Protection Society, 120, 170
African traditional diplomacy, 147, 149
　See also Rolong, the
Ahyonwaeghs. See Brant, John
Allen, Chadwick, 6, 183–184, 201
American Revolution, 10, 21, 28
Anishinaabeg, 108
　See also Ojibwe, the
Antwerp, Verplanck Van, 112–113
Appiah, Kwame Anthony, 9n13
Armstrong, Isobel, 100

Bagone-giizhig the younger, 124
Bathurst, Lord, 38–39
Beattie, William, 49
Beecher, Catharine, 97, 98n97
Belgrave, Michael, 202
Belmessous, Saliha, 14
Beloved Women, 96, 102
Bergren, Katherine, *The Global Wordsworth*, 204–206
Berlant, Lauren, 98
Bigger6 collective, 19
Borrows, John, 4, 41–42, 136
Boudinot, Elias
　Address to the Whites, An, 73
　editorial practices, 61, 63, 72, 87, 90–93
　and Hemans's poetry, 72–78, 84–87, 90, 94, 98, 100–101
　personal background, 61–62, 66
　See also *Cherokee Phoenix*
Brant, John
　engagement with Campbell, 21–23, 36, 41, 42–44, 45–50
　personal background, 37–38, 55, 55–56n85
　political mission to Britain, 23, 32, 36, 38–41, 52, 55
Brant, Joseph
　derogatory depictions of, 22, 35–36, 43, 48–49, 52–53
　Grand River negotiations, 29–31, 40, 52
　personal background, 27–28, 31, 56
　See also "Monster Brandt"
Brittain, Henry, 186–187
Browne, Thomas Gore, 181
Burritt, Elihu, 103, 125n71
Burton, Antoinette, 13
Busby, James, 176, 177–178
Butler, Marilyn, 195
Buzard, James, 139
Byron, George Gordon
　"Age of Bronze, The," 129
　Childe Harold's Pilgrimage, 104, 127–129

Byron, George Gordon *(continued)*
  and Copway, 127–133, 135–136, 138–139
  Don Juan, 128n85, 129n151, 133
  Giaour, The, 133, 173, 194–195, 200
  and lines cited by Kōhere, 184–185, 186, 195–196, 200–201
  poetic digressions, 130–131, 134

Campbell, Robert, 98
Campbell, Thomas
  engagement with John Brant, 21–23, 36, 41, 42–44, 45–50
  and justice v. aesthetics, 46, 50–54, 58, 59
  See also *Gertrude of Wyoming* (Campbell)
Chander, Manu Samriti, 15, 19
Chaw-win-is, 46, 48, 54
Cherokee Phoenix
  appeals for sympathy in, 63, 72, 83–84, 87, 98–102
  establishment of, 66, 70
  other names of, 74n35
  tropes of hearth and home in, 74–81, 89–92, 98
  See also Boudinot, Elias; Hemans, Felicia
Cherokees, the
  diplomatic traditions, 66–67
  Eastern Cherokees, 65, 75
  National Council, 65–66, 96
  quoting of past exchanges, 67–69, 71, 87–92
  and removal, 62–63, 75–76, 81–83, 94, 96–97
  and treaties, 64–65, 81, 88, 96
  Western Cherokees, 65, 81, 88
  white activist support for, 97–99
  women's authority in, 95–97, 102
  See also Boudinot, Elias

Childe Harold's Pilgrimage (Byron), 104, 127–131
Chippewa. See Ojibwe, the
Claus, William, 37
Cobden, Richard, 126
Colenso, William, 178
colonial diplomacy. See settler-imperial diplomacy
colonization
  and injustice, 51, 95, 158–159, 204–205
  and power, 10, 69, 205–207
  and Romantic literature, 10–12, 196–197
condolence ceremony model, 25, 26–27, 33–35, 37, 41
Copway, George
  and Byron, 127–133, 135–136, 138–139
  European trip, 120–127, 136–137
  Kahgega, 118, 120, 134, 140
  personal background, 103, 116–117, 119–121, 135
  rhetorical style, 104–107, 117, 125n75, 130–131, 134–135, 141
  Running Sketches, 104–107, 119, 127–133, 135, 137–139, 140–141
  Traditional History, The, 117–118, 133–134
Corntassel, Jeff, 46, 48, 54
cosmopolitanism, 7, 131, 187
cross-cultural communication
  relationship-building, 2, 3, 9, 27, 66–67, 126
  Western discourses, utilization of, xiv, 8–9, 66, 71–72n28, 109, 192

daffodil gap, the, 204–208, 215
"Daffodils (the other version), The" (Figiel), 208, 209

"Daffodils—from a native's perspective, The" (Figiel), 209–212
Dean, Janet, 99
Declaration of Independence (1835), 176, 177
Deloria, Vine, Jr., 14, 206
Demson, Andrew, 72n30
Deserted Village, The (Goldsmith), 144–145, 154–159, 161–165, 169–170
DeVries, Laura, 57
Dodge, Henry, 113

Eaton, John H., 76, 78
Edmonds, Penelope, 4n4
Elbourne, Elizabeth, 36, 52, 55
Eshkibagikoonzh, 114, 124

Fanon, Frantz, 7
feminine rhetoric, 98–102
Festa, Lynn, 11–12
Figiel, Sia, 207–212
Firth, Raymond, 201
Flat Mouth, 114, 124
Flint, Kate, 23, 59, 105
Fulford, Tim, 23, 105

Galagina. *See* Boudinot, Elias
Gaul, Theresa Strouth, 63, 70, 85, 87
Gertrude of Wyoming (Campbell)
  Campbell's source notes, 32–33, 34–35, 48–52
  dispute in *Christian Recorder*, 43–44, 52
  and Haudenosaunee diplomatic traditions, 33–35
  influence of, 36, 42–43, 51–53, 53–54n80, 57
  "Monster Brandt" in, 22, 35, 48–49, 50–51n71
  scenario, 21–22, 32–36
  See also Campbell, Thomas

Giaour, The (Byron), 173, 185–186, 194–196, 200–201
Global Wordsworth, The (Bergren), 204–205
Goldsmith, Oliver, 144–145, 154–159, 161–165, 169–170
Goslee, Nancy Moore, 94
Gourlay, Robert, 53
Grand River lands, 29–32, 37–40, 44, 56–57
Green, Sarah, 23n3

Haire, Karen, 159
Haldimand, Frederick, 29–30, 32, 38–40, 45, 56
Hall, Catherine, 197
Hall, James, 55–56n85
Hansen, Julia, 51–52
Harper, R.J., 58
Harris, John, 170
Haudenosaunee, the, 24
  diplomatic traditions, 24–27, 34–35, 37, 41
  political affiliations, 21, 28–29
  quoting of past exchanges, 27, 37–40
  See also Brant, John; Brant, Joseph
Helu-Thaman, Konai, 212–213
Hemans, Felicia
  affective discourse, 91–92, 94, 98, 100–102
  "Dreams of Heaven," 93
  "Evening Song of the Tyrolese Peasants," 79, 80–81, 87
  "Indian with His Dead Child, The," 85–87
  "Lines to an Orphan," 80
  "Meeting of the Ships, The," 84–85
  "Nature's Farewell," 81–82, 83, 88
  "Parting Song, A," 83–84
  "Ruined House, The," 78–79

Hemans, Felicia *(continued)*
"Song," 83
"Sunbeam, The," 80
"Treasures of the Sea, The," 89
"Two Homes, The," 74–78
"Voice of the Waves, The," 93
"Woman and Fame," 89–90
"Wounded Eagle, The," 82
Hill, G. Ava, 56
Hobson, William, 177, 178, 179
Hofmeyr, Isabel, 13
Hole in the Day, 124
Hone Heke, 178, 219–220
Hongi Hika, 176, 220
Horatius (Macaulay), 174, 184, 186–187, 189–190, 196–197
Hutchings, Kevin, 23

imperialism. *See* colonization
imperial-settler diplomacy. *See* settler-imperial diplomacy
Indian Removal Act (1830), 62–63, 94, 109
Indians' Advocate. See *Cherokee Phoenix*
Indigenous autonomy:
  intellectual sovereignty, 13, 208, 212
  political sovereignty, 26, 57, 123, 176–177, 206–207
Indigenous diplomatic strategies:
  and multiple genres, xiv, 4–6, 15, 22, 144, 154
  quoting of past exchanges, xiv, 3, 13, 27, 38–40, 67–69, 116, 182
  relationship-building, 2, 3, 9, 27, 66–67, 126
  sympathy/justice appeals, 87, 98–102, 150–151, 161, 163, 189
  values, mobilization of, 2, 7, 11, 61, 72, 169
  and Western discourses, xiv, 8–9, 66, 71–72n28, 109, 192
  See also Romantic poetry

Iroquois. *See* Haudenosaunee, the

Jackson, Andrew, 88–90
Jameson, Anna, 50–51n71
Jones, Daniel, 164

Kahgega, 118, 120, 134, 140
Kahgegagahbowh. *See* Copway, George
Katteuha, 102
Kaul, Suvir, 162n51
Kawatupu, Renata Paraire, 182
Kelderman, Frank, 14–16, 107
Kerr, Robert Johnson, 21, 38–40
Kōhere, Mokena, 180–181, 185, 190–192
Kōhere, Rēweti:
  Byron/Macaulay/Māori connections, 184–185, 187, 189–190, 193, 197, 200–201
  and Marangairoa 1D Block, 185–186, 188–192
  personal background, 174
  petitions, 186, 188–189
  rhetorical style, 174–175, 184–185, 188–190, 193–194, 201
  Story of a Maori Chief, The, 190–192
  translated verses, 173n2, 174n3
Kohimārama Conference (1860), 180
Kohl, Johann Georg, 139–140
Krupat, Arnold, 69–70
Kugel, Rebecca, 123, 126

Lancaster, Barry, 50
Leask, Nigel, 196
Lootens, Tricia, 87, 99
Lopenzina, Drew, 41
Lyons, Scott Richard, 13, 106, 118, 134

Macaulay, Thomas Babington:
  Horatius, 174, 184, 186–187, 189–190, 197

image of London in ruins, 198
Lays of Ancient Rome, 196
Maghegabo, 113
Mahuta, Robert Te Kotahi, 199–200
Maitland, Peregrine, 32
Māori cultural concepts, 184, 188, 189, 192
Māori diplomacy
  and British Crown, 176–180
  diplomatic traditions, 176, 178, 190, 193, 200
  and land confiscation, 180, 186, 187
  petitions, 182–183, 186, 188–189
  and settlers, 175–180, 192, 220–221
  and Treaty of Waitangi, xiii–xiv, 175, 177–184
  See also Kōhere, Rēweti
Mar, Tracey Banivanua, 6
Marangairoa 1D Block, 185–186, 188–192
Marsh, Selina Tusitala, 214–217
Martin, Meredith, 196–197
Martini, Elspeth, 119n52
Matjila, D.S., 159
Mellor, Anne K., 101
Miles, Tiya, 95, 96
Miller, Cary, 124
Mississaugas, the, 29, 31–32, 40
Mkhize, Khwezi, 152, 155, 161
Mohawks. *See* Haudenosaunee, the
Mole, Tom, 138
Molema, Seetsele Modiri, 148
"Monster Brandt"
  mischaracterization of, 22, 35, 48–49, 50–51n71
  ongoing impact, 36, 42–43, 51–53, 53–54n80, 57
  See also Brant, Joseph
Montague, John, 161n50, 163
Montshiwa, 145–146, 169, 170
Morgan, Cecilia, 120, 125n75

"My friend Mr. Ambassador" (Figiel), 208–209

Nanye'hi (Nancy Ward), 96
Native American communication, 9, 14, 70
Native Land Court, 181, 185–186, 188
Native Lands Act (1862), 181
Native Life in South Africa (Plaatje)
  appeals for sympathy, 151, 153, 161, 167, 172
  and *Deserted Village*, 144–145, 154–159, 161–165
  disparate quotations, 152–154
  Romantic rhetoric, 159, 161, 171
Natives' Land Act (1913), 144, 148
Newey, Vincent, 162
Ngāti Porou
  Kōhere, Mokena, 180–181
  Marangairoa 1D Block, 185–186, 188–192
  See also Kōhere, Rēweti
Nichols, John D., 110
Norton, John, 31, 37, 48

Oconostota, 68
Odendaal, André, 148n16
Ojibwe, the, 103n1
  diplomacy prior to War of 1812, 108–109
  diplomatic traditions, 112–113, 123–124, 137–138
  print culture, 107, 108, 135
  quoting of past exchanges, 113–116
  removal v. reservations, 111–112, 114–115, 118–119
  and transatlantic politics, 122–123, 125, 127, 134–135
  treaty diplomacy after 1820, 109–116, 119
  See also Copway, George

Old Raven, 68
Opondo, Sam Okoth, 153–154
Orange, Claudia, 176, 180, 181n25

Pasifika poets
  Figiel, Sia, 207–212
  Helu-Thaman, Konai, 212–213
  Marsh, Selina Tusitala, 214–217
Payajik, 113
Payne, John Howard, 69
Peace Congress (1850), 107, 121–126, 129, 130, 137
Penner, Robert, 121, 134–135
Perdue, Theda, 95
Peterson, Bhekizizwe, 167
Peyer, Bernd, 105, 121, 127, 130
Phoenix. See *Cherokee Phoenix*
Pinch, Adela, 7n9
Pine Tree Treaty (1837), 109–110, 112–113
Plaatje, Solomon T.
  mission to England, 143–144, 149–150, 163–166, 169n70
  Native Life in South Africa, 144–145, 151–159, 161–164, 167, 171–172
  personal background, 143, 145, 147–148, 150–151
  and petitions, 167–169
  rhetorical style, 152–156, 166, 168–169, 172
  Sechuana Proverbs, 165–166
  Sechuana Reader, A, 164
  Shakespeare, affinity with, 160
"Pua and Daffodils" (Figiel), 207–208

racist typologies, 35, 52, 55–56n85, 57–58, 122, 157
Ramsey, Alexander, 111, 114
Reder, Deanna, 106
Remmington, Janet, 144
Richardson, Robbie, 35

Ridge, John, 90
Rolong, the, 145–147
  See also Plaatje, Solomon T.
Romantic poetry
  and colonization, 10–12, 196–197
  diplomatic power of, 15–16, 22–23, 42, 139, 203
  as diplomatic texts, 2, 4, 19, 61, 144, 175, 201
  and failed promises, 87, 172, 197, 213, 216
  tenets of, 105–106
  themes of, 11, 74, 159, 171, 184, 216
  time period of, 10, 145, 175
  values in, 2, 11, 20, 61, 72
  See also specific poems
Romantic studies, xiii, 4n4, 12–13, 16, 19, 59
Rothstein, David, 91–92
Round, Phillip H., 71
Running Sketches (Copway)
  and Byron, 127–133, 136, 138–139
  diplomatic function of, 119, 135, 140–141
  disparate quotations in, 104–107, 130

Saler, Bethel, 108
Salmond, Anne, 193
Sandy Lake tragedy, 112, 114
SANNC, 143, 148–150
Schalkwyk, David, 172
Scott, Jill, 54
Scott, Margaret Ann, 96–97
settler responsibilities, 19–20, 221
settler-imperial diplomacy, xiii–xiv, 3, 5, 55, 69, 177
Shagobai, 113
Shannon, Timothy J., 26
Shelley, Percy Bysshe, 15

Sigourney, Lydia, 97–100
Simpson, Audra, 57
Simpson, David, 23
Six Nations. *See* Haudenosaunee, the
Smithers, Gregory D., 66
"Socrates," 90
South African Native National Congress, 143, 148–150
Stabler, Jane, 130–131, 134
Starfield, Jane, 165–166
Stock, Paul, 129
Story of a Maori Chief, The (Kōhere), 190–192
Strachan, John, 43, 53
Stuart, Henry, 110–111

Taonui, Makoare, 179
Taylor, Zachary, 111, 115
Te Toa Takitini, 173–174, 186–187, 196
Te Waitaheke, Nopera, 182
Tekarohoken, Henry, 38, 44, 45n62, 55
Thayendanegea. *See* Brant, Joseph
Tiffin, Helen, 7, 13, 204–206
T'lakwadzi, 46, 48, 54
Traditional History (Copway), 117–118, 133–134
Trail of Tears, 63, 79
Treaty of Fort Stanwix (1768), 27–28
Treaty of Holston (1791), 64, 81
Treaty of La Pointe (1842), 110–111
Treaty of Long Island (1777), 68
Treaty of Prairie du Chien (1825), 109
Treaty of St. Peters (1837), 109–110, 112–113
Treaty of Waitangi (1840)
 and claim negotiations, xiii–xiv
 Māori v. Crown perspectives, 177–180
 in public discourse, 175, 179–184
 two texts, 177, 181, 183–184
Treaty of Washington (1828), 81, 87–88
truth and reconciliation, 46–48, 50, 54, 59
Tshidi Rolong. *See* Rolong, the
Tūhaere, Pāora, 182
Turner, Dale, 8–9

"Unity" (Marsh), 214–217

Valaskakis, Gail Guthrie, 57
verbatim quotation of past exchanges
 diplomatic power of, xiv, 38–40, 67–69
 reasons for, xiv, 1, 3–5, 13, 27
 written v. oral records, 111, 112–116, 117, 178–179, 182–183
Vizenor, Gerald, 135
Voss, A. E., 156

Waikato (chief), 176, 220
wampum, 24, 26, 29, 34, 37, 67
War of Independence, American, 10, 21, 28
Washington, George, 88
Watie, Buck. *See* Boudinot, Elias
Watkins, Daniel P., 200
Weaver, Jace, 127
whaikōrero, 178, 190, 193, 200
White, Bruce M., 113–114
White, Richard, 108–109
White Crow, 110
Willan, Brian, 151
Williams, Henry, 177–178
Williams, Robert A. Jr., 9–10, 137
Williams, Skyler, 58
Wilmot, Robert, 39
Wisecup, Kelly, 90

Witgen, Michael, 124
Wolfson, Susan, 101
women's voices
  Cherokee women, 95–97
  nineteenth-century white writers, 97–102
  Pasifika poets, 207–217

Wordsworth, William
  and daffodil gap, 204–208, 215
  repurposing of "Daffodils," 207–213, 214

Young Beaver, 80–81, 83
Yuan, Yin, 195

www.ingramcontent.com/pod-product-compliance
Lightning Source LLC
Chambersburg PA
CBHW030533230426
43665CB00010B/879